Walter W. Skeat

Lancelot of the Laik

A Scottish Metrical Romance

Walter W. Skeat

Lancelot of the Laik
A Scottish Metrical Romance

ISBN/EAN: 9783744674508

Printed in Europe, USA, Canada, Australia, Japan

Cover: Foto ©Thomas Meinert / pixelio.de

More available books at **www.hansebooks.com**

The Romans

of

Lancelot of the Laik.

BERLIN : ASHER & CO., 13, UNTER DEN LINDEN.

NEW YORK : C. SCRIBNER & CO.: LEYPOLDT & HOLT

PHILADELPHIA : J. B. LIPPINCOTT & CO.

𝕷𝖆𝖓𝖈𝖊𝖑𝖔𝖙 𝖔𝖋 𝖙𝖍𝖊 𝕷𝖆𝖎𝖐 :

A SCOTTISH METRICAL ROMANCE,

(ABOUT 1490–1500 A.D.)

RE-EDITED

FROM A MANUSCRIPT IN THE CAMBRIDGE UNIVERSITY LIBRARY,

WITH AN

INTRODUCTION, NOTES, AND GLOSSARIAL INDEX,

BY

THE REV. W. W. SKEAT, M.A.,

LATE FELLOW OF CHRIST'S COLLEGE, CAMBRIDGE; AND TRANSLATOR OF THE SONGS AND
BALLADS OF UHLAND.

[Second and Revised Edition, 1870.]

LONDON:
PUBLISHED FOR THE EARLY ENGLISH TEXT SOCIETY
By KEGAN PAUL, TRENCH, TRÜBNER & CO., LIMITED,
DRYDEN HOUSE, 43, GERRARD STREET, SOHO, W.
1865.

[Reprinted 1889, 1905.]

Original Series, 6.

RICHARD CLAY & SONS, LIMITED, LONDON AND BUNGAY.

PREFACE.

I.—DESCRIPTION OF THE MS., ETC.

A FORMER edition of the present poem was printed for the Maitland Club, in 1839, and edited by Joseph Stevenson, Esq. It has saved me all trouble of transcription, but by no means, I am sorry to say, that of correction. Those who possess the older edition will readily perceive that it differs from the present one very frequently indeed, and that the variations are often such as considerably to affect the sense. Many of the errors in it (such as *casualtyee* for *casualytee, grone,* for *gone, reprent* for *repent*) are clearly typographical, but there are others which would incline me to believe that the transcription was too hastily executed; several passages being quite meaningless. Near the conclusion of Mr Stevenson's preface we read : " The pieces which have been selected for the present volume[1] are printed with such errors of transcription as have crept into them by the carelessness of the scribe;" a statement which certainly implies that there was no intention on his part of departing from the original. Yet that he sometimes unconsciously did so to such an extent as considerably to alter (or destroy) the sense, the reader may readily judge from a few examples :—

[1] The volume contains other poems besides " Sir Lancelot."

LINE.	EDITION OF 1839.	TRUE READING OF THE MS.
26.	fatil (*fatal*),	fatit (*fated*).
285.	unarmyt (*unarmed*),	enarmyt (*fully armed*).
682.	can here,	cam nere.
700.	rendit (*rent*),	vondit (*wounded*).
764.	refuse (*refusal*?),	reprefe (*defeat*).
861.	felith (*feeleth*),	fetith (*setteth*).
1054.	vyt,	rycht.
1084.	speiris,	spuris.
1455.	cumyng (*coming*),	cunyng (*skill*).
1621.	he war,	be war (*beware*).
1641.	promyſ,	punyſ (*punish*).
2010.	ane desyne,	medysyne.
2092.	born,	lorn (*lost*).
2114.	havin,	harm.
2142.	Hymene (!),	hyme (*him*).
2219.	such,	furth (*forth*).
2245.	al so y-vroght,	al foly vroght.
2279.	chichingis (!),	thithingis (*tidings*).
2446.	love,	lore (*teaching*). Etc.

Several omissions also occur, as, *e. g.*, of the word "off" in l. 7, of the word "tressore" in l. 1715, and of four whole lines at a time in two instances; viz., lines 1191-4, and 2877-80. It will be found, in fact, that the former text can seldom be safely quoted for the purposes of philology; and I cannot but think Mr Stevenson's claim of being accurate to be especially unfortunate; and the more so, because the genuine text is much simpler and more intelligible than the one which he has given.

The original MS. is to be found in the Cambridge University Library, marked Kk. 1. 5. It formerly formed part of a thick volume, labelled "Tracts;" but these are now being separated, for greater convenience, into several volumes. The MS. of "Lancelot" has little to do with any of the rest as regards its subject, but several other pieces are in the same hand-writing; and, at the end of one of them, an

abstract of Solomon's proverbs, occur the words, " Expliciunt
Dicta Salamonis, per manum V. de F."[1] This hand-writing,
though close, is very regular, and my own impression certainly
is that the scribe has almost always succeeded in preserving
the sense of the poem, though there is much confusion in the
dialectal forms, as will be shewn presently.

The present text is as close a fac-simile of the MS. as can
be represented by printed letters, every peculiarity being preserved as far as practicable, even including the use of *y* for *þ*
(or *th*) ; so that the reader must remember that *yow* in l. 94
stands for *thow*, and *yis* in l. 160 for *this*, and so on; but this
ought not to cause much difficulty. The sole points of differ-
ence are the following :

1. In the MS. the headings "Prologue," " Book I. " etc.,
do not occur.

2. The lines do not always begin (in the MS.) with a
capital letter.

3. The letters *italicized* are (in the MS.) represented by
signs of contraction. One source of difficulty is the flourish
over a word, used *sometimes* as a contraction for *m* or *n*. I
have expanded this flourish as an *m* or *n* wherever such letter
is manifestly required ; but it also occurs where it is best to
attach to it no value. In such instances, the flourish occurs
most frequently over the last word in a line, and (except very
rarely) only over words which have an *m* or *n* in them. It
would thus seem that their presence is due to the fact of the
scribe wanting employment for his pen after the line had been
written, and that the flourish therefore appears over certain
words, not so much because the *n* is *wanting* in them, as
because it is *there already*. Such words have a special attrac-
tion for the wandering pen. Still, in order that the reader

---

[1] See Mr Lumby's editions of "Early Scottish Verse" and "Ratis Raving," both edited for the E. E. T. S. from this MS. Only the latter of these is
in the hand-writing of V. de F.

may know wherever such flourishes occur, they have all been noted down; thus, in l. 46, the stroke over the *n* in " greñ " means that a long flourish occurs drawn over the whole word, and the reader who wishes to expand this word into " grene " or " grenn " may easily do it for himself, though he should observe that the most usual form of the word is simply "gren," as in lines 1000, 1305.

In a few nouns ending in -*l*, the plural is indicated by a stroke drawn through the doubled letter; as in *perillis*, *sadillis*, etc.; and even the word *ellis* (else) is thus abbreviated.

4. I am responsible for all hyphens, and letters and words between square brackets; thus, "with-outen" is in the MS. "with outen;" and "knych[t]ly" is written "knychly." Whenever a line begins with a capital letter included between two brackets, the original has a blank space left, evidently intended for an illuminated letter. Wherever illuminated letters actually occur in the MS., they are denoted in this edition by large capitals.

5. We find, in the MS., both the long and the twisted *s* (f and s). These have been noted down as they occur, though I do not observe any law for their use. The letter "ß" has been adopted as closely resembling a symbol in the MS., which apparently has the force of double *s*, and is not unlike the " *sz* " used in modern German hand-writing. It may be conveniently denoted by *ss* when the type "ß" is not to be had, and is sometimes so represented in the "Notes."

6. The MS. is, of course, not punctuated. The punctuation in the present edition is mostly new; and many passages, which in the former edition were meaningless, have thus been rendered easily intelligible. I am also responsible for the headings of the pages, the abstract at the sides of them, the numbering of the folios in the margin, the notes, and the glossary; which I hope may be found useful. The greatest

care has been taken to make the text accurate, the proof-sheets having been compared with the MS. *three times* throughout.[1]

II.—DESCRIPTION OF THE POEM.

The poem itself is a loose paraphrase of not quite fourteen folios of the first of the three volumes of the French Romance of Lancelot du Lac, if we refer to it as reprinted at Paris in 1513, in three volumes, thin folio, double-columned.[2] The English poet has set aside the French Prologue, and written a new one of his own, and has afterwards translated and ampli-fied that portion of the Romance which narrates the invasion of Arthur's territory by "le roy de oultre les marches, nomme galehault" (in the English *Galiot*), and the defeat of the said king by Arthur and his allies.

The Prologue (lines 1-334) tells how the author undertook to write a romance to please his lady-love; and how, after deciding to take as his subject the story of Lancelot as told in the French Romance, yet finding himself unequal to a close translation of the whole of it, he determined to give a para-

---

[1] This refers to the edition printed in 1865. In executing the present re-print, the proof-sheets have been once more compared with the MS., and a very few insignificant errors have been thus detected and rectified.

[2] "As to the Romance of Sir Lancelot, our author [Gower], among others on the subject, refers to a volume of which he was the hero; perhaps that of Robert de Borron, altered soon afterwards by Godefroy de Leigny, under the title of *Le Roman de la Charrette*, and printed, with additions, at Paris by Antony Verard, in the year 1494.

> For if thou wilt the bokes rede
> Of Launcelot and other mo,
> Then might thou seen how it was tho
> Of armes," etc. (GOWER: *Confessio Amantis*, Book iv.)

Quoted from Warton's English Poetry, vol. ii., p. 234, *ed.* 1840. I quote this as bearing somewhat on the subject, though it should be observed that *Le Roman de la Charrette* is not the same with *Lancelot du Lac*, but only a romance of the same class. Chaucer also refers to Lancelot in his Nonnes Prestes Tale, l. 392; and it is mentioned in the famous lines of Dante (*Inf.* v. 127)—
> "Noi leggevamo un giorno per diletto
> Di Lancilotto, come amor lo strinse," &c.

phrase of a portion of it only. After giving us a brief summary of the earlier part by the simple process of telling us
what he will *not* relate, he proposes to begin the story at the
point where Lancelot has been made prisoner by the lady of
Melyhalt, and to take as his subject the wars between Arthur
and Galiot, and the distinction which Lancelot won in them;
and afterwards to tell how Lancelot made peace between these
two kings, and was consequently rewarded by Venus, who

> " makith hyme his ladice grace to have " (l. 311).

The latter part of the poem, it may be observed, has not come
down to us. The author then concludes his Prologue by beseeching to have the support of a very celebrated poet, whose
name he will not mention, but will only say that

> " Ye fresch enditing of his laiting toung
> Out throuch yis world so wid is yroung," etc.[1] (l. 328.)

The first Book introduces us to King Arthur at Carlisle.[2]
The king is visited by dreams, which he imagines to forebode
misfortune ; he therefore convokes all his clerks, and inquires
of them the meaning of the dreams, proposing to hang them in
the event of their refusal. Thus strongly urged, they tell him
that those on whom he most relies will fail him at his need ;
and when he further inquires if this evil fate can be averted,
they answer him very obscurely that it can only be remedied
by help of the water-lion, the leech, and the flower ; a reply
which the king evidently regards as unsatisfactory. Soon after
an aged knight, fully armed, enters the palace, with a message
from King Galiot, requiring him to give " tribute and rent."
Arthur at once refuses, somewhat to the astonishment of the
knight, who is amazed at his hardihood. Next arrives a
message from the lady of Melyhalt, informing Arthur of the

---

[1] He does not necessarily imply that the poet invoked was still alive ; and
we might almost suppose Petrarch to be meant, who was more proud of his
Latin poem called " Africa " than of his odes and sonnets. See Hallam's
Literary History (4 vols.), vol. i., p. 85. But this is pure conjecture.
[2] But the French has " Cardueil." See l. 2153.

actual presence of Galiot's army. We are then momentarily introduced to Lancelot, who is pining miserably in the lady's custody. Next follows a description of Galiot's army, at sight of the approach of which King Arthur and his "niece," Sir Gawain, confer as to the best means of resistance. In the ensuing battle Sir Gawain greatly distinguishes himself, but is at last severely wounded. Sir Lancelot, coming to hear of Sir Gawain's deeds, craves leave of the lady to be allowed to take part in the next conflict, who grants him his boon on condition that he promise to return to his prison. She then provides for him a red courser, and a complete suit of red armour, in which guise he appears at the second battle, and is the "head and comfort of the field;" the queen and Sir Gawain beholding his exploits from a tower. The result of the battle convinces Galiot that Arthur is not strong enough at present to resist him sufficiently, and that he thus runs the risk of a too easy, and therefore dishonourable, conquest; for which excellent reason he grants Arthur a twelvemonth's truce, with a promise to return again in increased force at the expiration of that period. Sir Lancelot returns to Melyhalt according to promise, and the lady is well pleased at hearing the reports of his famous deeds, and visits him when asleep, out of curiosity to observe his appearance after the fight.

In the Second Book the story makes but little progress, nearly the whole of it being occupied by a long lecture or sermon delivered to Arthur by a "master," named Amytans, on the duties of a king ; the chief one being that a king should give presents to everybody—a duty which is insisted on with laborious tediousness. Lines 1320-2130 are almost entirely occupied with this subject, and will be found to be the driest part of the whole narrative. In the course of his lecture, Amytans explains at great length the obscure prophecy mentioned above, shewing that by the water-lion is meant God the Father, by the leech God the Son, and by the flower the Virgin

Mary. Though the outline of a similar lecture exists in the
old French text, there would seem to be a special reason for the
length to which it is here expanded. Some lines certainly seem
to hint at events passing in Scotland at the time when the poem
was composed. Thus, "kings may be excused when of tender
age" (l. 1658); but when they come to years of discretion
should punish those that have wrested the law. Again we
find (l. 1920) strong warnings against flatterers, concluding
(l. 1940) with the expression,

> "Wo to the realme that havith sich o chans!"

Such hints may remind us of the long minorities of James II.
and James III.; and, whilst speaking on this subject, I may
note a somewhat remarkable coincidence. When King Arthur,
as related in Book I., asks the meaning of his dream, he is told
that it signifies that "they in whom he most trusts will fail
him" (l. 499); and he afterwards laments (l. 1151) how his
"men fail him at need." Now when we read that a story is
current of a prophetess having told James III. that he was
destined to "fall by the hands of his own kindred,"[1] and
that that monarch was in the habit of consulting *astrologers*[2]
(compare l. 432) as to the dangers that threatened him, it seems
quite possible that the poem was really composed about the year
1478; and this supposition is consistent with the fact that the
hand-writing of the present MS. copy belongs to the very end
of the fifteenth century.

Towards the end of the Second Book, we learn that the
twelvemonth's truce draws near its end, and that Sir Lancelot
again obtains permission from the lady to be present in the
approaching combat, choosing this time to be arrayed in
"armys al of blak" (l. 2426).

---

[1] Tytler's History of Scotland (Edinburgh, 1841), vol. iv., p. 216.
[2] The French text does not say anything about "astronomy." We may
especially note the following lines, as *not* being in the French, viz., lines 1473-
1496, 1523-1542, 1599-1644, 1658-1680, and the long passage 1752-1998.

In the Third Book Galiot returns to the fight with a host thrice as large as his former one. As before, Gawain distinguishes himself in the first encounter, but is at length so "evil wounded" that he was "the worse thereof evermore" (1. 2706). In the second combat, the black knight utterly eclipses the red knight, and the last thousand (extant) lines of the poem are almost wholly occupied with a description of his wonderful prowess. At the point where the extant portion of the poem ceases, the author would appear to be just warming with his subject, and to be preparing for greater efforts.

In continuance of the outline of the story, I may add that the French text[1] informs us how, after being several times remounted by Galiot, and finding himself with every fresh horse quite as fresh as he was at the beginning of the battle, the black knight attempted, as evening fell, to make his way back to Melyhalt secretly. Galiot, however, having determined not to lose sight of him, follows and confronts him, and earnestly requests his company to supper, and that he will lodge in his tent that night. After a little hesitation, Lancelot accepts the invitation, and Galiot entertains him with the utmost respect and flattery, providing for him a most excellent supper and a bed larger than any of the rest. Lancelot, though naturally somewhat wearied, passes a rather restless night, and talks a good deal in his sleep. Next day Galiot prays him to stay longer, and he consents on condition that a boon may be granted him, which is immediately acceded to without further question. He then requests Galiot to submit himself to Arthur, and to confess himself vanquished, a demand which so amazes that chieftain that he at first refuses, yet succeeds in persuading Lancelot to remain with him a little longer. The day after, preparations are made for another battle, on which occasion Lancelot wears Galiot's armour, and is at first mistaken for him, till Sir Gawain's acute vision detects that the armour

[1] See Appendix.

really encases the black knight. As Lancelot now fights on
Galiot's side, it may easily be imagined how utter and complete
is the defeat of Arthur's army, which was before victorious
owing to his aid only; and we are told that Arthur is ready to
kill himself out of pure grief and chagrin, whilst Sir Gawain
swoons so repeatedly, for the same reason, as to cause the most
serious fears to be entertained for his life. At this sorrowful
juncture Lancelot again claims his boon of Galiot, who, in the
very moment of victory, determines at last to grant it, and
most humbly sues for mercy at the hands of Arthur, to that
king's most intense astonishment. By this very unexpected
turn of affairs, the scene of dolour is changed to one of un-
alloyed joy, and peace is immediately agreed upon, to the
satisfaction of all but some true-bred warriors, who preferred
a battle to a peace under all circumstances. Not long after,
Galiot discovers Lancelot with eyes red and swollen with much
weeping, and endeavours to ascertain the reason of his grief,
but with small success. After endeavouring to comfort
Lancelot as much as possible, Galiot goes to visit King Arthur,
and a rather long conference takes place between them as they
stand at Sir Gawain's bedside, the queen being also present.
In the course of it, Galiot asks Arthur what price he would
pay to have the black knight's perpetual friendship; to which
Arthur replies, he would gladly share with him half of everything that he possessed, saving only Queen Guinevere. The
question is then put to Gawain, who replies that, if only his
health might be restored, he would wish to be the most beauti-
ful woman in the world, so as to be always beloved by the
knight. Next it is put to Guinevere, who remarks that Sir
Gawain has anticipated all that a lady could possibly wish, an
answer which is received with much laughter. Lastly, Arthur
puts the question to Galiot himself, who declares that he would
willingly, for the black knight's sake, suffer that all his honour
should be turned into shame, whereat Sir Gawain allows him-

self to be outbidden. The queen then obtains a brief private conference with Galiot, and prays him to obtain for her an interview with the black knight, who promises to do what he can to that end. He accordingly sounds the black knight upon the subject, and, finding him entirely of the same mind, does all he can to promote their acquaintance, and is at last only too successful; and at this point we may suppose the Scottish Romance to have stopped, if indeed it was ever completed. For some account of the Romance of Lancelot, I may refer the reader to Professor Morley's English Writers, vol. i., pp. 568—570, and 573; to "Les Romans de la Table Ronde," par M. Paulin Paris; and to the Prefaces to the "Seynt Graal," edited by Mr Furnivall for the Roxburghe Club, 1861, and "La Queste del Saint Graal," also edited by the same for the same club in 1864. In the last-named volume short specimens are given from thirteen MSS. at Paris, ten of which contain the Romance of Lancelot. There are also manuscript copies of it in the British Museum, viz., MSS. Harl. 6341 and 6342, Lansdowne 757, and MS. Addit. 10293.

III.—THE DIALECT OF THE POEM.

In coming to discuss the dialect, we find everywhere traces of considerable confusion; but it is not at all easy to assign a satisfactory reason for this.[1] Certain errors of transcription soon shew that the scribe had before his eyes an older copy, which he mis-read. Thus, in l. 433, we find " set," where the older copy must have had "fet," and which he must have misread as "fet;" and again, in lines 2865, 2883, he has, by a similar confusion between "f" and "f," written "firft" instead of "fift." It is most probable that the older copy was

[1] For many valuable remarks upon the dialect of the poem I am indebted to Mr R. Morris.

written in the Lowland Scottish dialect (the whole tone of
the poem going to prove this), as shewn by the use of *ch* for
gh, as in *bricht* for *bright*, (unless this be wholly due to the
scribe) ; by the occurrence of plurals in -*is*, of verbal preterites
and passive participles in -*it*, and of words peculiarly Scottish,
such as *syne* (afterwards), *anerly* (only), *laif* (remainder), *oft-
syss* (oft-times), etc.   Moreover, the Northern *r* is clearly
indicated by the occurrence of such dissyllables as *gar-t*, 2777,
lar-g, 2845, *fir-st*, 2958, 3075 ; with which compare the sig-
nificant spellings *harrmful*, 1945, and *furrde*, 2583.   But, on
the other hand, it would appear as if either the author or the
copyist had no great regard for pure dialect, and continually
introduces Southern and Midland forms, mixing them together
in an indiscriminate and very unusual manner.   We find, for
example, in line 1765,

> " B*eith* larg and iff*is* frely of thi thing,"

the Scottish form *iffis* (give) and the Southern *beith* in close
conjunction ; and we find no less than six or seven forms of
the plural of the past tense of the verb "to be ;" as, for
example, *war* (3136), *veir* (818), *ware* (825), *waren* (3301),
veryng (2971), *waryng* (443), etc.   If we could suppose that
the scribe was not himself a Scotchman, we might in some
measure account for such a result ; but the supposition is
altogether untenable, as the peculiar character of the hand-
writing (resembling that found, not in English, but in
French MSS.) decides it to be certainly Scottish ; as is also
evident from the occurrence, in the same hand-writing, of a
Scotticised version of Chaucer's " Flee from the press."

The best that can be done is to collect a few instances of
peculiarities.

1. The broad Northumbrian forms *a, ane, baith, fra, ga, haill,
hame, knaw, law, sa, wat*, although occasionally retained, are
also at times changed into *o, one, boith, fro, go, holl, hom, know*,

low, so, and *wot.* Thus, at the end of l. 3246, we find *haill,* which could not have been altered without destroying the rime; but in l. 3078, we find it changed, in the middle of the line, into *holl.* In l. 3406, we find *sa,* but only three lines further on we find *so* twice.

So, too, we not only find *tane* (taken), *gais* (goes), but also the forms *tone* and *goſ.* See lines 1071, 1073.

2. The true plural form of the verb is shewn by lines 203, 204,   " Of quhois fame and worschipful dedis
                Clerkis into diuerſ bukis *redis,*"

where alteration would have ruined the rime utterly; and the same termination (-*is*) is correctly used in the imperative mood, as,   ——" ſo *giffis* ws delay " (l. 463);
       " And of thi wordis *beis* trew and stable" (l. 1671);

but the termination -*ith* is continually finding its way into the poem, even as early as in the fourth line,

       " *Uprisith* arly in his fyre chare ; "

and in the imperative mood also, as,

       " *Remembrith* now it stondith one the poynt" (l. 797).

The most singular point of all, however, is this—that, not content with changing -*is* into -*ith* in the 3rd person singular, the scribe has done the same even in the 2nd person, thus producing words which belong to no pure example of any distinct dialect. Observe the following lines :—

       " O woful wrech, that *levis* in to were !
         To schew the thus the god of loue me sent,
         That of thi seruice no thing is content,
         For in his court yhoue [= thou] *lewith* in disspar,
         And vilfully *sustenis* al thi care,
         And *schapith* no thinge of thine awn remede,
         Bot *clepith* ay and *cryith* apone dede," etc. (ll. 84-90).

Here *levis* is altered into *lewith,* not only unnecessarily, but quite wrongly. For similar mistakes, see ll. 1019, 1369, 1384,

2203. For examples of correct usage, see ll. 1024, 1337, 1796, 2200, 2201.

3. But the terminations which are used in the most confused manner of all are -*en*, -*yne*, and -*ing* or -*yng*. Thus we find the non-Scottish infinitives, *telen* (494), *makine* (191) ; the constant substitution of -*ing* for -*and* in the present participle ;[1] a confusion between the past participial ending -*ine* (more correctly -*yn*), and the present ending -*and*, thus producing such forms as *thinkine* (34), and *besichyne* (418) ; and also a confusion between -*ing* and the past participial ending -*en*, as *fundyng* for *funden* (465), *fallyng* for *fallen* (1217, 1322, 3267), *swellyng* for *swollen* (1222), and *halding* for *halden* (2259). We even find -*ing* in the infinitive mood, as in *awysing* (424), *viting* (to know, 410), *smyting* (1326), *warnnyng* (1035), *passing* (2148), *fchewing* (2736), etc. ; and, lastly, it occurs in the plural of the indicative present, instead of the Midland -*en ;* as in *passing* (1166), *biding* (2670), and *levyng* (3304).[2]

It may safely be concluded, however, that the frequent occurrence of non-Scottish infinitives must not be attributed to the copyist, since they are probably due rather to the author ; for in such a line as

"Of his desir to viting the sentens " (l. 410),

the termination -*ing* is required to complete the rhythm of the line.

In the same way we must account for the presence of the prefix *i*-, as in the line

" Quharwith that al the gardinge was I-clede " (l. 50).

---

[1] We find the true forms occasionally, as *obeisand* (641), *plesand* (1731), *thinkand* (2173), *prekand* (3089), and *fechtand* (3127). Compare the form *seruand* (122).

[2] " The Scottish pronunciation of -*ing* was already, as it still is, -*een ;* and the writer, knowing that the correct spelling of *dwellin*, for example, was *dwelling*, fancied also that *fallen*, *halden* (Sc. *fallyn*, *haldyn*) were *fallyng*, *haldyng*. Lyndesay and Gawain Douglas often do the same. Compare *gardinge* (l. 50), *laiting* (l. 327)."—J. A. H. Murray.

This prefix never occurs in vernacular Scottish; but we may readily suppose that this and other numerous Southern forms of words are due (as in Gawain Douglas and Lyndesay) to the author's familiarity with Chaucer's poems, as evinced by the similarity of the rhythm to Chaucer's, and by the close resemblance of several passages. Compare, for instance, the first seventy lines of the Prologue with the opening passages of "The Flower and the Leaf," and "The Complaint of the Black Knight;" and see notes to ll. 432, 1608. Indeed, this seems to be the only satisfactory way of accounting for the various peculiarities with which the poem abounds.

Mr J. A. H. Murray, in his remarks printed in the preface to Mr Lumby's edition of "Early Scottish Verse," comes to a similar conclusion, and I here quote his words for the reader's convenience and information. "There is no reason, however, to suspect the scribe of *wilfully* altering his original; indeed, the reverse appears manifest, from the fact that the 'Craft of Deyng' has not been assimilated in orthography to 'Ratis Raving,' but distinctly retains its more archaic character; while in 'Sir Lancelot,' edited by Mr Skeat for the Early English Text Society, from the handwriting of the same scribe, we have a language in its continual Anglicisms quite distinct from that of the pieces contained in this volume, of which the Scotch is as pure and unmixed as that of the contemporary Acts of Parliament. With regard to the remarkable transformation which the dialect has undergone in Sir Lancelot, there seems reason, therefore, to suppose that it was not due to the copyist of the present MS., but to a previous writer, if not to the author himself, who perhaps affected *southernism*, as was done a century later by Lyndesay and Knox, and other adherents of the English party in the Reformation movement. The Southern forms are certainly often shown by the rhyme to be original, and such a form as *tone* for *tane* = taken, is more likely to have been that of a Northerner trying to write

Southern, than of a Southern scribe, who knew that no such word existed in his dialect. The same may be said of the *th* in the second person singular. A Scotch writer, who observed that Chaucer said *he liveth*, where he himself said *he lyres,* might be excused for supposing that he would also have said *thou liveth* for the Northern *thow lyres;* but we can hardly fancy a Southern copyist making the blunder.'

4. We find not only the Northumbrian forms *sall* and *suld,* but also *shall, shalt,* and *shuld.*

5. As regards pronouns, we find the Scottish *scho* (she) in l. 1169; but the usual form is *sche.* We find, too, not only the broad forms *thai, thair, thaim,* but also *thei* (sometimes *the*), *ther,* and *them.* As examples of forms of the relative pronoun, we may quote *who, quho, whois, quhois* (whose), *quhom, quhome* (whom), *quhat, qwhat* (what), and *whilk, quhilk, quhich, quich, wich* (which). *Wich* is used instead of *who* (l. 387), and we also find *the wich,* or *the wich that,* similarly employed. The nominative *who* does not perhaps occur as a *simple* relative, but has the force of *whoso,* or *he who,* as e. g., in l. 1102; or else it is used interrogatively, as in l. 1172.

6. Many other peculiarities occur, which it were tedious to discuss fully. It may suffice, perhaps, to note briefly these following. We find both the soft sound *ch,* as in *wich, sich,* and the hard sound *k,* as in *whilk, reke* (reach), *streke* (stretch), etc.; which are the true Northern forms.

Mo is used as well as *more.*

Tho occurs for *then* in l. 3184; and for *the* in l. 247.

At occurs as well as *that; atte* as well as *at the,* 627, 1055.

The short forms *ma* (make), *ta* (take), *sent* (sendeth), *stant* (standeth), are sometimes found; the two former being Northumbrian.

Has is used twice as a *plural* verb (ll. 481, 496).[1]

---

[1] "The plural in Scottish always ends in -*s* after a noun or when the verb is separated from its pronoun; we still say *the men hes, the bairns sings, them*

ȝha (yes) occurs in l. 2843; but we also meet with ȝhis, or yis; with reference to which Mr Morris writes:—"The latter term was not much in favour with the people of the North. Even now yes sounds offensive to a Lancashire man. 'Hoo cou'd naw opp'n hur meawth t' sey eigh (yea) or now (no); boh simpurt on sed iss; th' dickons iss hur on him too.—Tim Bobbin.'" In fact, the distinction between ȝha and ȝhis, which I have pointed out in William of Palerne (Glossary, s. v. ȝis), viz., that ȝha merely assents, whilst ȝhis shews that the speaker has an opinion of his own, is in this poem observed. Thus, in l. 2843, ȝha = "yes, I admit that I do;" but in l. 514, yis = "yes, but you had better do so;" in l. 1397, ȝhis = "yes, indeed I will;" and in l. 3406, ȝis = "yes, but I cannot accept your answer."[1] The true distinction between thou and ye (William of Palerne, Pref. p. xli) is also generally observed. Thus the Green Bird, in the Prologue, considers the poet to be a fool, and calls him thou; but the clerks, in addressing Arthur (l. 498) politely say ye. And again, Amytans, when rebuking Arthur, frequently calls him thou, without any ceremony. Cf. ll. 659, 908, 921, 2839, &c.

As regards the vocabulary, we find that some Northumbrian terms have been employed, but others thrown aside. Thus, while we find the Northumbrian words thir (these), traist (trust), newis (neives, fists), radour (fear), etc., we do not, on the other hand, meet with the usual Scottish word mirk, but observe it to be supplanted by dirk (l. 2471). So, again, eke is used in the sense of also, instead of being a verb, as more usual in Northern works. We may note, too, the occurrence of frome as well as fra, and the Scottish form thyne-furth (thenceforth) in l. 2196.

'at cums, not have, sing, come. Notice the frequent use of th for t, as in l. 497, Presumyth = presumit, presumed, it being presumed."—J. A. H. Murray. [Or, presumyth may be the pl. imperative, as in Remembrith (l. 797), already noticed.—ED.]

[1] "This ȝis is the common form in the Scottish writers, though ay is largely the modern vernacular."—J. A. H. Murray.

The spelling is very various. We find even four forms of one word, as *cusynace, cusynece, cusynes, cwsynes;* and, as examples of eccentric spelling, may be quoted *qsquyaris* (squires, l. 3204), whilst in l. 3221 we find *squar.*

Both in the marginal abstract and in the notes I have chiefly aimed at removing minor difficulties by explaining sentences of which the construction is peculiar, and words which are disguised by the spelling. For the explanation of more uncommon words, recourse should be had to the Glossarial Index.

APPENDIX.

EXTRACTS FROM THE FRENCH ROMANCE OF
"LANCELOT DU LAC."

As it seems impossible to do justice to the story of Lancelot without giving due attention to the famous French Romance, and since a portion of the French text is really necessary to complete even that fragment of it which the Scottish author proposed to write, the following extracts have been made with the view of shewing (1) the general outline of the earlier part of the story, (2) the method in which the Scottish author has expanded or altered his original, and (3) the completion of the story of the wars between Arthur and Galiot.[1]

I. Headings of the chapters of the French Romance, from its commencement to the end of the wars with Galiot.

[The commas are inserted by the present editor, and the expansions marked by italics.]

¶ Cy commence la table du premier volume de la table ronde lancelot du lac.

¶ Comment apres la mort de vterpandragon roy du royaulme de logres, & apres la mort aramon, roy de la petite bretaigne, le roy claudas de la terre Descosse mena guerre contre le roy ban de benoic et le roy boort de gauues tant quil les desherita[2] de leurs terres. Fueillet. i.

Claudas, king of Scotland, deprives king Ban and king Boort of their lands.

---

[1] The extracts are from the Paris edition of 1513, 3 vols. folio, a copy of which is in the King's Library in the British Museum. There are also two other editions in the Museum, one in the Grenville Library, 3 vols. Paris, 1494, folio; the other in one folio volume, Paris, 1520.   [2] See ll. 1447-1449.

Claudas besieges Ban in the Castle of Trible.

¶ Comment le roy claudas assiegea le chasteau de trible auquel estoit le roy ban de benoic, et comment ilz parlementerent ensemble. f.   i.

King Ban, his wife, and his son Lancelot repair to the court of Arthur.

¶ Comment le roy ban de benoic, accompaigne de sa femme et de son filz lancelot, auecques vng seul escuyer, se partirent du chasteau de trible pour aller querir secours deuers le roy Artus a la grant bretaigne. Fueillet   ii.

The Castle of Trible is treacherously given up to Claudas.

¶ Comment apres ce que le roy ban fut party de son chasteau de trible, le seneschal a qui il auoit baille la garde trahit ledit chasteau, et le liura es mains du roy claudas. Fueillet.   ii.

King Ban dies of grief, and Lancelot is taken away by the lady of the lake.

¶ Comment le roy ban mourut de dueil quant il veit son chasteau ardoir et brouyr. Et comment la dame du lac emporta son filz lancelot.[1] Fueillet.   iiii.

¶ Comment la royne helaine, apres que le roy fut mort et elle eut perdu son filz, se rendit nonnain en labbaye du monstier royal. Fueillet.   v.

¶ Comment le roy de gauues mourut | & comment la Royne sa femme, pour paour de claudas, sen partit de son chasteau pour aller au monstier royal, ou sa seur

The two sisters, widows of kings Ban and Boort, retreat to a monastery.

estait rendue. et comment ses enfans Lyonnel et Boort luy furent ostez. Fueillet   vi.

¶ Comment la royne de Gauues, apres que son seigneur fut mort et que elle eut perdu ses deux enfans, se vint rendre au monastere ou estoit sa seur la royne de benoic. Fueillet   vi.

Merlin's love for the lady of the lake.

¶ Comment merlin fut engendre du dyable : Et comment il fut amoureux de la dame du lac. Fueillet vii.

Sir Farien secretly nourishes the two sons of king Boort, and is made seneschal to king Claudas.

¶ Comment le cheualier farien, qui auoit tollu a la royne de Gauues ses deux enfans, les emporta en sa maison | et les feist nourrir vne espace de temps. Et comment le roy claudas fut amoureux de la femme du dict Farien | et pource le fist son seneschal. Fueillet viii.

Claudas accuses Sir Farien of treason.

¶ Comment le roy claudas fist appeller son cheualier farien de trahison par ladmonnestement de sa femme, disant quil gardoit les deux enfans du roy boort de gauues Fueillet.   viii.

Claudas, in disguise, visits Arthur's court.

¶ comment le roy claudas en maniere de cheualier estrange, se partit du royaulme de gauues pour aller en la grant bretaigne a la court du roy artus pour veoir sa puissance & son gouuernement. Fueillet   x.

The lady of the lake informs Lancelot that he is a king's son.

¶ Comment la dame du lac bailla a lancelot vng maistre pour linstruyre comme il appartenoit a filz de roy. Fueillet   xii.

¶ Comment la royne helaine alloit faire chascun iour

[1] Lines 215, 220.

son dueil au lieu ou son seigneur mourut | et de la
alloit au lac ou elle perdit son filz.   Fueillet   xv.

¶ Comment le bon Religieux qui auoit dit nouuelles
a la royne helaine de son filz lancelot, print conge de   .
elle, et sen vint au roy artus en la grant bretaigne.
Fueillet   xvi.

¶ Comment la dame du lac enuoya sa damoyselle a   The lady of the
la court du roy claudas, pour delyurer les deux enfans   lake seeks to de-
au roy boort que claudas tenoit en prison. Fueillet xvii.   king Boort.

¶ Comment farien, seneschal du roy claudas par le
commandement de son seigneur, alla querir en prison
les deux filz au roy de Gauues.   Fueillet   xviii.

¶ Comment les deux enfans au roy de gauues   Lyonnel and
blecerent le roy claudas, & occirent dorin son filz | et   Boort wound
comment la damoyselle du lac les emmena en semblance   and slay his son
de deux leuriers. fueil.   xix.   Dorin.

¶ De la grant ioye et du grant honneur que la dame
du lac fist aux deux enfans quant elle les veit en sa
maison.   Fueillet   xx.

¶ Comment le roy claudas mena tres grant dueil   Claudas bewails
pour la mort de dorin son filz que boort auoit occis.   his son's death.
Fueillet   xx.

¶ Comment farien et le peuple de la cyte de gauues
sesmeurent contre le roy claudas a cause que il vouloit
faire mourir les deux filz au roy boort de gauues.
Fueillet.   xxi.

¶ Comment le roy claudas se partit de gauues | et
comment ceulx dudit lieu le vouloient occire, se neust   Farien saves
este farien le bon cheualier. f.   xxiii.   Claudas' life.

¶ Comment le roy claudas se deffendit vaillamment
contre ceulx de Gauues qui le vouloyent occire.   Fueillet.   xxv.

¶ Comment lyonnel et boort perdirent le boire et le
manger pource quilz ne scauoyent nouuelles de leur
maistres | lesquelz estoyent demourez auec le roy claudas
| & comment la dame du lac enuoya vne sienne damoy-
selle a gauues pour les amener.   Fueillet.   xxvii.

¶ Comment, par le conseil des barons de gauues :   Leonce and Lam-
leonce & lambegues sen allerent auecques la damoyselle   begues go to seek
pour veoir leurs seigneurs lyonnel et boort. Fueillet xxviii.   Boort.

¶ Comment la dame du lac sen retourna apres ce
quelle eut monstre a leonce et a lambegues les enfans du
roy de gauues leurs seigneurs, et comment lesditz cheualiers sen retournerent a gauues.   Fueillet   xxx.

¶ Comment le roy claudas retourna a gauues, pour   Claudas medi-
soy venger de la honte quon luy auoit faicte, et pour la   tates revenge.
mort de son filz.   Fueil.   xxxi.

¶ Comment lappointement fut fait entre le roy
claudas et les barons, par le moyen de farien et lambegues son nepueu. fueillet. xxxiii.

Death of Farien.·

¶ Comment farien | sa femme, et son nepueu
lambegues sen partirent pour aller veoir lyonnel et
boort, qui estoyent au lac | & comment farien mourut.
Fueillet xxxv.

The widow of
king Boort sees
her children and
Lancelot in a
vision, and dies.

¶ Comment les deux roynes menerent saincte vie au
monstier royal | et comment celle de gaues veit ces
deux enfans & lancelot en aduision | et comment elle
trespassa de ce siecle. Fueillet. xxxv.

Arthur holds a
tournament, and
Banin, son of
king Ban, is the
victor.

¶ Comment le roy artus assembla le iour de pasques
tous ses barons, & tint grant court a karahes, et comment banin le filleul au Roy ban emporta le pris du
behourdys celluy iour. Fueillet. xxxvi.

The lady of the
lake sends Lance-
lot to Arthur to
be knighted, and
provides for him
white armour.

¶ Comment la dame du lac se pourpensa de mener
lancelot au roy artus pour le faire cheualier,[1] et elle luy
bailla armes blanches, et partit du lac a tout quarante
cheualliers pour le conuoyer. Fueillet xxxvii.

Of the wounded
knight who came
to Arthur's court.

¶ Comment vng cheuallier naure, lequel auoit vne
espee fichee en la teste et deux troncons de lance parmy
le corps,[2] vint a la court du roy artus | et comment la
dame du lac le mena deuant le roy artus, et luy prya
quil le fist cheualier. Fueillet xxxix.

Lancelot is
knighted.

¶ Comment messire yuain, a qui le roy Artus auoit
recommande lancelot, alla faire sa requeste audit roy
artus, que le lendemain il fist ledit lancelot cheualier, et
comment ledit lancelot defferra le cheualier naure.[3]
Fueillet. xli.

How the white
knight defended
the lady of No-
halt,

¶ Comment la dame de noehault[4] enuoya deuers le
roy artus, luy supplier quil luy enuoyast secours contre
le Roy de norhombellande qui luy menoit guerre. Et
comment Lancelot requist au roy artus quil luy donnast
congie dy aller | & il luy octroya. Fueillet xlii.

and won the
battle for her.

¶ Comment le nouueau cheualier aux armes blanches
vainquit la bataille pour la dame de noehault. Fueillet xliii.

¶ Comment lancelot apres ce quil se fut party de la
dame de noehault, se combatit auec vng cheualier qui
lauoit mouille. Fueillet xlv.

How Lancelot
conquered the
"Sorrowful
Castle."

¶ Comment lancelot conquist vaillamment par sa
force et proesse le chasteau de la douloureuse garde que
nul aultre ne pouoit conquerre.[5] Fueillet xlv.

How Arthur
hears of it, and
sends Gawain to
see if it is true.

¶ Comment les nouuelles vindrent au roy artus que
la douloureuse garde estoit conquise par la cheualier

---

[1] Line 223.   [2] Lines 237-245.   [3] Lines 249-252.
[4] Line 255.   [5] Lines 257-259.

aux armes blanches | Et le roy y enuoya messire gauuain pour en scauoir la verite. Fueillet xlviii.

¶ Comment messire Gauuain fut mys en prison | et comment le roy et la royne entrereut en la premiere porte de la | et la veirent des tumbes ou il y auoit escript que monseigneur gauuain estoit mort, et plusieures aultres cheualiers. Fueillet. xlix.

Gawain is imprisoned, and supposed to be dead.

¶ Comment vne damoyselle de lhostel de la dame du lac feist assauoir au cheuallier blanc que monseigneur gauuain & ses compaignons estoyent emprisonnez par celluy qui auoit este seigneur de la douloureuse garde. Fueillet l.

Lancelot hears of Gawain's imprisonment,

¶ Comment le blanc cheualier se combatit encontre celluy qui auoit este seigneur de la douloureuse garde, qui tenoit en prison messire gauuain et ses compaignons.[1] Fueillet. l.

and delivers him and his companions.

¶ Comment le cheuallier blanc emmena le cheualier conquis en vng hermitaige. et comment ledit cheualier conquis luy rendit audit hermitage gauuain & ses compaignons. f. lii.

¶ Comment messire gauuain et ses compaignons sen vindrent par deuers le roy artus qui estoit a la douloureuse garde. Et comment le roy et la royne furent ioyeulx quant ilz les virent. Fueillet. liii.

Gawain returns to Arthur and his Queen at Douloureuse Garde.

¶ Comment le cheuallier blanc retourna a labbaye ou il auoit laisse ses escuyers | et comment il sceut lassemblee qui deuoit estre entre le roy artus et le roy doultre les marches, & comment il conquist le cheualier qui disoit mieulx aymer le cheualier qui auoit naure que celluy qui lauoit este.[2] Fueillet. liiii.

Lancelot hears of the war to come between Arthur and Galiot.

¶ Comment messire gauuain se mist en queste pour trouuer le blanc cheuallier.[3] Et comment la meslee dentre les gens au roy des cent cheualiers et les gens de la dame de noehault fut appaisee. Fueillet lv.

Gawain goes to seek the white knight,

¶ Comment le blanc cheualier vainquit lassemble dentre les deux roys | et comment il fut naure du roy des cent cheualiers. Fueillet. lvi.

who is wounded in the battle against Galiot by the king-of-a-hundred-knights.

¶ Comment apres que le cheualier qui auoit gangne le tournoyement dentre le roy doultre les marches sen fut alle, le roy artus & la royne genieure se partirent pour aller en leurs pays. Fueillet lvii.

Arthur and Queen Genure return home.

¶ Comment messire gauuain se combatit a brehainsans-pitie, et le rua par terre. et comment apres ilz sen allerent a la douloureuse garde : & comment les deux pucelles que messire Gauuain menoit luy furent tollues. Fueillet. lviii.

---

[1] Lines 263, -4.   [2] See ll. 244, -5.   [3] Line 267.

Lancelot ends the adventures of the "Sorrowful Castle."

¶ Comment lancelot print congie de son mire | et comment il mist a fin les aduentures de la douloureuse garde. Fueillet lx.

Lancelot is again victorious in the combat between Arthur and Galiot.

¶ Comment messire gauuain recouura les deux pucelles qui luy auoyent este tollues, Et comment lancelot vainquit la seconde assemblee dentre le roy artus & le roy doultre les marches. Fueillet lxi.

Gawain returns to Arthur's court.

¶ Comment messire gauuain retourna a la court du roy artus apres la seconde assemblee dentre le roy artus & le roy doultre les marches, et comment lancelot vainquit le cheualier qui gardoit le gue. Fueillet lxiii.

[*Here begins the Scotch Translation.*]

Arthur's evil dreams.

¶ Comment le roy Artus songea plusieurs songes | et apres manda tous les saiges clercs de son royaulme pour en scauoir la signifiance.[1] Fueillet lxiiii.

Galiot defies Arthur.

¶ Comment le roy doultre les marches, nomme gallehault, enuoya deffier le roy artus[2] | et comment Lancelot occist deux geans empres kamalot.[3] Fueillet lxv.

Lancelot is assailed by forty knights, and imprisoned by the lady of Melyhalt.

¶ Comment lancelot occist vng cheualier qui disoit moins aymer le cheualier naure que celluy qui lauoit naure.[4] | et comment il fut assailly de .xl. cheualliers, et mys en prison de la dame de mallehault.[5] Fueillet lxviii.

Lancelot, released from prison, is again victorious against Galiot.

¶ Comment gallehault assembla au roy artus vng iour durant que lancelot estoit en prison[6] | et comment le lendemain lancelot fut deliure de prison[7] | et vainquit lassemblee dentre les deux roys.[8] Fueillet lxvii.

Arthur is reproved by Amytans, and Galiot proposes a truce for a year.

¶ Comment le roy artus fut reprins de ses vices, et moult bien conseille par vng cheualier qui suruint en son ost[9] | Et comment gallehault donna tresues au roy Artus iusques a vng an.[10] Fueillet lxix.

Lancelot returns to the lady of Melyhalt.

¶ Comment lancelot, apres ce quil eut vaincu lassemblee, retourna en la prison de la dame de mallehault[11] | et comment elle le congneut, a son cheual et par les playes quil auoit, que cestoit celluy qui auoit vaincu lassemblee.[12] Fueillet lxxii.

Gawain, with 39 comrades, departs to seek the red knight.

¶ Comment messire gauuain, soy quarantiesme de compaignons, se mist en queste pour trouuer le cheuallier qui auoit porte lescu vermeil a lassemblee dentre le roy artus et Gallehault.[13] Fueillet lxxii.

The lady of Melyhalt accepts Lancelot's ransom.

¶ Comment la dame de mallehault mist a rancon le cheuallier quelle tenoit en prison, et le laissa aller quant elle veit quelle ne peult scauoir son nom.[14] fu. lxxiii.

[1] Lines 363-527. [2] Lines 540-592. [3] Line 280.
[4] Lines 233-252. [5] Lines 281-292 [6] Lines 634-894.
[7] Lines 895-974. [8] Lines 975-1138. [9] Lines 1275-2130.
[10] Lines 1543-1584. [11] Lines 1139-1152. [12] Lines 1181-1274.
[13] Lines 2161-2256. [14] Lines 2347-2442.

¶ Comment messire gauuain et ses compaignons retournerent de leur queste[1] | et comment apres les treues faillies galehault vint assembler contre le roy artus, & tous ses gens en furent moult troublez.[2] fu.　　lxxiiii.

The truce ended, Galiot again attacks Arthur.

¶ Comment gallehault suyuit le cheuallier aux noires armes,[3] & fist tant par belles parolles quil lemmena en son ost, dont le roy artus et tous ses gens en furent moult troublez. Fueillet　　lxxviii.

Galiot gains over the black knight.

¶ Comment lancelot par sa prouesse conquist tout, et fist tant que gallehault crya mercy au roy artus. fu.　　˙-　　lxxix.

Lancelot induces Galiot to submit to Arthur.

¶ Comment gallehault fist tant que la royne vit lancelot | & comment ilz se arraisonnerent ensemble. fu. lxxxi.

The Queen and Lancelot meet.

¶ Comment la royne congneut lancelot apres ce quil eut longuement parle a elle, & quil luy eut compte de ses aduentures. & comment la premiere acointance fut faicte entre la royne & lancelot par le moyen de galehault. fu.　˙　　lxxxii.

The Queen knows Lancelot from his adventures that he tells her.

¶ Comment la premiere acointance fut faicte de galehault & de la dame de malehault par le moyen de la royne de logres, & comme[nt] lancelot & galehault sen alloyent esbatre & deuiser auecques leurs dames. fu.　　lxxxiiii.

Galiot becomes acquainted with the lady of Melyhalt.

II. The Chapter of the French romance from which the translator has taken the beginning of his First Book is here given, in order to shew in what manner he has treated his original.　It begins at Fol. lxiii. *a*, col. 1.

Comment le roy artus songea plusieurs songes, et apres manda tous les sages clercz de son royaulme pour en scauoir la signifiance.

Arthur's evil dreams.

OR dit le compte que le roy artus auoit longuement seiourne a cardueil. Et pource ny auenoit mie grandement de aduentures, il ennuya moult aux compaignons du Roy de ce quilz auoient si longuement seiourne, & ne veoient riens de ce quilz souloyent veoir. Principallement keu le seneschal en fut trop ennuye Et en parloit moult souuent, et disoyt deuant le roy que trop estoit ce seiour ennuyeulx, & trop auoit dure. Le roy luy demande " Keu | que vouldriez vous que nous feissons ? " " Certes," fait keu, " ie conseilleroye que nous allissions a kamalot | car la cite est plus aduan-

King Arthur being at Carduell,

his knights are annoyed at meeting with no adventures.

Sir Kay counsels that they should go to Camelot.

---

[1] Lines 2504-2530.　　　　[2] Lines 2531-3268.
[3] Lines 3343-3487.

tureuse que vous ayez | et la nous verrions souuent et orrions choses de merueilles que nous ne voyons pas icy. Nous auons seiourne ia icy plus de deux moys, et oncques ne y veismes gueres de choses aduenir." " Or alons donc," fait le roy, " a Kamalot, puis que vous le conseillez." Lendemain deust partir le roy | mais la nuyct luy aduint vne merueilleuse aduenture. Il songa que tous les cheueulx de sa teste cheoient, et tous les poilz de sa barbe, dont il fut moult espouente. Et par ce demoura encores en la ville. La tierce nuyt apres il songa que il luy estoit aduis que tous les dois luy cheoient fors les poulces, & lors fut plus esbahy que deuant.

A Lautre nuyt songea il que tous les ortelz des piedz luy cheoient fors les poulces. de ce fut si trouble que plus ne peult. " Sire," fait son chappelain a qui il lauoit dit, " ne vous chaille | car songes ne sont pas a croire ;" le roy le dit a la royne, et elle respond tout ainsi que luy auoit fait son chappelain. " En verite," dist il, " ie ne laisseray pas la chose ainsi " | il fait mander ses euesques et archeuesques quilz soient a luy au .ix iour ensuyuant a kamalot, & quilz amainent auec eulx tous les plus sages clercz quils pourroient auoir et trouuer. A tant se part de cardueil & sen va par les chasteaulx et par les citez | tant que au neufniesme iour est venu a kamalot, et aussi sont venus les clercz du pays. Il leur demande conseil de son songe, et ilz elisent dix des plus sages : le roy les fist bien enserrer, et dist que iamais nen sortiroient de prison deuant quilz luy auroient dit la signifiance de son songe. Ilz esprouuerent la force de leur science par neuf iours, et puis vindrent au roy, & dirent quilz nauoient riens trouue. " Ainsi maist dieu," dit le roy, "ia ainsi neschapperez." Et ils demandent respit iusques au troisiesme iour ensuyuant, et il leur donne. Les .iii iours passez, ilz reuiennent deuant le roy, et dient que ilz ne peuent riens trouuer | et demandent encores autre delay | et ilz ont. Et de rechief vindrent pour demander aultres troys iours de dilacion, ainsi que le roy auoit songe de tierce nuyt en tierce nuyt. " Or sachez," fait le roy, "que iamais plus nen aurez." Quant vint au tiers iour ilz dirent quilz nauoient rien trouue ; " ce ne vault rien," fait le roy, "ie vous feray tous destruire se vous ne me dictes la verite ;" et ils dirent. " Sire nous ne vous en scairions que dire " Lors se pense le roy quil leur fera paour de mort. Il fait fair vng grant feu, & commanda en leurs presences que les .v. y fus-

The king consents to go;

but the same night dreams that all his hair falls off, which delays him.
The third night after he dreams that all his fingers fall off except his thumbs.

Again, that all his toes fall off except his great toes.

The Queen and his chaplain disregard the dreams;

but Arthur sends for his bishops, archbishops, and their wisest clerks;

whom he imprisons till they shall tell him what the dreams mean.

After trying for nine days, they fail.

They twice obtain a delay of three days.

The king threatens to slay them.

Five are to be burnt, and five hung.

sent mis, et que les autres cinq soyent penduz | mais
priueement deffent a ses baillifz quilz ne les menassent
que iusques a la paour de mourir. Quant les cinq qui
furent menez aux fourches euerent les cordes entour *The five who are to be hung, having the cords round their necks, offer to speak out.*
leurs colz, ils eurent paour de mourir, et dirent, que se
les aultres cinq le vouloyent dire, ilz le diroyent. La
nouuelle vint au .v. que len menoit ardre | et ilz dirent
que, se les autres le vouloyent dire, ils le diroyent | ils
furent amenez ensemble deuant le roy, et les plus sages
dirent | "sire, nous vous dirons ce que nous auons *They stipulate not to be held as liars if their interpretations fail.*
trouue | mais nous ne vouldrions mie que vous nous
tenissiez a menteurs se il ne aduenoit | car nous vould-
rions bien quil nen fust rien, et voulons, comment quil
en aduiengne, que vous nous asseurez que ia mal ne
nous en aduiendra ;" et il leur promet. Lors dist lung
de eulx qui pour tous parla. "Sire, sachez que ceste *The dreams mean that he will lose his land and his honour.*
terre et tout honneur vous conuiendra perdre et ceulx
en qui plus vous fiez vous fauldront ; telle est la sub-
stance et signifiance de voz songes." De ceste chose fut
le roy moult effraye, "Or me dictes," fait il, "sil est *Arthur asks if anything can avert such fate.*
chose qui men peult garantir." "Certes," fait le
maistre, nous auons veu une chose | Mais cest si grande
merueille que on ne le pourroyt penser, et ne la vous
osons dire." "Dictes," fait il, "seurement | car pis ne
me pouez vous dire que vous mauez dit." "Sire, riens *He is told, "nothing, except the savage lion and the leech without medicine, by help of the counsel of the flower."*
ne vous peult garder de perdre tout honneur terrien fors
le lyon sauluaige, et le mire sans medecine, par le conseil de la fleur, & se nous semble estre si grande folie
que nous ne losions dire | Car lyon sauluaige ne y peult
estre, ne mire sans medecine | ne fleur qui parlast |" le
roy est moult entreprins de ceste chose: mais plus en
fait belle chiere que le cueur ne luy apporte. Ung iour *Arthur goes to the chase.*
alla le roy chasser au boys bien matin | et mena auec
luy messire gauuain, keu le seneschal, et ceulx qui lui
pleust. Si laisse icy le compte a parler de luy, et
retourne a parler du cheualier dont messire Gauuain
aporta le nom en court.

QVant[1] le cheuallier qui lassemblee auoyt vaincu *Lancelot on his wanderings.*
se partast de la ou il se combatist a son hoste,
il erra toute iour sans autre aduanture trouuer. Il se
logea la nuyt chiez une veufue dame a lyssue dune
forest a cinq lieues angleches pres de kamelot. Le
cheualier se leua matin, et erra, luy et ses escuyers et sa *He meets an esquire,*
damoyselle, tant quil encontra vng escuyer. "Varlet,"
fait il, "scez tu nulles nouuelles?" "Ouy," fait il, *and asks him, "what news?"*

[1] There is no trace of the rest of this chapter in the Scottish poem.

"The queen,"
he says, "is at
Camelot."
"ma dame la royne est icy pres a kamalot." "quelle royne" fait il "Le femme au roy artus," fait lescuyer.

Lancelot goes on
till he sees a large
house, a lady, and
her damsel.
Le cheuallier sen part, et cheuauche tant quil treuue vne maison forte, et voit vne dame en son surcot, qui regardoit les prez et la forest | & auoit auec elle vne

He regards her
fixedly.
damoiselle. Le cheuallier se arreste, et regarde la dame moult longuement tant quil oublie tout autre chose. Et maintenant passa vng cheuallier arme de toutes

An armed knight,
passing, asks him
what he is regard-
ing so closely.
armes, qui luy dist. "Sire cheualier, que attendez vous?" et celluy ne respond mot | car il ne la pas ouy. Et le cheualier le boutte, et luy demande quil regarde.

He replies, that
he looks at what
pleases him.
"Je regarde," fait il, "ce que me plaist: Et vous nestes mie courtois, qui de mon penser me auez iecte." "Par

The knight asks
if he knows who
the lady is,
la foy que vous deuez o dieu," fait le cheuallier estrange, scauez vous bien qui la dame est que vous regardez?" "Je le cuyde bien scauoir," fait le bon cheualier. "Et

and he replies
that he knows it
is the queen.
qui este elle," fait lautre. "Cest ma dame la royne." "Si maist dieu, estrangement la congnoissez, deables vous font bien regarder dames." "Pourquoy," faict il. "Pource que vous ne me oseriez suyuir par deuant la Royne la ou ie yroye." "Certes," faict le bon cheuallier, "se vous osiez aller la ou ie vous oseray suyuir, vous aurez passez de couraige tous les plus grans oseurs qui oncques furent." A tant sen part le cheualier. Et

The stranger
takes Lancelot
home to lodge
with him,
le bon cheuallier va apres. Et quant ilz ont vne piece alle, lautre luy dist, "vous he[r]bergerez ennuyt auec moy, et le matin ie vous meneray la ou ie vous diz;" et le bon cheuallier luy demande sil conuient ainsi faire. "Oy" | fait il. Et il dist que donc lottroyera il. Il

and he is well
entertained.
geut la nuyt chez le cheualier sur la riuiere de kamalot, et fut moult bien herberge, et sa pucelle | et ses escuyers.

III. Our last extract will shew exactly where the Scottish poem suddenly ceases, and how the story was probably continued. For the latter purpose, four chapters of the French Romance are added beyond the point where the Scotch ends; and it is possible (judging from lines 306-312 of the Prologue) that the author did not intend to go very much further. The passage begins, in the French copy, at Fol. lxxvii. b, col. 1; and, in the Scotch poem, at l. 3427.

Lors descent de son cheual, et la baille au cheualier.

Galiot gives
Lancelot his own
horse,
Et celluy si y monte sans arrest. Et gallehault monta sur vng autre, et vient a son conroy | Si prent auec

soy les dix mille, et dit quilz voisent assembler deuant;
" et vous," fait il au roy vend, "viendres apres, si ne
assemblerez mie si tost comme ceulx cy seront assem-   *and gives orders to his own men.*
blez | mais quant les derrains de ceulx de dela seront
venus, vous assemblerez, & moy mesmes vous iray
querir." A tant amaine les dix mille pour assembler,[1]
Et quant il fut entre en la bataille il fist sonner ses   *He commands the trumpets to be sounded.*
busines tant que tout en retentissoit.[2] Quant le noir
cheuallier les ouyt venir, si luy sembla que grant effort
de gens eut la, si se retrait vng pou vers les siens, et les
appella entour luy, & leur dist. "Seigneurs, vous estes   *Lancelot harangues his men.*
tous amys du roy. Or y perra comment vous le ferez."[3]
Et messire yuain, qui les vit venir, dist a ses gens,
"Or soyes tous asseurs que nous ne perdrons au iourd-   *Sir Yvain comforts Arthur's soldiers.*
huy par force de gens."[4] Et ce disoit il pource quil
cuidoit que les gens gallehault fussent tous venus.[5]

Qvant les .x.m. de gallehault sassemblerent, si
fut grande la noise, et moult en abbatent a
leur venir | mais quant messire yuain vint, si reconforta
moult les gens du roy artus | et tous les fuyans re-
tournent auec luy. Et gallehault sen va arriere a son   *Galiot orders charge.*
conroy, et commande quilz cheuauchent fermement | et
quilz se frappent es gens du roy artus[6] de telle maniere[7]
que nul dentreulz ne demeure a cheual "Vous estes
tous frays. Or y perra comment vous le ferez." A
tant cheuauchent les conroys deuers leurs gens, Car ilz
auoyent ia du pire. Et quant le conroy de Gallehault   *Galiot's reserve arriving, his men awhile prevail.*
fut venu, si changa moult laffaire | Car moult y auoyt
grant effort de gens. Et fut a leur venue le cheualier
noir mis a terre.[8] Et aussi les six compaignons qui
toute iour auoyent este pres de luy.[9] Lors vint galle-
hault, qui le remonta sur le cheual mesmes ou son corps   *Galiot again remounts Lancelot.*
seoit.[10] Et si tost comme il fut monte, il sen reuint a la
meslee aussi frays comme il auoit le iour este. Et
quant il vint aux coups donner, tous ceulx qui le veoyent
sen esmerueilloyent, Ainsi dura la bataille iusques a la
nuyt. Et quant il vint au soir ilz se departirent | et   *Night arriving, the hosts retreat.*
toutesfoys les gens du roy Artus en eurent du meilleur.
Le bon cheualier se departit de lost le plus coyement   *Lancelot tries to depart unobserved,*
quil peut,[11] et sen alla par vng chemin entre les prestz
et vng tertre, et cuyda que nul ne le veist | mais Galle-

---

[1] Line 3432.   [2] Lines 3435-3440.
[3] Lines 3441-3476.   [4]Lines 3477-3480.
[5] Lines 3481-3484.   [6] Lines 3485, 6.
[7] Line 3487 *and last.*   [8] Compare lines 3365-3368.
[9] Lines 3369, 70.   [10] Compare lines 3391-3426.
[11] Compare line 1140.

but is followed by Galiot,

hault sen print tres bien garde, et picqua tant son
cheual qui luy fut au deuant par vne adresse, et le vint
rencontrer au pied du tertre. Si le salue, et dit ' que
dieu le conduit.' Et celuy le regarde en trauers, et luy
a a moult grant peine rendu son salut. "Bel amy,"
fait galehault, "qui estes vous?" "Sire," fait il, "ie
suis vng cheualier, ce poucz vous veoir." "Certes," fait
galehault, "cheualier estes vous meilleur qui soit | &
vous estes lhomme du monde que plus ie vouldroye

who prays him to lodge with him for that night.

honnourer,[1] et si vous suis venu prier que vous herbergez
ceste nuyt auec moy." Et il luy dist ainsi comme sil
ne lauoit huy veu, "Qui estes vous, sire, qui me auez
prie de me he[r]berger?" "Je suis gallehault, le sire
de ces gens icy, vers qui vous auez au iourdhuy garanty
le royaulme de logres, lequel ie eusse ia conquis se ne
fust vostre corps." "Comment" (fait il) "vous estes
ennemy de monseigneur le roý artus, et me priez de

Lancelot at first refuses, till Galiot agrees to do whatever Lancelot may require of him,

herberger? | Auec vous ne herbergeray ie mie en ce
point." "Haa sire," faict gallehault, "plus feray ie
pour vous, et si nay mye a commencer. Et ie vous
prie que vous y herbergiez par tel conuenant que ie
feray tout ce que me scaurez requerre." A tant se
arresta le cheuallier, et dist a gallehault; "Sire, vous
promettez assez | mais ie ne scay comment il est du
rendre" | et gallehault luy dist. "Sire, se vous he[r]-

and promises to entertain him sumptuously;

whereupon they return together to Galiot's camp.

bergez ennuyt auec moy, ie vous donneray tout ce que
vous oserez diuiser de bouche, et bien vous en feray
seur," Et lors luy fiance, & apres luy promet bailler
bons plaiges; Adonc sen vont tous deux en lost.

¶ Comment gallehault suyuit le cheuallier aux
noires armes, et fist tant par belles parolles quil
lemmena en son ost, donc le roy artus & tous
ses gens en furent moult troublez.

Gawain, seeing Lancelot with Galiot,

MEssire gauuain auoyt veu aller le cheuallier au
noir escu, & le eust voulentiers suiuy sil eust
peu monter a cheual. Lors regarde contre val la riuiere,

tells the Queen that now they are all lost;

et voit gallehault et le cheuallier noir qui retournoyent
pour venir a lost, et dist a la royne, "Haa dame, or
pouons nous bien dire que nous sommes gens perdus |
regardez que gallehault a conquis par scauoir," Et elle
regarde, & voyt que cest le cheuallier noir que gallehault
emmaine; si en est tant iree quelle ne peut dire mot.
Et messire gauuain se pasme en pou dheure plus de

and swoons away more than three times.

trois fois. Le roi artus vint leans | et ouyt le cry que
chascun disoit, "il est mort, il est mort." Si vint a
luy, et lembrassa, et commenca a plorer moult tendre-

[1] Compare lines 2845-8.

ment. Et reuient monseigneur Gauuain de pasmoison ;
Et quant il veit le roy artus, il commence a le blasmer,
et dit. "Ores est venu le terme que les clercz vous
disrent. Regardez le tresor que vous auez huy perdu.
celluy vous toldra terre qui toute iour la vous a garantie
par son corps, et se vous fussiez preudhomme vous
leussiez retenu, ainsi comme a fait le plus preudhomme
qui viue, qui par cy deuant lemmaine." Lors voit le
roy gallehault, qui emmenoit le cheuallier, dont il a tel
dueil que a pou quil ne est cheut | mais de plorer ne se
peut tenir, et toutesfois faict il la plus belle chere quil
peut pour son nepueu reconforter. Et si tost que il vit
en la salle, il fist grant dueil | aussi fist chascun preud-
homme. .

He tells Arthur that his time of misfortune is come ;

for their protector is lost.

Arthur also sees Galiot, and is deeply grieved, but tries to comfort his nephew.

TAnt sont allez gallehault et le cheualier quilz
sont venus empres lost, Adonc luy dist le
cheualier, "Sire, ains que ie entre dedans vostre ost,
faictes moi parler aux deux plus preudhommes que vous
ayez et esquelz vous fiez le plus." Et gallehault lottroye. Lors sen va en son tref, et prent deux des
hommes du monde ou plus il se fie, et leur dist, " Venez
auec moy et vous verrez le plus riche homme du
monde." "Comment," font ilz, "nestes vous mie le
plus riche qui soit au monde?" "Nenny," dist il |
"mais ie le seray ains que ie dorme." Ces deux estoyent
le roy premier conquis | et le roi des cent cheualliers.
Quant ilz virent le cheuallier, si lui firent moult grant
ioye | Car ilz le congneurent bien par ses armes. Et le
cheuallier leur demanda qui ilz estoient | et ilz se nom-
merent sicomme vous auez ouy | et il leur dist.
"Seigneurs, vostre sire vous faict moult grant honneur |
Car il dit que vous estes les deux hommes du monde
que plus il ayme, et entre luy et moy a vne conuenance
que ie vueil que vous oyez | Car il ma fiance que pour
en nuyt herberger auec luy me donnera ce que ie luy
vouldray demander." Et gallehault dist | " vous dictes
verite." "Sire," faict le cheuallier, "ie vueil encores
auoir la seurte de ses hommes." Et gallehault dist,
"Dictes moy comment." "Ilz me fianceront," fait le
cheuallier, "que se vous me faillez de conuenant, ilz
vous guerpiront et sen viendront auec moy la ou ie
diray," Et gallehault dit que ainsi le veult | et il le fait
fiancer. Lors appella gallehault le roy premier conquis
a vne part, et luy dist. "Allez auant & dictes a mes
barons quilz assemblent maintenant a monstre si hon-
norablement comme ilz pourront, et gardez que en mon
tref soient tous les deduys que len pourra trouuer en

Galiot and Lance-lot arrive at Ga-liot's camp,

and Lancelot asks to speak with the two men whom Galiot most trusts.

Galiot takes him to the " first-con-quest " king and the king of a hun-dred knights, and

Lancelot repeats to them his com-pact with Galiot,

and takes their pledge that they will forsake Galiot if he breaks his agree-ment, and will go with himself (Lancelot).

Galiot orders all kinds of entertainments to be brought to his tent.

tout lost." Lors sen va celluy au ferir des esperons, & fist le commandement de son seigneur. Et gallehault tient le cheualier aux parolles, luy & son seneschal, tant que le commandement fust fait. Si ne demoura gueres que encontre eulx vindrent deux cens barons qui

Twenty-eight kings, beside dukes and counts, come to the feast, and honour Lancelot as the flower of the knighthood of the world.

tous estoient hommes de gallehault, .xxviii. roys, et les autres estoient ducz et contes ; la fut le cheuallier tellement honnoure que oncques si grant feste ne fut pour vng homme mescongneu comme len fit pour luy a celle fois | et disoient grans & petis, "Bien viengnez, la fleur de la cheualerie du monde" | et il en auoit grant honte. Ainsi vindrent iusques au tref de gallehault, si ne pourroient estre comtez les dedluys et les instrumens qui leans estoient. A telle ioye fut receu, et quant il fut desarme,

Lancelot is richly attired, and nobly served.

gallehault luy fit apporter vne robe moult riche, et il la vestit. quant le manger fut prest, ilz se assirent a table, et furent noblement scruis, et le cheualier fut moult honnoure.

After supper four beds are prepared, one larger than the rest, for Lancelot.

APres manger commanda gallehault a faire quatre litz desquelz lung estoit plus grant que les aultres. Quant les litz furent si richement atournez, gallehault maine le cheuallier coucher. Et dist. "Sire, vous gerrez icy ;" "Et qui gerra de la ?" fait le cheualier. "Quattre sergens," faict gallehault, "qui vous seruiront | Et ie iray en vne chambre par dela, affin que vous soyez icy plus en paix." "Haa, Sire, pour dieu," faict il, "ne me faictes gesir plus ayse que ces aultres cheualiers | car tant ne me deuez a vilennir." "Nayez

Galiot awhile departs, and Lancelot falls asleep.

garde," faict galehault, "Car ia pour chose que vous faciez pour moi vous ne serez tenu a villain." A tant sen part gallehault. Et le cheuallier commence a penser au grant honneur que gallehault luy faisoit. Si lenprise moult | puis se coucha, et tantost il sendormit | car

Galiot then returns, and lies near Lancelot,

moult estoit las ; Et quant gallehault sceut quil fut endormy, le plus coyement quil peut se coucha en vng autre lit empres luy | et es deux aultres litz se coucherent deux cheualiers, et nestoyent en la chambre que

and hears how his guest murmurs in his sleep.

eulx quatre, sans plus. La nuyt se plaint moult le cheualier en son dormant, et gallehault loit bien, car il ne dormoit gueres. Ains pensa toute la nuyt a le retenir.

Next day they go to hear mass,

Lendemain le cheualier se leua et alla ouyr messe ; et ia estoit gallehault leue | car il ne voulut mie que le

and Lancelot then demands his arms, wishing to depart.

cheualier laperceust. Quant ilz vindrent du monstier, le cheualier demanda ses armes, & gallehault demande pourquoy. Et il dist quil sen vouloit aller. Et gallehault luy dist. "Beau doulx amy, demourez | et ne cuydez mye que ie vous vueille deceuoir. Car vous

noserez ia riens demander que vous nayez. Et sachez
que vous pourriez bien auoir compagnie de plus riche
homme que ie suis | mais vous ne laurez iamais a
homme qui plus vous ayme." "Sire," faict le cheuallier, "ie demoureray donc puis quil vous plaist. Car
meilleure compaignie que la vostre ne pourroye ie mye
auoir | Mais ie vous diray presentement le don pour-
quoy ie demoureray auec vous | et se ie ne lay, ie ny
demoureray ia." "Sire," fait gallehault, "dictes seure-
ment et vous laurez, se cest chose que ie puisse acomplir ;" Et le cheuallier appella ses deux plaiges et dist
deuant eulx, "Je vous demande," fait il, "que si tost
que vous serez au dessus du roy artus, que vous luy
alliez crier mercy si tost comme ie vous en semondray."
Quant gallehault lentent, si en est tout esbahy, et commence a penser. Et les deux roys luy dirent. "A
quoy pensez vous icy endroit, de penser nauez mestier |
car vous auez tant couru que vous ne pouez retourner."
"Comment," faict Gallehault, "cuydez vous que ie me
vueille repentir | se tout le monde estoit mien si luy
oseroye ie bien donner. mais ie pensoye a vng seul mot
quil a dit | mais ia dieu ne maist," dist il, "se vous
nauez le don | car ie ne pourroye riens faire pour vous
ou ie peusse auoir honte. Mais ie vous prye que ne me
tollez vostre compagnie pour la donner a aultruy ;" et
le cheualier luy creanca. Ainsi demoura | et ilz se
asseirent au manger qui estoit appreste. Si font moult
grant ioye par tout lost du cheualier qui est demoure.
Ainsi passerent celle nuyt. Lendemain gallehault et
son compaignon allerent ouyr messe, et gallehault luy
deist | "Sire, il est huy iour dassembler ; voullez vous
armes porter ?" "Ouy," dist il. "donc porterez vous
les miennes," fait gallehault, "pour le commencement."
Et il dist quil les porteroit voulentiers | "mais vous ne
porterez armes," feist il a gallehault, "si non comme
mon sergent ?" "Non," dist il. Lors firent apporter
les armes, & armerent le cheuallier du fort haulbert, &
des chausses qui trop estoyent longues & lees ; Lors se
armerent les gens de gallehault. et pareillement les gens
du roy Artus, & passerent les lices de telz y eut. Touteffoys le roy auoyt deffendu que nul ne les passast. Si
y eut de bonnes ioustes en pou dheure | si se assembler-
ent tous les ostz deuant la lice, & commencerent a faire
armes. Le roy artus estoit a son estandart, et auoit
commande que ilz menassent la royne a sauluete se la
descomfiture tournoit sur eulx | quant tous les ostz
furent assemblez et le bon cheualier fust arme, si cuida

Side notes:

Galiot induces him to stay,

but again promises to do for him whatever he asks.

Lancelot then demands that Galiot shall submit himself to Arthur.

Galiot is confounded, and ponders, but then grants Lancelot's request.

Lancelot remains with him another night.

Next day, the hosts are again armed for battle.

Lancelot is at first mistaken for Galiot; but is recognized by Gawain.

chascun que ce fust gallehault, & disoyent tous. "Voicy gallehault, voicy gallehault" | messire gauuain le congneust bien & dist. "Ce nest mye gallehault | ains est le cheualier aux armes noires, le meilleur cheualier du monde" | & si tost comme ilz furent assemblez, oncques

Arthur's men cannot stand against Lancelot.

ne se tint le roy Artus ne ses gens depuis que le cheualier y fut arriue | et trop se desconfortoyent du bon cheualier qui contre eulx estoit, si furent menez iusques a la lice. car trop estoient grans gens auec gallehault. au partir des lices ce tindrent vne piece et souffrirent longuement | mais le souffrit ny peut riens valoir. Grant fut le meschief des gens au roy artus. et dit le compte que le cheualier neust mie moins de peine de tenir les gens de gallehault que ilz ne passassent oultre la lice quil auoit de chasser les gens au roy Artus. Et nompourtant moult les auoit supportez | & il les eut mis oultre a force sil eust voulu | mais il demoura emmy le pas pour les aultres detenir. Lors regarda tout entour

Lancelot calls upon Galiot to keep his compact.

de luy, et commenca a hucher | "gallehault, gallehault." et gallehault vient grant alleure, et dist. "bel amy, que voulez vous?" "quoy," faict il, "ie vueil que mon conuenant me tenez;" "Par ma foy," fait gallehault, "ie suis tout prest de lacomplir puis quil vous plaist."

Galiot rides forward, and finds Arthur ready to kill himself for grief, the Queen being escorted away by a guard of forty knights, and Gawain wishing to die.

Lors picque le cheual des esperons & vient iusques a lestandart ou le roy artus estoit, qui faisoit si tresgrant dueil que a peu quil ne se occioit pource quil estoit desconfit. Si estoit ia la royne montee, et lemmenoyent quarante cheualliers. Et monseigneur gauuain, que on vouloit emporter en lictiere | mais il dit quil aymeroit mieulx mourir en ce point que veoir toute cheualerie morte et honnye : si se pasma tellement que len cuydoit bien que il mourust incontinent.

How Lancelot makes Galiot cry mercy to Arthur.

¶ Comment lancelot par la prouesse conquis tout, et fist tant que galehault cria mercy au roy artus.

Quant le cheualier veit gallehault prest dacomplir son conuenant, il iura bien que oncques si loyal compaignon ne fut trouue. Il en a telle pytie quil en souspire moult fort, & dit entre ses dens. "Haa dieu,

Galiot demands to see King Arthur,

qui pourra ce desseruir?" & gallehault cheuauche iusques a lestandart et demande le roy artus. Il vient auant moult dolent & esmaye comme celluy qui tout honneur et toute ioye terrienne cuyde auoir perdue ; Et quant gallehault le voit, si luy dit. "sire, roy artus, venez auant, & nayez paour | car ie vueil a vous parler." et quant le roy louyt, il sesmerueille moult que ce peult

and, at sight of him, dismounts, kneels to him,

estre ; Et de si loing comme galehault le voit venir, il descend de son cheual et se agenouille, et dit. "Sire,

ie vous viens faire droit de ce que ie vous ay meffait ;
si men repens, et me metz en vostre mercy." and submits himself to him
humbly.

QVant le roy lentend, il a mcrueilleuscment gra*n*t
ioye, et lieue les mains vers le ciel, louant Dieu
de ceste aduanture | et se le roy fait bonne chere, en-
cores la faict meilleure Gallehault. et il se lieue de
genoulx, & sentrebaisent, en font moult grande chere
lung a lautre. lors dist Gallehault | " sire, faictes vostre
plaisir de moy | car ie metz en vostre saisine mon corps
pour en faire ce que il vous plaira. Et sil vo*us* plaist,
ie yray retraire mes gens arriere, & puis r̃euiendray a
vous incontinent." "Allez doncq*ues*," fait le roy | "car
ie vueil parler a vous." A tant sen part gallehault &
reuient a ses gens | & les en faict aller. Et le roy
enuoya apres la royne, qui sen alloit faisant grand dueil.
et les messages cheuauchent tant que ilz lattaingnent |
et sont venus a elle, & luy comptent la ioye que aduenue
leur est. Et elle ne le peult croire tant q*u*elle voy les
enseignes que le roy luy enuoye. ta*n*t coururent les
nouuelles que mo*n*seigne*ur* gauuain le sceut, lequel en
eut grant ioye sur tous les aultres, et dist au roy.
"Sire, comment a ce este ?" "Certes, ie ne scay," fait
il : "mais ie croy que telle a este le plaisir de nostre
seigneur." moult est grande la ioye, & moult se esmerueille chascun co*m*ment ce peult estre aduenu. Gallehault dist a son compaignon. "que voulez vous que ie
face ? iay fait vostre c̃ommandement ; & le roy ma dit
que ie retourne | mais ie vous conuoyeray aua*n*t iusques
a voz tentes." "Haa sire," fait le cheualier, "aincoys
vous irez au roy & luy porterez le plus grant honneur
que vous pourrez. Et tant auez fait. pour moy que ie
ne le pourroye desseruir | mais tant vous prye, pour
dieu | et pour lamour que vous auez a moy, que nul ne
sache ou ie suis " | ainsi sen vont parlant iusqu*es* a leurs
tentes. chascun scait que la paix est faicte | mais
plusie*ur*s en sont dolens | car mieulx aymassent la
guerre que la paix. lors sont descenduz les deux
compaignons, et si tost quilz furent desarmez, Gallehault print vne de ses meilleures robbes pour aller a la
court. et feist cryer par tout son ost q*ue* chascun sen
allast, fors tant seullement ceulx de son hostel. Apres
appella les deux roys, et leur baille son compaignon, &
leur commande quilz facent autant de luy comme de
son corps mesmes. A tant monte Gallehault, et sen
va a la court du roy artus. Et le roy luy vint alen-
contre, et la royne qui ia estoit retournee, & la dame de
malehault auec plusieurs dames & damoyselles. A tant

Arthur, over-
joyed, praises
God.

Galiot, first ask-
ing Arthur's
leave, dismisses
his troops to their
tents.

The Queen and
Sir Gawain re-
joice greatly.

Lancelot prays
Galiot not to re-
veal where he is,
and they return
to their tents.

Galiot commits
his guest to the
care of the two
kings, and de-
parts to speak
with Arthur.

Arthur and Galiot go together to the tower where Gawain lies ill.

vont en la bretesche ou monseigneur gauuain gisoit
malade. et quant il sceut que gallehault venoit, il
sefforce de belle chere faire, comme celluy qui oncques
mes ne lauoit veu de si pres. lors luy dist | "bien
soyez vous venu comme de celluy dont ie desiroye moult
lacointance | car vous estes lhomme du monde qui plus

Gawain welcomes Galiot.

doibt estre prise & ayme a droit de toutes gens. Et ie
cuyde que nul ne scait si bien congnoistre preudhomme
comme vous & bien y a paru." Ainsi parle messire
gauuain a gallehault, & il luy demande comment il luy
est | et Gauuain dist. "Jay este pres de mort. mais
la grant amour qui est entre vous & le roy ma guery."

The Queen, the King, and Gawain rejoice at Galiot's coming,

Moult font grant ioye le roy artus & la royne & mon-
seigneur gauuain de la venue de gallehault | et tout le
iour ont parle de amour et daccointance. Mais du noir
cheualier ne tiennent ilz nulles parolles | ains passent le
iour a resiouyr lung lautre tant quil vint au vespre.
Lors demande gallehault congie de ses gens aller veoir.

but he, soon after, departs to see Lancelot for a short time, promising to return.

Et le roy le luy donne | "mais vous reuiendrez," fait il,
"incontinent;" et gallehault le luy octroye | si sen-
reuient a son compaignon & luy demande comment il a
lepuis fait | et il luy respondit que bien; "Sire," fait
gallehault, "comment feray ie |: le roy ma moult prie
que ie retourne a luy, & il me feroit mal de vous laisser

Lancelot tells Galiot to do whatever Arthur wishes.

en ce point." "Haa, sire cheualier, pour dieu mercy,
vous ferez ce que monseigneur le roy vouldra. car iamais
a plus preudhomme que il est ne eustes accointance.
Mais ie vueil que vous me donnez vng don." Et galle-

He charges Galiot again not to ask his name, but to tell him about Arthur.

hault luy dist. "Demandez ce quil vous plaira | car ie
ne vous escondiroye iamais;" "Sire," fait il, "ie vous
remercye. Vous me auez donne que vous ne me de-
manderez mon nom deuant que ie le vous diray." "Et
ie men tiendray a tant puis que vous le voulez," dit
gallehault. "Et ne doubtez pas que ce eust este la
premiere chose que ie vous eusse demande, si men
tairay a tant." Lors luy demanda de laccointance du
roy artus | mais il ne nomme mie la royne | et galle-
hault dit que "le roy est moult preudhomme, & moult
me poyse que ie ne lay congneu pieca | Car moult en

Galiot praises the Queen,

feusse amende | mais ma dame la royne est sy vaillante
que oncques plus honneste dame ne vey." et quant le
cheualier ouyt parler de la royne, si se embronche et

and Lancelot sheds tears.

commence a souspirer durement. et gallehault le regarde et se esmerueille moult pource que les larmes luy
cheoyent des yeulx, si commence a parler daultre chose.

Quant ilz ont longuement parle ensemble, le cheualier noir luy dist. "Allez, si ferez a monsei-

gneur le roy compaignie, et si escoutez sy vouz orrez de
moy nulles parolles, & vous me compterez demain ce
que vous aurez ouy." "Voulentiers, sire," faict galle-
hault | lors le accolle, et dit aux roys. "Je vous baille
en garde cest homme comme le cueur de mon ventre."
Ainsi sen va gallehault & le cheuallier demeure en la
garde de deux preu[d]hommes du pays de Gallehault |
mais il ne fault mye demander sil fust honnore | car
len faisoit assez plus pour luy quil neust voulu. celle
nuyt geurent les deux roys au tref gallehault pour
lamour du cheualier & luy firent entendant quilz ny
coucheroyent mye | & ilz le firent coucher ainsi que
Gallehault auoit fait lautre nuyt. Au commencement
dormit le cheualier moult fort, et quant vint a mynuit
si commenca a soy tourner, et commenca a faire vng
dueil si grant que tous ceulz qui entour luy estoyent sen
esueillerent. Et en son refrain disoit souuent. "Haa
chetif, que pourray ie faire?" Et toute nuyt demena
tel deuil. Au matin se leuerent les deux roys le plus
coyement quilz peurent | & moult se merueillent quil
pouoit auoir. daultre part fut gallehault leue, & vint a
son tref veoir son compaignon. Il demande aux deux
roys que son compaignon fait. Et ilz luy dient quil
auoit toute nuyt mene grant dueil. Lors entre en la
chambre ou il estoit, et si tost comme il le ouyt venir
il essuye ses yeulx ; Adonc gallehault, cuidant que il
dormist, saillist dehors de la chambre incontinent ;
apres le cheualier se leua. Et gallehault vit que il
auoit les yeulx rouges et enflez. Adonc le prent par la
main, et le tyre a part, et luy dist. "Beau doulx compaignon, pourquoy vous occiez vous ainsi? dont vous
vient ce dueil que vous auez toute nuyt demene, & le
desplaisir que vous auez? Je vous prye pour dieu que
vous me diez la cause, et ie vous ayderay se nul homme
mortel y peult conseil mettre ;" & commence a plourer
si durement comme sil veist mort la chose du monde
que mieulx aymast. Lors est gallehault moult a
malayse et luy dit, "Beau doulx compaignon, dictes
moy vostre mescheance | car il nest nul homme au
monde, sil vous auoit riens forfait, que ie nen pourchas-
sasse vostre droit." Et il dist que nul ne luy a riens
meffait. "beau doulx amy, pourquoy menez vous
doncques si grant dueil? Vous poise il que ie vous ay
fait mon maistre & mon compaignon?" "Haa," fait il,
"vous auez assez plus fait pour moy que ie ne pourroye
desseruir, ne riens du monde ne me met a malaise que
mon cueur, qui a toute paour que cueur mortel pourrait

Lancelot asks
Galiot to return
to Arthur, and
to report to him
all the conversa-
tion.

Lancelot sleeps
with the two
kings in Galiot's
tent;

but awakes at
midnight, and
makes a great
moaning.

Galiot comes to
see after Lance-
lot,

finds him with his
eyes red and
swoln,

and conjures him
to tell him what
the matter is.
Lancelot cries bit-
terly,

and says that it is
his heart, which
has all the dread
that it is possible
for mortal heart
to have.

auoir. Si doubte moult que vostre grant debonnairete
ne me occie." De ceste chose est gallehault moult a
malayse, si reconforte son compaignon. Apres allerent
ouyr masse. Quant vint que le prestre eut fait trois
parties du corps de nostre seigneur, gallehault se trait
auant, et tient son compaignon par la main, & luy
monstre le corps de nostre seigneur que le prestre tenoit
entre ses mains; Puis luy dist. "doncques ne croyez
vous pas bien que cest le corps de nostre saulueur?"
"Voirement le croy ie bien," fait le cheualier. Et
gallehault luy dist. "beau doulx amy, or ne me
mescreez mye que ces trois parties de chair que ie vois
en semblance de pain, ia ne feray en ma vie chose que
ie cuyde qui vous ennuye : mais toutes les choses que
ie scauray qui vous plairont, pourchasseray a mon
pouoir." "sire," fait il, "grant mercys." A tant se
taisent iusques apres la messe | et lors demanda galle-
hault a son compaignon quil fera ; "Sire," fait il,
"vous ne laisserez mie le roy en ce point | ains yrez luy
faire compaignie." "Sire," faict il, "grant mercys;"
A tant sen part de luy, si le rebaille aux preudhommes
de la court du roy artus. si font de luy grant signeurie
sicomme ilz peuent.

ET quant vint apres disner, sy furent le roy & la
royne & gallehault appuyez au lict de messire
gauuain, tant que messire gauuain dist a gallehault.
"Sire, or ne vous poise dune chose que ie vous de-
manderay." "Certes," fait galehault, "non fera il."
"sire, celle paix qui fut entre vous & mon oncle, par
qui fut elle, par la chose au monde qui plus vous
aymez?" "Sire," fait il, "vous me auez tant coniure
que ie le vous diray. Vng cheualier la fist." "Et qui
est le cheualier?" fait messire gauuain. "Si maist
dieu," fait gallehault, "ie ne scay." "Qui fut celluy
aux noires armes?" deist messire gauuain. "Ce fut,"
fait il, "vng cheualier ;" "Tant," fait il, "en pouez
vous bien dire | mais acquitter vous conuient." "Je
me suis acquite de ce que me coniurastes. Ne plus ne
vous en diray ores | ne rien ne vous en eusse ores dit,
se vous ne me eussiez coniure." "Par dieu," faict la
royne, "ce fut le cheuallier noir | mais faictes le nous
monstrer." "Qui | moy, dame?" faict gallehault, "ie
le vous puys bien monstrer sicomme celluy qui riens
nen scait!" "Taisez vous," fait la royne, "il est
demoure auec vous, & hier porta voz armes." "Dame,"
fait il | "il est vray | mais ie ne le vys oncques puis
que ie party du roy a la premiere fois." "comment,"

fait le roy, "ne le cognoissiez vous mye | ie cuydoye
que il fust de vostre terre." "Si maist dieu, non est,"
fait gallehault. "certes," fait le roy, "ne de la myenne
non est il mye" | Moult tindrent longuement gallehault   and Galiot will
a parolle le roy et la royne pour auoir le nom du cheua-   not disclose the
lier | mais plus nen peurent traire. et messire gauuain   knight's name,
craint quil ne ennuye a gallehault, si dist au roy.   "Or
en laissez a tant le parler. certes le cheualier est
preudhomme, & pleust a dieu que ie luy ressemblasse."
Moult loe messire gauuain le cheualier. Si en ont la
parolle laissee | et gallehault la recommence et dit.
"Sire, veistes vous oncques meilleur cheuallier que   but asks Arthur
celluy au noir escu?" "certes," fait le roy, "ie ne vy   if he ever saw a
oncques cheualier de qui ie aymasse mieulx laccointance   better knight, and
pour cheualerie;" "Non" | fait gallehault. "Or me   give to know him
dictes," faict gallehault, "par la foy que vous deuez a   henceforth.
ma dame qui cy est, combien vous vouldriez auoir donne
pour auoir son accointance a tousioursmais?" "Si   " Half of all I
maist dieu," faict il, "ie luy partiroye la moytie de tout have, except my
ce que ie pourroye auoir, fors seullement de ceste dame." wife," says
"Certes," fait gallehault, "assez y mettriez. Et vous,   Arthur.
messire gauuain, se dieu vous doint sante que tant   "And what would
desirez, quel meschief en feriez vous pour auoir com-   you give, Ga-
paignie a si preudhomme?" Et quant messire gauuain   wain?"
lot, si pense vng petit comme celluy qui ne cuyde
iamais auoir sante. "Se dieu me donnoit la sante que   " I should like to
ie desire | ie vouldroye orendroit estre vne des plus   turn woman if
belles dames du monde, par conuenant quil me aymast   he would love me
tous les iours de sa vie." "par ma foy," fait gallehault, all his life."
"assez y auez mis." "Et vous, madame, quel meschef
feriez vous par conuenant que vng tel cheualier fust
tousiours en vostre seruice?" "par dieu," fait elle,   " I can offer no
"messire gauuain y a mis toutes les offres que dame y   more than Ga-
peult mettre." Et monseigneur gauuain & tous aultres   wain," says the
se commencerent a rire. "Gallehault," fait messire   Queen.
gauuain, "qui tous nous auez adiurez par le serment
que ie vous coniuray, ores qui vouldriez vous y auoir
mys?" "Si maist dieu," faict gallehault, "ie y voul-   " Well," says
droye auoir tourne mon honneur a honte, par tel si que   Gallot, "I would
ieusse a tousioursmais vng si bon cheualier en ma com-   turn all my
paignie." "Sy maist dieu," faict messire gauuain,   honour into
"plus y auez mys que nous." et lors se pensa messire   shame, for his
gauuain que cestoit le noir cheualier qui le paix auoit   sake."
faicte | car pour luy auoit tourne son honneur a honte,   So Gawain con-
quant il veit quil estoyt au dessus. Et le dist gauuain   cludes that it was
a la royne, & se fut la cause dont gallehault fut plus   the Black Knight
prise ; Moult tindrent longuement parolles du cheualier. who brought
                                                           about the peace.

The Queen walks away with Galiot, tells him she loves him much, and prays him to let her see the Black Knight.

et la royne sadressa, et dist quelle sen voulloit aller vers la bretesche pour veoir les prez, et gallehault la conuoye : si le print la royne par la main & luy dist. "Galle-hault, ie vous ayme moult, & il est vray que vous auez le cheualier en vostre baillie, & par aduenture il est tel que ie le congnois bien ; si vous prie si cher que vous auez mamour, que vous faciez tant que ie le voye." "Dame," fait gallehault, "ie nen ay encores nulle saisine | & ne le vy puis que la paix fut faicte de moy & du roy. Et se il estoit or en mon tref, si y conuien-

He promises to do all he can for her;

droit il aultre voulente que le vostre & que la mienne. Et bien saichez que tant me auez coniure que ie mettray tout le pouoir que ie pourray. comment vous pourrez

and the Queen says, "I shall be sure to see him if you try,

parler a luy ?" "se vous en faictes vostre pouoir," fait elle, "ie le verray bien, & ie men attens a vous, et faictes tant que ie soye vostre a tousiours : car cest vng des hommes du monde que ie verroye plus voulentiers." "Dame," fait il, "ie en feray mon pouoir." "Grant

for he is in your custody. Send and get him."

mercys," fait elle. "Or gardez que ie le voye au plus tost que vous pourrez | car il est en vostre baillie, ie le scay bien | et se il est en vostre terre, enuoyez le querre." Atant sen part gallehault & sen vient au roy.

Arthur wishes Galiot's people and his own to be brought nearer to one another.

Et monseigneur gauuain & le roy lui dient. "galle-hault, ie suis deliure de mes gens, ores faictes approcher voz gens des nostres, ou ie feray approcher les nostres des vostres | Car nous sommes a priuee mesgnie." "Sire," faict gallehault, "ie feray approcher les miens daultre part de cest riuiere si que mon tref sera endroit le vostre, et sera vne nef appareillee en quoy nous pas-serons dicy la et de la icy." "Certes," fait le roy, "moult auez bien dit."

Galiot returns to Lancelot,

Lors sen va Gaillehault en sa tente, et trouue son compaignon moult pensif. Il luy demande comment il a puis fait ; Et il dist, "bien, se paour ne me mestriast." et gallehault dist, "de quoy auez vous telle paour ?" "que ie ne soye congneu," dist il. "or nen ayez mie paour, car vous ny serez ia congneu, se

tells him what the King, Gawain, and the Queen have said of him,

vostre voulente ne y est ;" Lors luy compte les offres que le roy et messire gauuain ont faict pour luy, et ce que la royne dit | et comment la royne la tenu a grant parlement de le veoir | et comme il luy respondit. "et saichez que elle na de nully si tres grant desir de veoir comme de vous. Et monseigneur la Roy ma prye que ie face mes gens approcher | car nous sommes trop loing

and asks him what answer he shall give the Queen.

lung de lautre. Or me dictes que vous voulez que je face | car il est en vostre plaisir." "Je loue que vous facez ce que monseigneur le roy vous prye ;" "Et a ma

dame que respondray ie, beau doulx amy ?"   "Certes,"
fait il, "ie ne scay."   Lors commence a souspirer.   Et   *Lancelot sighs,*
gallehault luy deist.   "Beau doulx amy, ne vous
esmayez point | mais dictes moy comment vous voulez
quil soit | car bien saichez quil sera ainsi comme vous
vouldrez | et ie aymeroye mieulx estre courrouce a la
moytie du monde que a vous tout seul.   ores me dictes
quil vous en plaist."   "Sire," faict ledit cheualier, "ce   *and says, "What-*
que vous me louerez | car ie suis en vostre garde   *ever you advise."*
desormais."   "Certes," fait gallehault, "il me semble   *"There will be*
que pour veoir ma dame la royne il ne ·vous peult   *no harm in seeing*
empyrer."   Lors apperceut galehault assez de son penser,   *her," answers*
& le tient si court quil luy octroye ce quil demande | *Galiot.*
"mais il conuiendra," faict il, "que il soyt faict celce-   *Lancelot says the*
ment, que nul ne le saiche | fors moy et vous."   Et   *matter must be*
gallehault dit que il ne se soulcye point.   "Or dictes,"   *managed secret-*
(fait le cheualier a gallehault,) "a ma dame que vous   *ly ; and they agree*
me auez enuoye querre."   "Sur moy en laissez le sur-   *that Galiot shall*
plus," dit Gallehault.   Lors sen part a tant, et com-   *tell the Queen he*
manda ses trefz a tendre la ou il auoit en conuenant au   *has sent to seek*
roy | et son seneschal fist son commandement.   *for Lancelot.*

¶ Comment gallehault fist tant que la royne veit   *How Guinevere*
    Lancelot, Et comment ilz se araisonnerent en-   *and Lancelot*
    semble, et parlerent de plusieurs choses.   *meet and talk.*

A Tant sen partit gallehault & sen vient au tref   *The Queen asks*
   du roy, & si tost comme la royne le voit, si luy   *Galiot what he*
courut a lencontre, & luy demande comment il auoit   *has done for her.*
exploycte la besongne.   "dame," faict il, "ie en ay
fait tant que ie craing que lamour de vostre pryere ne
me tolle la chose du monde que ie ayme plus."   "Sy
maist dieu," faict elle, "vous ne perderez riens par moy
que ie ne vous rende ou double | mais que y pouez
vous," fait elle, "perdre ?"   "Celluy mesmes que vous
demandez," fait gallehault | "Car ie doubte quil ne se
courrouce, et que ie ne le perde a tousiours."   "Certes,"
faict elle, "ce ne pourray ie pas rendre | mais ia par
moy ne le perderez, se dieu plaist.   Et touteffoys dictes
moy quant il viendra" | "dame," fait il, "quant il   *"Sent to seek for*
pourra | car ie lay enuoye querre, et croy que il ne   *your knight,"*
demourra mye longuement."   De leur conseil entendit   *says he.*
ung peu la dame de mallehault qui sen prenoit garde et
nen faisoit mye semblant.   Lors sen partit gallehault et   *Galiot returns to*
vient a ses gens qui estoyent logez la ou il auoit com-   *his men,*
mande.

Q Vant il fut descendu, il parla a son Seneschal et   *and tells his Sen-*
   luy deist | "quant ie vous enuoyeray querir,   *eschal to bring*
venez a moy, vous & mon compaignon en ce lieu la."   *Lancelot when he*
   sends for him.

Et le roy des cent cheualiers, qui son seneschal estoit,
dist que moult voulentiers feroit son commandement &
Galiot then goes
back to the
Queen, says he
thinks she will
see her knight
that evening, and
appoints to meet
her in an Orchard
below. son plaisir.   Lors salua Gallehault son compaignon, et
sen retourna a la court.   Et quant la royne veit gallehault qui estoit venu, elle luy dist que il gardast bien
et loyaulment ce quil luy auoit promis.   Et il luy dist |
" dame, ie cuyde que vous verrez ennuyt ce que vous
auez tant desire."   Quant elle ouyt ce, si en fut moult
ioyeuse, et moult luy ennuya ce iour pour sa voulente
acomplir du desir que elle auoit de parler a celuy ou
toutes ses pensees estoyent.   Lors luy deist Gallehault,
"nous yrons apres soupper en ce vergier la aual " | et
After supper the
Queen goes to the
Orchard, elle luy octroye.   Quant ce vint apres souper, si appelle
la royne | la dame de mallehault | et dame Lore de car-
dueil, une sienne pucelle, et sen vont tout droit la ou
and Galiot sends
for his Seneschal
and the Knight, gallehault auoyt dit | et gallehault prent ung escuyer
et luy dist.   " Va et dy a mon seneschal que il viengne
la ou ie luy commanday."   Et celuy y va.   Apres ne
who come. demoura guaires que le seneschal y vint, luy et le cheualier.   Ilz estoyent tous deux de grant beaulte ; Quant
ilz approcherent, si congneut la dame de mallehault le
cheualier comme celluy que elle auoyt eu maint iour en
sa baillie.   Et pource quelle ne vouloit mye que il la
congneut, se embroncha, et ilz passent oultre. le seneschal les salue.   Et gallehault dit a la royne.   " Dame,
The Queen at first
cannot think that
either is the black
knight, lequel vous semble il que se soit?" | et elle dit.   " Certes,
ilz sont tous deux beaulx cheuallliers | mais ie ne voy
corps ou il puisse auoir tant de prouesse que le noir
cheualier auoit." " or saichez, dame, que cest lung de ces
deux " | a tant sont venuz auant, et le cheuallier tremble
si que a peine peult saluer la royne, & la royne sen
esmerueille. lors se agenouillent eulx deux, et le cheua-
but one is so
bashful that she
fixes on him, lier la salue | mais cest moult pourement | car moult
estoit honteux.   Lors se pense la royne que cest il.   Et
gallehault dit au seneschal.   " allez, si faictes a ces dames
compaignie."   Et celluy fait ce que son sire luy com-
seats him by her,
smiles on him,
says she has so
longed to see him, mande.   A doncques la royne prent le cheualier par la
main & le assiet iouxte elle.   Sy luy fait moult beau
semblant & dit en riant.   " Sire, moult vous auons desire, tant que, dieu mercy et gallehault, vous voyons. et
nonpourtant encores ne croy ie mye que ce soit celluy
and now he must
tell her who he is.
" I don't know,"
he answers. que ie demande | & gallehault ma dit que cestes vous |
& encores vouldroye scauoir qui vous estes par vostre
bouche mesmes, se vostre plaisir y estoit."   Et celuy
dit que il ne scait | et oncques ne la regarda au visaige.
Et la royne ce esmerueille que il peult auoir, tant quelle
souspeconne une partie de ce quil a.   Et gallehault, qui

le voigt si honteux, pense quil veult dire a la royne son Galiot leaves the two to them-selves, penser seul a seul. lors sen vient messire gauuain celle part, et fait rasseoir les damoyselles pour ce que leuees sestoient encontre luy. Puis commence*n*t a parler de maintes choses. ·Et la Royne dit au cheuallier, "Beau sire, and the Queen asks the knight, "Are not you he who wore the black armour, and overcame everyone?" pourquoy vous celez vous de moy? Certes il ne y a cause pourquoy; nestes vo*us* mie celluy qui porta les noires armes, et qui vainquist lassemblee?" "Dame, nenny" | "et nestes vous pas celluy qui porta lendemain les armes a gallehault?" "Dame, ouy;" "Do*n*c estes vous celluy qui vainquistes lassemblee qui fut faicte le premier iour par deuers nous et par[1] deuers Gallehault?" "Dame, non suis." Quant la royne ot "No, I am not," saith he, ainsi parler le cheualier, a donc apperçoit elle bien quil ne veult mie congnoistre quil eust vaincue lassemblee, si len prise mieulx la royne | car quant vng homme se refusing to praise himself. loe luy mesmes, il tourne son honneur a honte | et quant aultruy le loe, adonc il est mieulx prise. "Or me dictes," fait la royne a lancelot | "q*ui* vous fist "Then who made you a knight, and when?" cheuallier?" "Dame," fait il, "vous;" "Moy?" fait elle, "Et quant?" "Dame," fait il, "vous remembrez vous point quant vng cheuallier vint a Kamalot, lequel "You, at Kamalot, when the pieces of a spear were drawn out of the wounded knight, estoyt naure de deux troncons de iance au corps, et dune espee parmy la teste, et que vng varlet vi*n*t a cou*r*t en vng vendredy, et fut cheualier le dymenche, et deffera le cheuallier?" "De ce," fait elle, "me souient il bien | et se dieu vous aist, feustes vous ce q*ue* la dame du lac amena en court vestu dune robe blanche?" "Dame, ouy." "Et pourquoy dictes vous donc que ie vous fis cheuallier?" "Dame," fait il, "ie dys vray | Car la coustume est telle que nul ne peut estre cheuallier sans ceindre espee. Et celluy de qui il tient lespee, and you girded on my sword, thus knighting me, le faict cheuallier; de vous la tiens ie. Car le roy ne la me donna onques. Pour ce dis ie que vous me feistes cheualier." De ce est la royne mo*u*lt ioyeuse | "ou vous en allastes vous au partir de cou*r*t?" "Dame, ie men and I went away to help the Lady of Noehault, and sent you two damsels. allay pour secourir la dame de noehault;" "Et durant ce temps me mandastes vous riens?" "Dame, ouy | ie vo*us* ennoyay peux pucelles." "Il est vray," dist la royne. "Et quant vous partistes de noehault, trouuastes vous nul cheuallier qui se reclamast de moy?" "Dame, ouy; vng Then I met a man, who said he was your knight, qui gardoit vng gue, et me dist que descendisse de dessus mon cheual et le vouloit auoir, et ie luy demanday a qui il estoit | et il dist a vous. Puis luy demanday apres, qui le commandoyt. Et il me dist quil nauoyt nul commandement que le sie*n*. Et adoncques remys le pied en lestrief et .

---

[1] The original has *pat*.

remontay | Car ie estoye ia descendu | et luy dis que il
ne lauoyt point, et me combatis a luy.   Et ie scay bien
que ie vous fis oultraige, si vous en crie mercy" | "Certes
a moy ne en feistes vous point | Car il nestoyt mye a
moy | et luy sceuz mauluais gre de ce quil ce reclama de
moy. Mais or me dictes on vous en allastes la ?" "Dame,
ie men allay a la douloureuse garde" | "& qui la con-
quist ?" "Dame, ie y entray" | "et ne vous y viz ie onc-
ques." "Ouy, plus de troys foys." "Et en quel temps ?"
fist elle. "Dame," fist il, "vng iour que ie vous deman-
day se vous vouliez leans entrer ; Et vous deistes ouy |
et estiez moult esbahye par semblant." "Et quel escu
portiez vous ?" "Dame, ie portay a la premiere foys
vng escu blanc a vne bande de belif vermeille.   Et
lautre foys vng ou il y auoyt deux bendes" | "Et vous
vys ie plus ?"   "Ouy, la nuyt que vous cuidiez auoir
perdu messire Gauuain et ses compaignons, et que les
gens cryoyent que len me prenist ; Je vins hors a tout
mon escu a troys bendes." "Certes," faict elle, "ce poise
moy | car se on vous eust detenu, tous les enchante-
ments feussent demourez | Mais or me dictes, fustes
vous ce qui iettastes messire Gauain de prison ?"
"Dame, ie y ayday a mon pouoir." "Certes," faict elle,
"en toutes les choses que vous me dictes ie nay trouue
si non verite. Mais or me dictes qui estoit en vne tour-
nelle dessus la chambre monseigneur." "Dame, cestoyt
vne pucelle que ie ne villennay oncques | Car ma dame
du lac la me auoyt enuoyee | si me trouua en ceste tour-
nelle | il fut assez qui la honnora pour moy.   Quant ie
ouy nouuelles de monseigneur Gauuain, si en fut moult
angoisseux, et men party de la Damoyselle qui auecques
moy debuoit venir, et luy priay que elle ne se remuast
tant que elle eust mon messaige ou moy.   Si fus si sur-
prins de tresgrant affaire que ie loubliay | et elle fut
plus loyalle uers moy que ie ne fus courtois vers elle |
car oncques ne se remua iusques a ce quelle eut mes
enseignes, et ce fut grant piece apres."

Comment la royne congneut Lancelot apres quil eut
        longuement parle a elle, et quil luy eut compte
        de ses aduentures.   Et comment la premiere
        acointance fut faicte entre lancelot et la royne
        genieure par le moyen de gallehault.

Q Vant la royne eut parle de la damoiselle, si scait
        bien que cest Lancelot. Si luy enquist de toutes
les choses quelle auoit ouy de luy, et de toutes le trouua
vray disant ; "Or me dictes," fait elle, "vous vy ie
puis ?" "Ouy, dame, telle heure que vous me eustes

and I fought him (for which I crave your pardon).

After that I took the Sorrowful Castle, and there I saw you thrice,

last when you thought you had lost Gawain and his companions,

and I helped to deliver him from prison."

The Queen asks the knight who was in the turret above his room there.

"A damsel whom I never dishonoured,

but I asked her not to leave till she saw my messenger or me, which I then forgot, and kept her there a very long time."

How the Queen knew Lancelot.

When she heard of this damsel the Queen knew it must be Lancelot,

bien mestier | car icusse este noye a kamalot se ne eussiez vous este." "Comment! feustes vous celluy que daguenet le fol print?" "Dame, prins fus ie sans faulte." "Et ou alliez vous?" "Dame, ie alloye apres vng cheuallier." "Et vous combatistes vous a luy" | "dame, ouy." "Et dillec ou allastes vous?" "Dame, ie trouuay deux grans villains que me occirent mon cheual | mais messire yuain, qui bonne aduenture ayt, men donna vng." "Ha, ha," fait elle, "ie scay bien qui vous estes; Vous auez nom lancelot du lac." Il se taist. "Par dieu," faict elle, "pourneant le celez | long temps a que messire Gauuain apporta nouuelles de vostre nom a court;" Lors luy compta comment messire yuain auoit compte que la damoyselle auoit dit | cest la tierce. "Et anten quelles armes portastes vous?" "Vnes vermeilles." "Par mon chef cest verite. Et auant hier pourquoy feistes vous tant darmes comme vous feistes?" Et il commenca a souspirer. "Dictes moy seurement | Car ie scay bien que pour aulcune dame ou damoyselle le feistes vous, et me dictes qui elle est, par la foy que vous me deuez." "Haa, dame, ie voy bien quil le me conuient dire, cestes vous." "Moy?" faict elle. "Voire, dame." "Pour moy ne rompistes vous pas les troys lances que ma pucelle vous porta?" "Car ie me mis bien hors du mandement, dame; ie fis pour elle ce que ie deuz, et pour vous ce que ie peux." "Et combien a il que vous me aymez tant?" "Des le iour que ie fus tenu pour cheuallier, et ie ne lestoye mye" | "Par la foy que vous me deuez, dont vindrent ces amours que vous auez en moy mises?" "dame," fait il, "vous le me feistes faire qui de moy feistes vostre amy, se vostre bouche ne me a menty." "Mon amy!" faict elle, "comment?" "Dame," fait il, "ie vins deuant vous quant ie eu prins congie monseigneur le roy | si vous commanday a dieu, et dis que ie estoye vostre cheuallier en tous lieux. Et vous me dictes que vostre amy et vostre cheuallier voulliez vous que ie feusse. Et ie dys, "a dieu! dame." Et vous distes "a dieu! mon beau doulx amy!" Ce fut le mot qui preudhomme me fera, se ie le suis, ne oncques puis ne fus a si grant meschef que il ne men remembrast. Ce mot ma conforte en tous mes ennuys. Cest mot ma de tous maulx guary. Cest mot ma fait riche en mes pouretez;" "Par ma foy," fait la royne, "ce mot fut en bonne heure dict | et dieu en soyt aoure | ne ie ne le prenoye pas acertes comme vous feistes, et a maint preudhomme ay ie ce dict ou ie ne pensay oncques riens que le dire. Mais la coustume est

and asks him if he was the knight whom Daguenet took. He answers "Yes;" and that two rascals killed his horse, and Ywain gave him another.

"Ah, then your name is Lancelot," says she,

"and for what lady or damsel did you do such feats of arms the day before yesterday?"

"For you, Lady; and for you I broke the three lances that your maiden brought me

for you had made me your *friend*, and said I was your knight in all lands, and bid me adieu as your own sweet friend.

That word has never left me, but always been my strength and wealth."

"Oh, but that was only an ordinary compliment," says Guinevere, to tease him.

telle des cheualliers que font a mainte dame semblant de telles choses dont a gueres ne leur est au cueur." Et ce disoit elle pour veoir de combien elle le pourroit mettre en malaise; Car elle veoit bien quil ne pretendoit a autre amour que a la sienne | mais elle se delectoyt a sa malaisete veoir, et il eut si grant angoisse que

This grieves Lancelot so that he nearly faints, at which Galiot is greatly grieved,

par vng pou quil ne se pasma | & la royne eut paour quil ne cheist, si appella gallehault, et il y vint acourant. Quant il voyt que son compaignon est si courrouce, si en a si grant angoisse que plus ne peut. "Haa, dame," fait gallehault, "vous le nous pourrez bien tollir, et ce seroit trop grand dommaige." "Certes, sire, se seroit mon;" "Et ne scauez vous pour qui il a tant fait

tells the Queen that Lancelot is the gallantest and truest of men,

darmes?" faict gallehault. "Certes, nenny," faict elle | "mais, se il est veoir ce qui ma este dict, cest pour moy;" "Dame, se maist dieu, bien len pouez croire | car aussi comme il est le plus preudhomme de tous les hommes | aussi est son cueur plus vray que tous aultres." "Voirement," fait elle, "diriez vous quil seroit preudhomme se vous scauiez quil a fait darmes puis quil fut cheuallier." Lors luy compte tout ainsi comment vous auez ouy | "et saichez quil a ce faict seullement pour moy," fait elle. Lors luy prie galle-

and prays her to have mercy on him. "What mercy?" says she;

hault, & dist. "Pour dieu, dame, ayez de luy mercy, et faictes pour moy ainsi comme ie fis pour vous quant vous men priastes." "Quelle mercy voulez vous que ien aye?" "Dame, vous scauez que ie vous ayme sur toutes, et il a fait pour vous plus que oncques cheualier ne fist pour dame, et sachez que la paix de moy et de monseigneur neust ia este faicte se neust il

"there is nothing he can ask of me that I will not do; but he will not ask."

este." "Certes," faict elle, "il a plus faict pour moy que ne pourroye desseruir, ne il ne me pourroyt chose requerre dont ie le peuisse esconduyre | mais il ne me requiert de riens | ains est tant melencolieux que merueilles." "Dame," fait gallehault, "auez en mercy; il est celluy qui vous ayme plus que soy mesmes. Si maist dieu, ie ne scauoye riens de sa voulente quant il vint, fors quil doubtoit de estre congneu, ne oncques plus ne men descouurit." "Je en auray," fait elle, "telle mercy comme vous vouldrez." "Dame, vous auez fait ce que ie vous ay requis; aussi doy ie bien faire ce que vous me requerez." Se dit la royne, "il ne

"He does not dare," answers Galiot, "but I will ask for him."

me requiert de riens." "Certes, dame," fait gallehault, "il ne ose | car len ne aymera ia riens par amours que len ne craigne | mais ie vous en prie pour luy, & se ie ne vous en priasse, si le deussiez vous pourchasser. Car plus riche tresor ne pourriez vous conquester." "Certes," fait elle, "ie le scay bien et ie en feray tout ce que vous commanderez." "Dame," fait Gallehault, "grant mercy. Je vous prie que vous luy donnez vostre amour, et le retenez pour vostre cheuallier a tousiours, et deuenez sa loyalle dame toute vostre vie | et vous le aurez fait plus riche que se vous luy auiez donne tout le monde." "Certes," faict elle, "ie luy ottroye que il soyt mien | et moy toute sienne, et que par vous soyent amendez tous les meffaitz." "Dame," faict Gallehault, "grant mercy. Or conuient il commencement de seruice;" "Vous ne deuiserez riens," fait la royne, "que ie ne face." "Dame," faict il, "grant mercy | donc baisez le deuant moy pour commencement de vrayes amours." "Du baiser," faict elle, "ie ne voy ne lieu ne temps | et ne doubtez pas," faict elle, "que ie le voulsisse faire aussi voullentiers quil feroit | mais ces dames sont cy qui moult se merueillent que nous auons tant fait, si ne pourroyt estre que ilz ne le vissent. Nompourtant, se il veult, ie le baiseray voullentiers." Et il en est si ioyeulx que il ne peult respondre si non tant quil dict. "Dame," faict il, "grant mercy" | "dame," faict Gallehault, "de son vouloir nen doubtez ia | Car il est tout vostre, bien le saichez, ne ia nul ne sen apperceuera; Nous troys serons ensemble ainsi comme se nous conseillions" | "Dequoy me feroye ie pryer" | faict elle | "plus le vueil ie que vous." Lors se trayent a part, et font semblant de conseiller. La Royne voyt que le cheuallier nen ose plus faire, si le prent par le menton, et baise deuant Gallehault assez longuement. Et la dame de Mallehauli (sic) sceut de vray que elle le baisoyt. Lors parla la Royne qui moult estoyt sage & vaillant dame. "Beau doulx amy," faict elle, "tant auez faict que ie suys vostre; Et moult en ay grant ioye. Or gardez que la chose soyt celee. Car mestier en est. Je suys une des Dames du monde dont len a greigneur bien dict, Et se ma renommee empiroyt par vous, il y auroyt layde amour et villaine | et vous, Gallehault, ie vous prye que mon honneur gardez | Car vous estes le plus saige | Et se mal men venoyt, ce ne seroyt si non par vous; Et se ien ay bien et ioye, vous me lauez donnee." "Dame," faict Gallehault, "il ne pourroyt vers vous mesprendre, et ien ay bien faict ce que vous me commandastes. Or vous prye que faciez ma voulente ainsi comme iay fait la vostre;" "Dictes," fait elle, "tout ce quil vous plaira hardyment | car vous ne me scauriez chose commander que ie ne face." "Dame," faict il, "donc mauez vous ottroye que ie

"Then I will grant it," says Queen Guinevere.

Galiot prays her to give Lancelot her love, and become his loyal lady all her life.

She promises to be Lancelot's,

and that she will do everything she is told.

"Then kiss Lancelot before me," says Galiot.

This Guinevere agrees to do, if Lancelot wishes it.

Galiot says there is no doubt about Lancelot's wish;

and as he is bashful, the Queen takes him by the chin, and kisses him before Galiot. (The Lady of Mallehault sees her.)

Guinevere tells Lancelot that she is his, but charges him to keep the matter secret,

and Galiot too.

Galiot promises this,

and asks Guinevere to make Lancelot his companion for ever.

seray son compaignon a tousiours." "Certes," fait elle, "se de ce vous failloit, vous auriez mal employe la peine que vous auez prinse pour luy et pour moy." Lors

She takes Lancelot's hand, gives him to Galiot,

prent le cheuallier par la main, et dict. "Gallehault, ie vous donne ce cheualier a tousiours sans ce que iay auant eu, et vous le me creancez ainsi" | et aussi le

and says she has given him Lancelot of the Lake, son of King Ban.

cheualier luy creance | "scauez vous," fait elle, "Gallehault, que ie vous ay donne lancelot du lac, le filz au roy ban de benoic ;" Ainsi luy a fait le cheualier congnoistre, qui moult en a grant honte. Lors a gallehault

This gives Galiot more joy than ever he had before, as he had often heard how Lancelot was the gallantest knight in the world.

greigneure ioye quil neust oncques | car il auoit maintesfois ouy dire, comme parolles vont, que cestoyt le meilleur cheualier et le plus preux du monde, et bien scauoit que le roy ban auoit este moult gentil homme, et moult puissant de amys et de terre.

Ainsi fut faicte la premiere acointance de la royne et de lancelot par gallehault | et Gallehault ne lauoit oncques congneu que de veue, et pource luy fait creancer quil ne luy demanderoit son nom tant quil luy dist, ou autre pour luy. Lors se leuerent tous troys, et il anuytoit durement. Mais la lune estoyt leuee, si

By the bright moonlight they recross the meads towards Lancelot's tent,

faisoit cler | Si que elle luysoyt par toute la praerie | Lors sen retournerent a vne part contrement les prez droit vers le tref le cheualier, & le seneschal et gallehault vint apres luy & les dames tant quilz vindrent

and Galiot sends Lancelot there, while he conducts the Queen to Arthur's tent,

endroit les tentes de gallehault. Lors enuoya Gallehault son compaignon a son tref, et prent conge de la royne, et gallehault la conuoye iusques au tref du Roy. Et quant le roy les veyt, si demanda dont ilz venoyent.

and tells him they have only been looking at the fields by themselves.

"Sire," fait Gallehault, "nous uenons de veoir ces pres a si peu de compaignie comment vous veez." Lors se assient, et parlent de plusieurs choses ; si sont la Royne et Gallehault moult ayses.

Av chef de piece se leua la royne, et sen alla en la bretesche ; gallehault la conuoya iusques la.

Galiot sees the Queen to her tower,

Puis la commande a dieu, et dist quil sen yroit gesir auec son compaignon. "Bien auez fait," dit la royne, "il en sera plus ayse" | A tant sen part gallehault, et vient au roy prendre congie, et dist quil ne luy desplaise, et que il yra gesir auec les gens pource quil ny

and then takes leave of Arthur and of Gawain,

auoyt geu de grant piece, et dist. "Sire, ie me doibz pener de faire leur voulente | car ilz me ayment moult." "Sire," fait messire gauuain, "vous dictes bien, et len doit bien honnorer telz preudhommes qui les a." Lors sen part gallehault et vient a son compaignon ; Ilz se

and goes to Lancelot's bed.

coucherent tous deux en vng lict, et deviserent la vne piece. Si nous laisserons ores a parler de gallehault &

de son compaignon, et dirons de la royne qui est venu
en la bretesche.

Q Vant gallehault fut party, la royne sen alla en
vne fenestre, et commence a penser a ce que
plus luy plaisoyt. La dame de mallehault saprocha
delle quant elle la vit seulle, et luy dist le plus priueement que elle peut. "Haa, dame! pourquoy ne est
bonne la compaignie de quatre?" La royne le ouyst
bien, si ne dit mot, et fait semblant que riens nen ouyt.
Et ne demoura gueres que la. dame dist celle parolle
mesmes; la royne lapella et dist. "Dame, pourquoy
auez ce dit?" "Dame," fait elle, "pardonnez moi, ie
nen diray ores plus | car par aduenture en ay plus dit
que a moy napartient | & len ne se doit mi faire plus
priuee de sa dame que len est | car tost en acquiert on
hayne." "Si maist dieu," fait la royne, "vous ne me
pourriez riens dire dont vous eussiez ma haine | ie vous
tiens tant a saige et a courtoyse, que vous ne diriez
riens qui fust encontre ma voulente | Mais dictes hardy-
ment | Car ie le vueil, et si vous en prie." "Dame,"
fait elle, "donc le vous diray ie | Je dy que moult est
bonne la compaignie de quatre; Jay huy veu nouueau
accointement que vous auez faict au cheuallier qui parla
a vous la bas en ce vergier. Et scay bien que cest la
personne du monde qui plus vous ayme, et vous ne auez
pas tort se vous laymez | car vous ne pourriez vostre
amour mieulx employer;" "Comment," fait la royne,
"le congnoissez vous?" "Dame," fait elle, "telle heure
a este ouen que ie vous en eusse bien peu faire refus
comme vous en pouez ores faire a moy | car ie lay tenu
vng an et demy en prison. Cest celluy qui vaincquit
lassemblee aux armes vermeilles | & celle de deuant
hier aux armes noires, les vnes & les autres luy baillay
ie; Et quant il fut auant hier sur la riuiere pensif, et ie
luy voulu mander que il fist vaillamment armes, ie ne
le faisoye sinon pour ce que ie esperoye quil vous aym-
ast; si cuydoye telle heure fust que il me aymast |
Mais il me mist tost hors de cuyder, tant me descouurit
de son penser." Lors luy compta comment elle lauoyt
tenu en prison an et demy | et pourquoy elle lauoit
prins. "Or me dictes," fait la royne, "quelle com-
paignie vault mieulx de quatre que de troys | car mieulx
est vne chose celee par trois que par quatre." "Certes
non est cy endroit, et si vous diray. Vray est que le
cheualier vous ayme, et aussi fait il gallehault, et desormais se conforteront lung lautre en quelque terre quilz
soient. Car icy ne seront ilz pas longuement: et vous

long, but you will; and if you have no one else to tell your thought to, you will be forced to keep your faith to yourself; but if you will let me be a fourth, we can comfort one another."

demourerez cy toute seule, et ne le scaura nul fors vous | ne si ne aurez a qui descouurir vostre pensee, si porterez ainsi vostre faix toute sculle | mais sil vous pleust que ie fusse la quarte en la compaignie entre nous deux dames, nous solacierons ainsi comme entre eulx deux cheualiers feront, si en seriez plus aise." "Scauez vous," fait la royne, "qui est le cheuallier?" "Se maist dieu," fait la dame, "nenny." "Vous auez bien ouy comment il se couurit vers moy." "Certes," faict la royne, "moult estes apparceuante, et moult conuiendroit estre sage qui vous vouldroit rien embler, & puis

Queen Guinevere agrees to this with great joy,

que ainsi est que vous lauez aperceu, et que vous me requerez la compagnie, vous laurez | mais ie vueil que vous portez vostre faix ainsi comme ie feray le mien." "Dame," faict elle, "ie feray ce que il vous plaira, pour ci haulte compaignie auoir." "En verite," faict la royne, "vous laurez | car meilleure compaignie que vous ne pourroye ie mye auoir." "Dame," fait elle, "nous serons ensemble toutes les heures quil vous plaira."

and tells the Lady that the knight is Lancelot of the Lake.

"Jen suys ioyeuse," faict la Royne. "Et nous affermerons demain la compaignie de nous quattre." Lors luy compte de Lancelot, comment il auoyt ploure quant il regarda deuers elle, "et ie scay que il vous congneut, et saichez que cest lancelot du lac, le meilleur cheuallier qui viue." Ainsi parlerent longuement entre elles deux | et font moult grant ioye de leur accointement

At night the ladies sleep together,

nouueau. Icelle nuyct ne souffrit oncques la Royne de logres que la dame de mallehault geust sinon auec elle | mais elle y geut a force. Car elle doubtoyt moult de gesir auec si riche dame ; Quant elles furent couchees si

and talk of their new loves,

commencerent a parler de leurs nouuelles amours ; La royne demanda a la dame de mallehault selle a[y]me nulluy par amours, et elle luy dict que nenny. "Saichez,

the Lady of Mallehault saying that she never loved but one, and then only in thought (and that was Lancelot).

dame, que ie naymay oncques que vne foys, ne de celle amour ne fis ie que penser ;" et ce dit elle de lancelot, quelle auoit tant ayme comme femme pourroit aymer homme mortel | Mais elle nen auoit oncques aultre ioye eue, non pourtant ne dit pas que ce eust il este. La

The Queen thinks she will make the Lady and Galiot fall in love with one another.

royne pensa quelle feroyt ses amours de elle et de gallehault, mais elle nen veult parler iusques a tant quelle scaura de gallehault sil la veult aymer ou non | car

Next morning they go to Arthur's tent and wake him, and then return over the meadows

autrement ne len requerroit elle pas. Lendemain se leuerent matin elles deux, & allerent au tref du roy, qui gisoit la pour faire a monseigneur gauuain et aux aultres cheualiers compaignie. La royne sesueilla, & dist, "que moult estoyt mauluais qui a ceste heure dormoyt." Lors se tournerent contreual les prez, et dames et damoyselles

auec elles.   Et ils allereut la ou laccointement damours where the meeting with Lancelot took place,
auoyt este faict, et dict la Royne a la dame de mallehault
toute laccointance de lancelot | et comme il estoit and the Queen tells the Lady of Mallehault all about it,
esbahy deuant elle, et riens ne luy laissa a dire.   Puis
commenca a louer gallehault, et dit que cestoit le plus and then praises Galiot as the wisest and best man in the world.
saige homme et le plus vertueulx du monde ; "Certes,"
fait elle, "ie luy compteray lacointance de nous deux
quant il viendra, et sachez que il en aura grant ioye.
Or allons | car il ne demourra gueres quil ne viengne."

The rubric of the next chapter is as follows :

   ¶ Comment la premiere acointance fut faicte de How Galiot became acquainted with the Lady of Melyhalt.
gallehault et de la dame de malehault par le moyen de
la royne de logres.   Et comment lancelot & gallehault
sen alloient esbatre et deuiser auec leurs dames.

It relates how Queen Guinevere requires Galiot to let her
dispose of his love as he had disposed of hers.   To this he consents, and she commends him to the Lady of Mallehault.
Next, they arrange for the promised *parlement de eulx quatre ;*
and the queen points out to Lancelot the lady who had so
many a day kept him in prison, i. e., the Lady of Mallehault.
At recognizing his old acquaintance, Lancelot feels somewhat
distressed, but is reassured by observing the new love-making
between her and Galiot.   Seated in a wood, the four "de-
mourerent grant piece, ne oncques ne tindrent parolles, fors
tant seullement de accoller & de baiser comme ceulx qui
voulentiers le faisoyent."
   We next hear of Gawain's recovery, and of the separation
of the party of four above spoken of.   Galiot takes Lancelot
home with him to his own country, whilst the Lady of Mallehault remains for a time with the queen and Arthur.   When
Lancelot is next spoken of, he is in Galiot's country, where we
will now leave him.

NOTES TO THE APPENDIX.

P. xxiii. *Descosse* = *d'Écosse*, of Scotland. In Old French, words are frequently run together; thus we have *labbaye* for *l'abbaye*, *sesmeurent* for *s'émeurent*, etc. Also the letter *s* is often replaced in modern French by an acute or circumflex accent; so that *Escosse* = *Écosse*; *chasteau* = *château*, etc. The word *si* often occurs below with a great variety of meanings, *viz.* I, he; and, also; so, thus; etc.

P. xxiv. *baille*, given, entrusted. *brouyr* (brûler), being burnt. *monstier*, monastery. *gauues*, so in the original throughout; *gaunes* is used in other romances.

P. xxv. *auecques* = *avec*, with.

P. xxvi. *aduision*, vision. *behourdys*, tournament. *naure*, wounded. *deffera* = *desferra*, un-ironed; it means that Lancelot drew the weapons out of the knight's wounds. *deuers*, "Préposition relative au temps et au lieu dont on parle; près, vers, contre, proche; de *versus*." Roquefort. *octroya*, permitted (authorized). *mouille*, *lit.* wetted; insulted.

P. xxvii. *veirent*, saw. *escript* (écrit), written. *lassemblee*, the gathering; *i.e.* the war, strife. *rua*, overthrew.

P. xxviii. *mire*, physician. *gue*, ford, pass. *tresues*, a truce; spelt *treues* on p. xxix.

P. xxix. *esbatre*, to divert oneself. In modern French, *s'ébattre*.

P. xxx. *orrions*, shall hear. *deust* = *dût*. *cheoient*, from *cheoir*, to fall. Compare *chûte*. *poilz*, hairs. *esbahy*, amazed. *ortelz*, toes. *chaille*; from *chaloir*, to be anxious about. *dilacion*, delay.

P. xxxi. *paour*, fear. *mire*, physician. *veufue*, old.

P. xxxii. *cheuauche*, rides. *boutte*, buts, pushes. *iecte* (jeté), cast. *cuyde*, I believe. *Si maist dieu*, so God aid me. Here *maist* is put for *m'aist*. *oncques*, ever. *ennuyt*, this night, to-night. *lottroyera*, will grant him his request. *conroy*, troops.

P. xxxiii. *derrains* (derniers), last. *busines*, trumpets. *Or y perra*, now it will appear. *cuidoit*, believed; from the old verb *quider*. *cheuauchent*, ride. *ia*, already. *tertre*, a small hill.

P. xxxiv. *adresse*, a cross-path. *huy*, just before ; *lit.* this day. Lat. *hodiè*. *se pasme*, swoons. *leans*, thither.

P. xxxv. *ores*, now. *huy*, to-day. *preudhomme*, a wise and prudent man. *lottroye*, permits him. *tref*, tent. *nenny*, no ! *ains*, before. *guerpiront*, will leave. *deduys*, amusements, diversions.

P. xxxvi. *leans*, there. *gerrez*, will lie. *las*, tired. *Ains*, but.

P. xxxvii. *semondray*, shall ask. *esbahy*, amazed. *tollez*, take away. *creanca*, promised. *lees*, wide, full. *lices*, lists.

P. xxxviii. *emmy le pas*, in the midst of the passage. *hucher*, to cry aloud.

P. xxxix. *lieue*, lifts. *saisine*, disposal. *enseignes*, tokens. *aincoys*, first of all.

P. xl. *oncques mes*, never. *a resiouyr (réjouir)*, in amusing. *escondiroye*, will refuse. *me poyse*, it troubles me. *pieca*, long ago. *se embronche*, covers his face.

P. xli. *sen esueillerent*, awoke thereat. *Adonc*, then. *riens jorfait*, anyway injured.

P. xlii. *ne me mescreez mye que*, do not doubt me more than.

P. xliii. *doint*, gives, were to give.

P. xliv. *mesgnie*, properly the *suite* or household of a prince ; see Roquefort s. v. *magnie* and *maignee*. *nef*, a boat. *loue*, advise.

P. xlv. *vous esmayez*, afflict yourself. *courrouce*, wroth, displeased.

P. xlvi. *vergier*, orchard. *aual*, below. *se embroncha*, she veiled herself, or, hid herself. *iouxte*, beside.

P. xlvii. *maintes*, many. *ot*, heard. *len prise mieulx*, esteemed it better. *loe*, praises. *deffera*, dis-ironed, drew the weapons out of. *lestrief*, the stirrup.

P. xlviii. *leans (la dédans)*, there. *belif*. We find in Cotgrave's French Dictionary, "*Belic*, a kind of red or geucles, in Blazon." *enseignes*, tokens, message.

P. xlix. *mestier*, serviceable. *dillec*, thence. *pourneant*, for nothing, in vain. *voire*, truly. *commanday a dieu*, commended to God, bade farewell.

P. li. *mestier en est*, there is need of it. *greigneur bien*, exceedingly well, very highly.

P. lii. *greigneure*, greater. *anuytoit*, became night. *ie me doibz pener*, I ought to take pains.

P. liii. *ouen*, this year.

The Romans

of

Lancelot of the Laik.

[PROLOGUE.]

THe foft morow ande The luftee Aperill,
   The wynt*er* set, the stormys in exill,
Quhen that the bry*cht and* frefch illumynare
Uprifith arly in his fyre chare   4
His hot courſ in to the orient,
And frome h*is* fpere his goldine ftremis sent
Wpone the grond, in ma*ner* off mefag,
One eu*er*y thing to valkyne thar curage,   8
That natur haith set wnd*er* hire mycht,
Boith gyrſ, and flour, *and* eu*er*y lufty vicht:
And namly thame that felith the affay
Of lufe, to fchew the kalendis of may,   12
Throw birdis fonge w*ith* opine wox one hy,
That feffit not one lufar*is* for to cry,
Left thai forʒhet, throw flewth of Ignorans,
The old wſage of lowis obſ*er*uans.   16
And frome I can the bricht face affpy,
It deuit me no langare fore to ly,

[Fol. 1.]
In April, when the fresh luminary upriseth,

and sendeth from his sphere his golden streams,

and when I espy his bright face.

1

Nore that loue schuld fleuth In to me finde,

I walk forth, be-
wailing my sad
life.
Bot walkine furth, bewalinge in my mynde　　　20
The dredful lyve endurit al to longe,
Sufferans in loue of forouful harmys ftronge,
The fcharpe dais and the hewy ȝerys,
Quhill phebus thris haith paffith al h*is* fperis,　　24
Vithoutine hope ore traiftinge of comfort ;
So be such meine fatit was my fort.

Thus in my faull Rolinge al my wo,

The sword of love
carves my heart.
My carful hart carwing cañ In two　　　　28
The derdful fuerd of lowis hot diffire ;
So be the morow set I was a-fyre
In felinge of the acceſ hot *and* colde,
That haith my hart in fich a fevir holde,　　　32
Only to me thare was noñe vthir eſ
Bot thinkine qhow I fchulde my lady pleſ.

The fcharp affay and ek the Inwart peine
Of dowblit wo me neulyng*is* cañ conftrein,　　36
Quhen that I have remembrit one my tho*ch*t

My lady knoweth
not how I am wo-
begone.
[Fol. 1 b.]
How sche, quhois bewte al my harm̄ haith wrocht,
Ne knouith not how I ame wo begoñe,
Nor how that I ame of hire fer*u*and*is* oñe ;　　40
And in my felf I cañ nocht fynde the meyne
In to quhat wyſ I fal my wo compleine.

I walked thus in
the field, and
came to a well-
beseen garden.
Thus in the feild I walkith to *and* froo,
As tho*ch*tful wicht that felt of no*ch*t bot woo,　　44
Syne to o gardinge, that weſ weil befeñ,
Of quiche the feild was al depaynt w*ith* greñ.
The tendyre and the lufty flour*is* new
Up thrōue the greñ vpone thar ftalk*is* grew　　48
Aȝhane the fone, and thare levis fpred,
Quharw*ith* that al the gardinge was I-clede ;
That pryapus, in to his tyme before,
In o luftear walkith nevir more ;　　　　52

It was closely
environed with
leaves.
And al about enweronyt and Iclofit
One fich o wyſ, that none w*ith*in fuppofit

Fore to be feñ with ony vicht thare owt ;
So dide the levis clof it[1] all about.   56
Thar was the flour, thar was the queñ alpheft,[2]
Rycht wering being of the nychtis reft,
Wnclofiñg gañe the crownel for the day ;
The brycht fone illumynit haith the fpray,   60 The sun illumin-
                                                          ed the sprays ;
The nychtis fobir ande the moft fchowris,
As criftoll terys withhong vpone the flouris,
Haith vpwarpith In the lufty aire,
The morow makith soft, ameyne, and faire ;   64
And the byrdis thar mychty voce out-throng,   the birds sang
                                                     till the woods re-
Quhill al the wood refonite of thar fonge,   sounded ;
That gret confort till ony vicht It wer
That pleffith thame of luftenes to here.   68
Bot gladneß til the thochtful, euer mo
The more he feith, the more he haith of wo.
Thar was the garding with the flouris ourfret,   the garden was
                                                     adorned with
Quich is in pofy fore my lady set,   72 flowers.
That hire Reprefent to me oft befor,
And thane alfo ; thus al day gan be for[3]
Of thocht my goft with torment occupy,
That I becañe In to one exafy,   76   [Fol. 2.]
                                                     I fell there into
Ore flep, or how I wot ; bot fo befell   an ecstasy or
                                                     sleep,
My wo haith done my livis goft expell,
And in fich wiß weil long I can endwr,
So me betid o wondir aventur.   80
As I thus lay, Rycht to my fpreit vas feñ
A birde, yat was as ony lawrare greñ,   and saw in my
                                                     dream a green
A-licht, and fayth in to hir birdis chere ;   bird, who said :
" O woful wrech, that levis in to were !   84
To fchew the thus the god of loue me fent,
That of thi feruice no thing is content,
For in his court yhoue lewith in diffpar,   " The God of
                                                     Love is discon-
And vilfully suftenis al thi care,   88 tent with thee.

---

[1] MS. "clofit."   [2] May we read " alcest " ?
          [3] MS. "befor."

And fchapith no thinge of thine awn remede,
Bot clepith ay and cryith apone dede.
Yhow callith the bird*is* be morow fro thar bour*is*,
Yhoue devith boith the erbis and the flour*is*,   92
And clepit hyme vnfaithful king of lowe,
Yow dewith hyme in to h*is* rigne abufe,
Yhow tempith hyme, yhoue doith thi felf no gud,

You are destitute of wit.

Yhoue are o moñ of wit al deftitude.   96
Wot yhoue no*ch*t that al liwis creatwre
Haith of thi wo i*n* to h*is* hand the cwre?

Though you call on trees, your lady hears not.

And fet yhoue clep one erbis and one treis,
Sche her*is* not thi wo, nore ȝhit fche feis;   100
For none may know the dirkneſ of thi tho*ch*t,
Ne blamyth h*er* thi wo fche knowith no*ch*t.
And It is weil according It be so
He fuffir harme, that to redreſ h*is* wo   104
Previdith not; for long ore he be fonde,
Holl of his leich, that fchewith not h*is* vound.

Ovid says it is better to shew, than to conceal love.

And of owid ye autor fchall yhow knaw
Of lufe that feith, for to confel or fchow,   108
The laft he clepith althir-beft of two;
And that is futh, and fal be eu*er* mo.
And loue alfo haith chargit me to fay,

[Fol. 2 b.]

Set yhoue prefume, ore beleif, ye affay   112
Of his f*er*uice, as It wil ryne ore go,
Prefwme It not, fore It wil not be so;
Al magre thine a f*er*uand fchal yow bee.

As touching thine adversity, seek the remedy."

And as tueching thine adu*er*fytee,   116
Complen and sek of the ramed, the cwre,
Ore, gif yhow likith, furth thi wo endure."
And, as me tho*ch*t, I anfuerde aȝaiñe

Then answered I:

Thus to the byrde, in word*is* fchort and plane: 120
" It ganyth not, as I have harde Recorde,
The f*er*uand for to difput w*ith* ye lord;

"Love knows the reason of my wo."

Bot well he knowith of al my vo the quhy,
And in quhat wyſ he hath me fet, quhar I   124

Nore may I not, nore can I not attane, ·
Nore to hir hienes dare I not complane."
" Ful ! " quod the bird, " lat be thi nyſ diſpare,

" Fool," said the bird, " despair not ;

For in this erith no lady is ſo fare.   128
So hie eſtat, nore of ſo gret empriſ,
That in hire ſelf haith viſdome ore gentrice,
Yf that o wicht, that worthy is to be
Of lovis court, fchew til hir that he   132
Seruith hire in lovis hartly wyſ,
That fchall thar for hyme hating or difpiſ.
The god of love thus chargit the, at fchort,

the God of Love charges thee to speak out your love, or else to write thy plaint ;

That to thi lady yhoue thi wo Report ;   136
Yf yhoue may not, thi plant fchall yhov vrit.
Se, as yhoue cane, be maner oft endit
In metir, quhich that no man haith fuffpek,
Set oft tyme thai contenyng gret effecc ;   140
Thus one fume wyſ yhow fchal thi wo dwclar.
And, for thir fedulis and thir billis are
So generall, and ek ſo fchort at lyte,
And fwme of thaim is loft the appetit,   144
Sum trety fchall yhoue for yi lady fak,

write, then, some treatise for her to read ;

That wnkouth is, als tak one hand and mak,
Of love, ore armys, or of fum othir thing,
That may hir one to thi Remembryng brynge ;   148
Qwich foundith Not one to no hewynes,

[Fol. 3.]

Bot one to gladneſ and to lufteneſ,
That yhoue belevis may thi lady pleſ,

one that may please her and get her thanks.

To have hir thonk and be cne to hir eſ ;   152
That fche may wit in feruice yhow art one.
Faire weil," quod fche, " thus fchal yhow the difpone,

Farewell, and be merry."

And mak thi felf als mery as yhoue may,
It helpith not thus fore to wex al way."   156
With that, the bird fche haith hir leif tak,
For fere of quich I can onone to wak ;

Thereon I awoke, and wondered what it might mean.

Sche was ago, and to my felf thocht I
Quhat may yis meyne ? quhat may this fignify ?   160

Is It of troucht, or of Illuſioune ?
Bot finaly, as in concluſioune,
Be as be may, I ſchal me not discharge,
Sen It apperith be of lovis charg ;　　　　164
And ek myne hart noñe othir biſſynes
Haith bot my ladice ſeruice, as I geſ ;

I determined to take in hand this occupation.

Among al vther*is* I ſchal one honde tak
This litil occupatioune for hire ſak.　　　　168
Bot hyme I pray, the my*ch*ty gode of loue,
That ſitith hie in to his ſpir abuf,
(At *com*mand of o wyſ quhois viſioune
My goſt haith takin this opvnioune,)　　　　172
That my lawboure may to my lady pleſ
And do wnto hir ladeſchip ſu*m* eſ,
So that my *tr*auell be no*ch*t tynt, and I
Quhat vther*is* ſay ſetith nothing by.　　　　176

I know it will but hurt my name, when men hear my feeble negligence.

For wel I know that, be this world*is* fam̃e,
It ſchal not be bot hurting to my nam̃e,
Quhen that thai here my ſebil negligens,
That empit is, and bare of eloquens,　　　　180
Of diſcreſſioune, and ek of Retoryk ;
The metire and the cu*n*ing both elyk
So fere diſcording frome per*f*eccioune ;

I submit my poem to the correction of the wise ;

Qu*hi*lk I ſubmyt to the correccioun*e*　　　　184
Of yai*m* the quhich that is diſcret *and* wyſ,
And ente*r*it is of loue in the ſeruice ;

[Fol. 3 b.]

Quhich knouyth that no lovare dare wit*h*ſtonde,
Quhat loue hyme chargit he mot tak one honde,　　　　188
Deith, or defam̃, or ony mane*r* wo ;
And at this tyme wit*h* me It ſtant ry*ch*t ſo,

for I dare not oppose Love's command.

As I that dar makine no demande
To quhat I wot It lykith loue *com*mande.　　　　192
Tueching his charg*is*, as wit*h* al deſtitut,
Wit*h*in my mynd ſchortly I conclud
For to fulfyll, for ned I mot do ſo.
Thane in my tho*ch*t rolling to and fro　　　　196

Quhare that I my*h*ct fu*m* wnkouth mate*r* fynde,

Quhill at ye laft it fell in to my mynd

At laft I thought of the ftory of "Lancelot of the Lake,"

Of o ftory, that I befor had fene,

That boith of loue and armys can conteñ,	200

Was of o kny*ch*t clepit lancelot of ye laik,

The fone of bane was, king of albanak ;

Of quhois fame *and* worfchipful dedis

Clerk*is* in to diuerf� buk*is* red*is*,	204

Of quhome I thynk her fu*m* thing for to writ

of whom I here think to write something.

At louis charge, and as I cane, endit ;

Set me*n* tharin fal by exp*er*iens

Know my confait, and al my negligens.	20Ɛ

Bot for that ftory is fo pafing larg,

But becaufe my ignorance cannot comprehend the French romance,

One to my wit It war fo gret o charg

For to tranflait the romans of that kny*ch*t ;

It paffith fare my cu*n*yng and my mycht,	212

Myne Ignorans may It not comp*re*hende ;

Quharfor thare one I wil me not depend

I fhall not tell how he was born ;

How he was borne, nor how his fad*er* deid

And ek his mod*er*, nore how he was denyed	216

Efter thare deth, p*re*fumyng he was ded,

Of al ye lond, nore how he fra that ftede

nor how he was nourifhed by the Lady of the Lake;

In sacret wyf⁰ wnwyft away was tak,

And nwrift *with* ye lady of ye lak.	220

Nor, in his ʒouth, think I not to tell

nor how he was brought to Arthur's court,

The aue*n*tour*is*, quhich to hyme befell ;

Nor how the lady of the laik hyme had

One to the court, quhare that he kny*ch*t was mad ;	224

None wift his nome, nore how that he was tak

[Fol. 4.]

By loue, and was Iwondit to the ftak,

And throuch *and* throuch perfit to ye hart,

and pierced to the heart by the beauty of Wanore (Guinevere),

That al his tyme he couth It not aftart ;	228

For thare of loue he ent*er*it in feruice,

Of wanore throuch the beute and franchis,

Throuch quhois feruice in armys he has vrocht

for whofe fervice he wrought many wonders;

Mony wonde*ri*s, and perell*is* he has socht.	232

i

Nor how he thor, in to his ȝoung curage,

nor how he made
a vow to revenge
a wounded
knight,
Hath maid awoue, and in to louis rage,

In the rewenging of o wondit knycht

That cumyne was in to the court that nycht ;   236

who had a broken
sword in his head,
and a truncheon
of a broken spear
in his body ;
In to his hed a brokin[1] fuerd had he,

And in his body alſo mycht men see

The tronſione of o brokine ſper that was,

Quhich no man out dedenyt to aras ;   240

Nor how he haith the wapnis out tak,

And his awow apone this wis can mak,

That he ſchuld hyme Reweng at his poware

One euery knycht that louith the hurtare   244

Better thane hyme, the quhich that vas Iwond.

Throw quich awoue in armys hath ben founde

a vow which
caused the death
of many a wight
warrior ;
The deth of mony wereoure ful wicht ;[2]

For, fro tho wow was knowing of the knycht,   248

Thare was ful mony o paſage in the londe

By men of armys kepit to withſtond

This knycht, of quhome thai ben al set afyre

Thaim to reweng in armys of deſir.   252

or how he and
Sir Kay were sent
to defend the lady
of Nohalt ;
Nor how that thane incontynent was fend

He and ſir kay togidder to defend

The lady of nohalt, nor how that hee

Gouernit hyme thare, nore in quhat degre.   256

Nor how the gret paſing vaſſolag

He eſcheuit, throue the outragouſ curag,

or how he con-
quered the Sor-
rewful Castle ;
In conquiryng of the sorowful caſtell.

Nor how he paſſith doune in the cauis fell,   260

And furth ye keys of Inchantment brocht,

That al diſtroyt quhich that thare vas vrocht.

[Fol. 4 b.]
or how he rescued
Sir Gawane and
his nine fellows ;
Nore howe that he reſkewit ſir gawane,

With his ix falouſ in to preſone tane ;   264

Nore mony vthere diuerſ aduenture,

Quhich to report I tak not in my cwre,

---

[1] MS. " abrokin."
[2] The MS. wrongly transposes ll. 247 and 248.

Nor mony affemblay that gawane gart be maid

To wit h*is* name ; nor how that he hyme hade   268

Wnwift, and hath the worfchip *and* empriſ ;

Nor of the kny*cht*i*s* in to mony,[1] diuerſ wyſ

Throuch his awoue that hath thare dethis found ;

Nor of the fufferans that by louis wounde   272

He in his trawel fufferith au*er* more ;

Nor in the quenis *pr*efens how tharfor

By camelot, in to that gret Revare,

He was ner dround.   I wil It not declare   276

How that he was in louis hewy tho*ch*t

By dagenet in to the court I-bro*ch*t ;

Nor how the kny*cht* that tyme he cane perfew,

Nor of the gyant*is* by camelot he flew ;   280

Nor wil I not her tell the man*er* how

He flew o kny*cht*, by nat*ur* of his wow,

Off melyholt ; nore how in to that toune

Thar came one hyme o gret confufione   284

Of pupil *and* [of] kny*cht*i*s*, al enarmyt,

Nor how he thar haith kepit hyme wnharmyt ;

Nor of his worfchip, nor of h*is* gret prowes,

Nor his defens of armys in the pres.   288

Nor how the lady of melyhalt y*at* fche

Came tó the feild, and pray[i]th hyme that he

As to o lady to hir[2] his fuerd hath ʒold,

Nor how he was in to hir keping hold ;   292

And mony vthir nobil deid alfo

I wil report quharfor I lat ourgo.

For quho thai*m* lykith for to fpecyfy,

Of one of thai*m* my*ch*t mak o gret ftory ;   296

Nor thing I not of his hye renōwn

My febil wit to makin menfioune ;

Bot of the wer*is* that was fcharp *and* ftrong,

Richt perellouſ, and hath enduryt long,   300

---

[1] We should perhaps omit "mony."   [2] MS. "his."

[Fol. 5.] Of Arthur In defending of his lond

Frome galiot, fone of the fair gyonde,

That broc*ht* of knyc*ht*i*s* o pafing confluens ;

wherein Lancelot won renown by his defence of Arthur ; And how lancelot of arthuri*s* hol defens   304

And of the veri*s* berith the renown ;

And how he be the wais of fortou*n*e

and at last made peace between the two princes. Tuex the two princ*is* makith the accorde,

Of al there mortall weri*s* to concorde ;   308

I shall also tell how Venus re-warded him. And how that venus, fiting hie abuf,

Reuardith hyme of trauell in to loue,

And makith hyme his ladice grace to have,

And thankfully his feruice cane refave ;   312

This is the mate*r* quhich I think to tell.

Bot ftil he mot ryc*ht* wi*th* the lady duell,

Quhill tyme cu*m* eft that we fchal of hy*m* fpek.

My summary must end for the present. This proceſ [now] mot clofine beñ and ftek ;   316

And furth I wil one to my mate*r* go.

But I pray for the support of a very great poet, Bot first I pray, and I befek also,

One to the moft conpilour to fupport,

Flour of poyet*is*, quhois nome I wil report   320

To me nor to noñ vthir It accordit,

whose name I may not men-tion; In to our rymyng his nam̃ to be recordit ;

For fum fuld deme It of prefumpfioune,

for our riming is but derision, when his excel-lence is remem-bered. And ek our rymyng is al bot deryfioune,   324

Quhen that reme*m*brit is his excellens,

So hie abuf that ftant in reue*r*ans.

Ye frefch enditing of h*is* laiting toung

The world knows his eloquence in inditing Latin; Out throuch yis world fo wid is yroung,   328

Of eloquens, and ek of retoryk ;

Nor is, nor was, nore neue*r* beith hyme lyk,

and none can ever gladden the world like him: This world gladith of h*is* fuet poetry.

His faul I blyſ conferuyt be for-thy ;   332

to him be the thanks for my success. And yf that ony lusty terme I wryt

He haith the thonk y*er*of, *and* this endit.

EXPLICIT P*R*OLOG*US*, ET INCIPIT P*R*IM*US* LIBER.

[BOOK I.]

Quhen [that] tytan, withe his lusty heit,

[Fol. 5 b.]

Twenty dais In to the aryeit 336

When Titan, be-
ing in Aries, had
apparelled the
fields,

Haith maid his courſ, and all with diuerſ hewis

Aparalit haith the feldis and the bewis ;

The birdis amyd the erbis *and* the flouris,

and birds began
to make their

And one the branchis, makyne gone thar bouris, 340

bowers;

And be the morow finging in ther chere

Welcum the lufty feſſone of the ȝere.

In to this tyme the worthi conqueroure

Arthure, wich had of al this worlde the floure 344

king Arthur was
at Carlisle.

Of cheuelry auerding to his crown,

So pafing war his knychtis in renoune,

Was at carlill ; and hapynnit ſo that hee

Soiornyt well long in that faire cuntree. 348

In to whilk tyme In to the court thai heire

His knights,
hearing of no ad-
venture, were an-
noyed.

None awenture, for wich the knyghtis weire

Anoit all at the abiding thare.

For-why, beholding one the fobir ayre 352

And of the tyme the pafing luftynes,

Can ſo thir knyghtly hartis to encreſ,

That thei fhir kay one to the king haith fende,

They therefore
sent Sir Kay to

Befeiching hyme he wold wichfaif to wende 356

pray the king to
go to Camelot.

To camelot the Cetee, whare that thei

Ware wont to heryng of armys day be day.

The king forſuth, heryng thare entent,

To thare defir, be fchort awyfment, 360

Ygrantid haith ; and ſo the king proponit

The king pro-
posed to do so on
the morrow.

And for to pas hyme one [1] the morne difponit.

Bot ſo befell hyme [on] that nycht to meit

An aperans, the wich one to his fpreit 364

---

[1] MS. "to pas one hyme one," with first " one " lightly
crossed out.

That night he
dreamt that his
hair all fell off;
It femyth that of al his hed ye hore
Of fallith and maid defolat ; wharfore
The king therof was penfyve in his mynd,
That al the day he couth no refting fynde,   368
which made him
delay his journey.
Wich makith hyme his Iorneye to delaye.
And fo befell apone the thrid day,
The bricht fone, pafing in the weft,
Haith maid his courß, and al thing goith to Reft ;   372
Again he dreamt,
tHat his bowels
fell out, and lay
beside him.
The king, fo as the ftory can dewyß,
He thoght aʒeine, apone the famyne wyß,
[Fol. 6.]
His vombe out fallith vith his hoil syde
Apone the ground, *and* liging hyme befid ;   376
Throw wich anon out of his flep he ftert,
Abafit and adred in to his hart.
He told the
queen, who an-
swered, "No man
should respect
vain dreams."
The wich be morow one to the qwen he told,
And fhe aʒeine to hyme haith anfuer ʒolde ;   380
" To dremys, *fir*, fhuld no man have Refpek,
For thei ben thing*is* weyn, of non affek."
" Well," q*uo*d the king, " god grant It fo befall ! "
The king next
shewed his dream
to a clerk,
Arly he roß, and gert one to hyme call   384
O clerk, to whome that al his hewynes
Tweching his drem fhewith he expreß,
who said, " Sir,
such things tes-
tify nothing."
Wich anfuer yaf and feith one to the kinge ;
" Shir, no Record lyith to fuch thing ;   388
Wharfor now, fhir, I praye yow tak no kep,
Nore traift in to the vanyteis of slep ;
For thei are thing*is* that afkith no credens,
But caufith of fum maner influe*n*s,   392
Empriß of thoght, ore fup*er*fleuytee,
Or than fum othir cafualytee."
" Yet," replied
he, " I shall not
leave it so."
" ʒit," q*uo*d the king, " I fal noc*h*t leif It so ;"
And furth he chargit mefinger*is* to go   396
Throgh al his Realm, *with*outen more demande,
He bade all the
bishops and
clergy come to
Camelot within
twenty days.
And bad them ftratly at thei fhulde comande
All the bifhopes, and makyng no delay
The fhuld appere be the tuenty day   400

At camelot, with al thar hol clergy
That moſt expert war, for to certefye
A mater tueching to his goſt be nyght;
The meſag goith furth with the lettres Right.   404

The king eft ſone, within a litill ſpace,
    His Iornay makith haith frome place to place,
Whill that he cam to camelot; and there
The clerkis all, as that the chargit were,   408
Affemblit war, and came to his preſens,
Of his deſir to viting the ſentens.
To them that war to hyme moſt ſpeciall
Furth his entent ſhauyth he al hall ;   412
By whois conſeil, of the worthieſt
He cheſith ten, yclepit for the beſt,
And moſt expert and wiſeſt was ſuppoſit,
To qwhome his drem all hail he haith diſcloſſit ;   416
The houre, the nyght, and al the cercumſtans ;
Beſichyne them that the ſignifycans
Thei wald hyme ſhaw, that he mycht reſting fynde
Of It, the wich that occupeid his mynde.   420
And one of them with ¹ al ther holl affent
Saith, "ſhire, fore to declare our entent
Vpone this matere, ye wil ws delay
Fore to awyſing one to the ix day."   424
The king ther-to grantith haith, bot hee
In to o place, that ſtrong was and hye,
He cloſith them, whare thei may no whare get,
Vn to the day, the wich he to them ſet.   428
Than goith the clerkis ſadly to awyſ
Of this mater, to ſeing in what wyſ
The kingis drem thei ſhal beſt ſpecefy.
And than the maiſtris of aſtronomy   432
The bookis longyne to ther artis ſet ; ²
Not was the bukis of arachell forget,

He goes to Came-
lot, and finds the
clerks assembled.

He discloses all
to the ten that are
most expert,

[Fol. 6 b.]

and beseeches
them to explain
the dreams.

One of them asks
for nine days to
advise upon the
matter.

The king com-
plies, but shuts
them up in a
strong place.

The masters of
astronomy fetch
their books,

---

¹ MS. "saith with" (with a very slight scratch through
"saith").   ² So in MS. Read "fet."

Of nembrot, of danȝhelome, thei two,

Of moyſes, *and* of herynes all soo ;   436

And ſeking be ther calcolaciou*n*e

To fynd the planet*is* diſpoſiciou*n*e,

The wich thei fond ware wonde*r* ewill yſet

The ſamyne nyght the king his ſweuen met.   440

So ner the point ſocht thei have the thing,

Thei fond It wonde*r* hewy to the king,

Of wich thing thei waryng in to were

To ſhew the king, for dreid of his danger.   444

Of ane accorde thei planly haue p*r*oponit

No worde to ſhow, and ſo thei them diſponit.

The day is cu*m*yng, and he haith fore them ſent,

Beſichyne them to ſhewing ther entent.   448

Than ſpak they all, and that of an accorde ;

" Shir, of this thing we can no thing Recorde,

For we can noght fynd in til our ſciens

Tweching this mater ony ewydens."   452

" Now," q*uo*d the king, " and be the glorius lorde,

Or we depart ye ſhall ſum thing recorde ;

So pas yhe not, nor ſo It ſall not bee."

" Than," q*uo*d the clerk*is*, " grant ws dais three."   456

The wich he grantid them, and but delay,

The term paſſith, no thing wold the ſay,

Wharof the king ſtondith heuy cherith,

And to the clerk*is* his viſag ſo apperith,   460

That all thei dred them of the king*is* myght.

Than ſaith o clerk, " si*r*, as the thrid nyght

Ye dremyt, ſo [now] giffis ws delay

The thrid tyme, and to the thrid day."   464

By whilk tyme thei fundyng haith the ende

Of this mater, als far as ſhal depend

To ther ſciens ; yit can thei not awyſ

To ſchewing to the king be ony wyſ.   468

The day is cum, the king haith them beſocht,

But one no wyſ thei wald declar ther thoght ;

Than was he wroth in to his felf and noyt,

And maid his wow that thei fhal[1] ben diftroyt.   472   The king vows to destroy them ;

His baronis he commandit to gar tak

Fyve of them one to the fir-ftak,

And vther fyue be to the gibbot tone ;

And the furth with the kingis charg ár gone.   ·   476

He bad them in to fecret wyß that thei   but secretly charges his knights not to harm them.

Shud do no harm, but only them affey.

The clarkis, dredful of the kingis Ire,

And faw the perell of deth and of the fyre,   480

Fyve, as thei can, has grantit to record ;

That vther herde and ben of ther accorde ;

And al thei ben ýled one to the king,

And fhew hyme thus as tueching of this thing.   484   They yield at last, and say,

" Shir, fen that we conftrenyt ar by myght

To fhaw that wich[2] we knaw no thing aricht ;

For thing to cum preferuith It allan

To hyme the wich is euery thing certañ,   488

Excep the thing that til our knawleg hee

Hath ordynat of certan for to bee ;

Therfor, fhir king, we your magnificens

Befeich It turne till ws to non offens,   492

Nor hald was nocht as learis, thoght It fall   " Hold us not as liars, though it happen not as we say.

Not in this mater, as that we telen fhall."

And that the king haith grantit them, and thei

Has chargit one, that one this wiß fall feye.   496

" Prefumyth, fhir, that we have fundyne so ;

All erdly honore ye nedis[3] moft for-go,   You must forego all earthly honour ;

And them the wich ye moft affy in-tyll   [Fol. 7 b.]
and those on

Shal failye ʒow, magre of ther will ;   500   whom you most rely, will fail you."

And thus we haue in to this matere founde."

The king, quhois hart was al wyth dred ybownd,

And afkit at the clerkis, if thei fynde

By there clergy, that ftant in ony kynde   504

---

[1] MS. "fhat."   [2] MS. "wich that."
[3] MS. "nedift ;" but see l. 518.

The king asks if his destiny can be altered.

Of poſſibilitee, fore to reforme

His deſteny, that ſtud in ſuch a forme;

If in the hewyne Is preordynat

On ſuch o wiſ his honor to tranſlat.   508

The clerkis faith, "forſuth, and we haue ſene

They reply, that the matter is dark.

O thing whar-of, if we the trouth ſhal meñ,

Is ſo obſcure and dyrk til our clergye,

That we wat not what It ſhal ſignefye,   512

Wich cauſith ws we can It not furth ſay."

" Yis," quod the king, " as lykith yow ye may,

For wers than this can nat be ſaid for me."

A master says, there is no help but in the true watery lion, and in the leech, and in the flower.

Thane ſaith o maiſtir, " than ſuthly thus finde we;   516

Thar is no thing ſal ſucour nor refkew;

Your worldly honore nedis moſt adew,

But throuch the watrye lyone and ek fyne,

On throuch the liche and ek the wattir fyne,   520

God knows what this should mean.

And throuch the confeill of the flour; god wot

What this ſhude meñ, for mor ther-of we not."

No word the king anſuerid ayane,

For al this reſone thinkith bot in weyne.   524

The king shews no outward grief,

He ſhawith outwart his contenans

As he therof takith no greuans ;

but is not rid of anxiety all night.

But al the nyght it paſſid nat his thoght.

The dais courſ with ful deſir he ſocht,   528

And furth he goith to bring his mynd in reſt

Next day he goes to the forest.

With mony O knyght vn to the gret foreſt ;

The rachis gon wn-copelit for the deire,

That in the wodis makith nois and cheir :   532

The knychtis, with the grewhundis in aweit,

Secith boith the planis and the ſtreit.

The chase.

Doune goith the hart, doune goith the hynd alſo ;

[In to the feld can ruſching to and fro]¹   536

The ſwift grewhund, hardy of aſſay ;

Befor ther hedis no thing goith away.

¹ A line must here be lost, but there is nothing to shew
this in the MS. The inserted line is imitated from l. 3293.

The king of hunting takith haith his fport,
And to his palace home he can Refort,   540 The king returns.
Ayan the noon ; and as that he was set
Vith all his noble knyght*is* at the met,   [Fol. 8.]
As they sit at
So cam ther in an agit knyght, *and* hee   meat, an aged
knight enters,
Of gret efftat femyt for to bee ;   544 fully armed.
Anarmyt all, as tho It was the gyf,
And thus the king he faluft, one this wif,
" **S**hir king, one to yow am y fende   The knight's
message is that
    Frome the worthieft that *in* world is kend, 548 king Galiot bids
Arthur to yield
That leuyth now of his tyme and age,   to him his king-
dom.
Of manhed, wifdome, *and* of hie curag,
Galiot, fone of the fare gyande ;
And thus, at fhort, he bid*is* yow your londe   552
Ye yald hyme our, w*ith*out Impedyment ;
Or of hyme holde, and if tribut and rent.
Th*is* is my charge at fhort, whilk if youe left
For to fulfill, of al he haith conqueft   556
He fais that he moft tendir fhal youe hald."
By fhort awys the king his anfuer yald ;   The king refuses.
" Shir knyc*ht*, your lorde wondir hie pretendis,
When he to me fic falutatioune send*is* ;   560
For I as yit, in tymys that ar gone,
Held neu*er* lond excep of god alone,
Nore neu*er* thinkith til erthly lord to yef
Trybut nor rent, als long as I may lef."   564
" Well," q*uod* the knyc*ht*, " ful for repentith me ;   The knight re-
plies, that his
Non may recift the thing the wich mone bee.   lord bids him de-
fiance, and will
To yow, fir king, than frome my lord am I   invade his land in
a month ;
With diffyans fent, and be this refone why ;   568
His purpos Is, or this day moneth day,
With all his oft, planly to affay
Your lond, w*ith* mony ma*n*ly man of were,
And helmyt knyc*ht*is, boith with fheld *and* fpere ; 572 not to return till
he has conquered ;
And neu*er* thinkith to retwrn home whill
That he this lond haith conqueft at his will ;

And ek vanour the quen, of whome that hee
Herith report of al this world that fhee   576
In fairhed and in wertew doith excede,
He bad me fay he think*is* to poffede."

" Schir," q*uod* the king, " your mefag me behuf*is*
Of refone and of curtafy excuff ;   580
But tueching to your lord *and* to his oft,
His powar [and] his mefag and his boft,
That pretendith my lond for to diftroy,
Thar-of as ȝit tak I non anoye ;   584

And fay your lord one my behalf, when hee
Haith tone my lond, that al the world fhal see
That It fhal be magre myne entent."

With that the kny*cht*, w*ith*outen leif, is went,   588
And richt as he was pafing to the dure,
He faith, " a gode ! ¹ what wykyt aduenture
Apperith !" w*ith* that his hors he nome,
Two knicht*is* kepit, waiting h*is* outcome.   592
The knicht is gon, the king he gan Inquere
At gawan, and at other kny*cht*is* fere,

If that thei knew or e*uer* hard recorde
Of galiot, and wharof he wes lorde ;   596
And ther was non among his kny*cht*is* all
Which anfuerd o word in to the hall.
Than galygantynis of walys rafe,

That trauelit in diuerß lond*is* has,   600
In mony kny*cht*ly auentur haith ben ;
And to the king he faith, " fir, I haue fen
Galiot, which is the fareft kny*cht*,

And hieft be half a fut one hycht,   604
That e*uer* I saw, and ek his me*n* accordith ;
Hyme lakid no*cht* that to a lord recordith.
For vifare of his ag is non than hee,
And ful of larges and humylytee ;   608

---

¹ MS. " agod⁎."

Au hart he haith of paſing hie curag,

And is not xxiiij ʒer of age,

And of his tyme mekil haith conquerit ;

Ten king*is* at his *command* ar ſterit. 612

He v*it*h his men ſo louit is, y geſ,

That hyme to pleſ is al ther beſynes.

Not ſay I this, ſir, in to ye entent

That he, nor none wnd*er* the firmament, 616

Shal pouere haue ayane your maieſteo ;

And or thei ſhuld, this y ſey for mee,

Rather I ſhall kny*ch*tly in to feild

Reſaue my deith anarmyt wnd*er* ſheld. 620

This ſpek y left ; "—the king, ayan the morn,

Haith varnit huntar*is* baith with hund *and* horne,

And arly gan one to the foreſt ryd,

With mony manly knyght*is* by h*is* ſid, 624

Hyme for to ſport and comfort w*it*h the dere,

Set contrare was the ſeſone of y*e* yere.

His moſt huntyng was atte wyld bore ;

God wot a luſtye cuntree was It thoore, 628

In the ilk tyme ! weil long this noble king

In to this lond haith maid his ſuiornyng ;

Frome the lady was send o meſinger

Of melyhalt, wich ſaith one this maner, 632

As that the ſtory ſhewith by recorde :

"TO yow, ſir king, as to hir foueran lorde,
My lady hath me chargit for to ſay

How that your lond ſtondith i*n* affray ; 636

For galiot, ſone of the fare gyande,

Enterit Is by armys in your land,

And ſo the lond and cuntre he anoyth,

That quhar he goith planly he diſtroyth, 640

And makith al obeiſand to his honde,

That nocht is left wnconqueſt i*n* that lond,

Excep two caſtell*is* longing to hir ewre,

Wich to defend ſhe may no*ch*t long. endure. 644

courageous, and
under xxiv years
of age.

Ten kings obey
him.

The king goes
again to the
chase.

He likes boar-
hunting best.
[Fol. 9.]

A messenger
comes from the
lady of Melyhalt,

to say that Galiot
has entered Ar-
thur's land,

and has conquer-
ed all but two
castles belonging
to his mistress.

Wharfor, fir, in word*is* plan *and* fhort,
Ye mon difpone your folk for to fupport."

The king pro-
mifes not to de-
lay, and inquires
the number of the
foe.

" Wel," q*uod* the king, " one to thi lady fay
The neid is myne, I fall It not delay ;   648
But what folk ar thei nemmyt for to bee,
That in my lond is cu*m*yne in fich degree ? "

" A hundred
thousand," is the
reply.

" An hundreth thoufand boith vith fheld *and* fpere
On hors ar armyt, al redy for the were."   652

" Wel," q*uod* the king, " and but delay this ny*ch*t,
Or than to morn as that the day is lycht,

The king says he
will set off that
very night.

I fhal remuf ; ther fhal no thing me mak
Impedyme*n*t, my Iorney for to tak."   656
Than feith his kny*ch*t*is* al w*ith* one affent.

His knights ad-
vise him to wait
till he has raised
an army.

" Shir, that is al contrar our entent ;
For to your folk this mater is wnwift,
And ye ar here our few for to recift   660
Jone power, and youre cuntre to defende ;
Tharfor abid, and for your folk ye send,
That lyk a king and lyk a weriour
Ye may fuften in armys your honoure."   664

" Now," q*uod* the king, " no langer that I jeme
My crowne, my fepture, nor my dyademe,
Frome that I here, ore frome I wnd*er*ftand,
That ther by fors be entrit in my land   668
Men of armys, by ftrenth of vyolens,

He refuses to
wait longer than
till the morrow.

If that I mak abid or refydens
In to o place langar than o ny*ch*t,
For to defend my cuntre *and* my ry*ch*t."   672

[Fol. 9 *b*.]

The king that day his mefage haith furth sent
Throuch al his realme, and fyne to reft is went.
Up goith the morow, wp goith the bry*ch*t day,
Wp goith the sone in to his frefh aray ;   676
Richt as he fpred his bemys frome northeft,

The king arises
next morning
without delay,

The king wprafs w*ith*outen more areft,
And by his awn confeil and entent,
His Iornaye tuk at fhort awyfment.   680

And but dulay he goith frome place to place
Whill that he cam nere whare¹ the lady was,
And in one plane, apone o reuer fyde,   and reaches a plain by the river side,
He lichtit doune, and ther he can abide ;   684
And yit with hymie to batell fore to go
Vij thousand fechteris war thei, and no mo.   having only seven thousand with him.

This was the lady, of qwhome befor I tolde,
    That lancilot haith in to hir kepinge holde ; 688 Lancelot, having been imprisoned by the lady of Melyhalt,
But for to tell his pafing hewyneffe,
His peyne, his forow, and his gret diftreffe
Of prefone and of loues gret fuppris,
It war to long to me for to dewys.   692
When he remembrith one his hewy charge
Of loue, wharof he can hyme not difcharge,
He wepith and he forowith in his chere,
And euery nyght femyth hyme o yere.   696
Gret peite was the forow that he maad,
And to hyme-felf apone this wif he faade :   laments his fate.

" Qwhat haue y gilt, allace ! or qwhat deferuit ?   Lancelot's lament ;
    That thus myne hart fhal vondit ben and carwit
One by the fuord of double peine and wo ?   701
    My comfort and my plefans is ago,   his pleasure is gone ;
To me is nat that fhuld me glaid referuit.

I curf the tyme of myne Natiuitee,   704   he curses his natal day ;
Whar in the heuen It ordinyd was for me,
    In all my lyue neuer til haue cef ;
    But for to be example of difef,
And that apperith that euery vicht may see.   708

Sen thelke tyme that I had fufficians
Of age, and chargit thoghtis fufferans,
    Nor neuer I continewite haith o day   he has never spent a single
    With-out the payne of thoghtis hard affay ; 712   day free from anxiety,
Thus goith my youth in tempeft and penans.

¹ MS. " whare that," with slight scratch through " that."

and is now in
prison;
[Fol. 10.]
And now my body is ln prefone broght ;
But of my wo, that in Regard is noght,
  The wich myne hart felith euer more.   716
and invokes
Death.
  O deth, allace ! whi hath yow me forbore
That of remed haith the fo long befoght !"

Thus neueremore he fefith to compleine,
This woful knyght that felith not bot peine ; 720
Thus the smart
of love's sorrow
pricketh him.
So prekith hyme the fmert of loues fore,
And euery day encreffith more and more.
And with this lady takine is alfo,
He is kept by her
from the exercise
of knighthood;
And kepit whar he may no whare go   724
To haunt knychthed, the wich he moft defirit ;
And, thus his hart with dowbil wo yfirite,
and there we let
him dwell.
We lat hyme duel here with the lady ftill,
Whar he haith laifere for to compleine his fyll. 728

Meanwhile,
Galiot besieged a
castle.
And galiot in this meyne tyme he laie
By ftrong myght o caftell to affay,
With many engyne and diuerf wais fere,
For of fute folk he had a gret powere   732
That bowis bur, and vther Inftrumentis,
His army had pa-
vilions, tents, and
iron-wheeled
chariots.
And with them lede ther palʒonis and ther tentis,
With mony o ftrong chariot and cher
With yrne qwhelis and barris long and fqwar ; 736
Well ftuffit with al maner apparell
That longith to o fege or to batell ;
Whar-with his oft was clofit al about,
That of no ftrenth nedith hyme to dout.   740
When he heard of
Arthur's coming,
And when he hard the cumyne of the king,
And of his oft, and of his gaderyng,
The wich he reput but of febil myght
Ayanis hyme for to fuften the ficht,   744
His confell holl affemblit he, but were,
ne assembled his
council,
Ten knightis with other lordis fere,
And told theme of the cuming of the king,
And afkit them there confell of that thing. 748

Hyme thoght that it his worſchip wold degrade,

If he hyme felf in propir perſone raide

Enarmyt ayane ſo few menye

As It was told arthur[is] fore to bee ;　752

And thane the kyng-An-hundereth-knychtis cold,

(And ſo he hot, for neuermore he wolde

Ryd of his lond, but In his cumpany

O hundyre knyghtis ful of chiuellry).　　756

He faith, "ſhir, ande I one hond [may] tak,

If It you pleſ, this Iorney ſhal I mak."

Quod galiot, "I grant It yow, but ye

Shal firſt go ryd, yone knychtis oſt and see."　760

With-outen more he ridith our the plan,

And ſaw the oſt and is returnyd ayañ ;

And callit them mo than he hade ſen, for why

He dred the repreſe of his cumpany.　764

And to his lord apone this wys faith hee,

" Shir, ten thouſand y ges them for to bee."

And galiot haith chargit hyme to tak

Als fell folk, and for the feld hyme mak.　768

And ſo he doith and haith them wel Arayt ;

Apone the morne his banaris war diſplayt.

Up goth the trumpetis with the clariounis,

Ayaine the feld blawen furth ther ſownis,　772

Furth goth this king with al his oſt anon.

Be this the word wes to king arthur gone,

That knew no thing, nor wiſt of ther entent,

But ſone his folk ar one to armys went ;　776

But arthur by Report hard saye

How galiot non armys bur that day,

Wharfor he thoght of armys nor of ſheld

None wald he tak, nor mak hyme for the feld.　780

But gawane haith he clepit, was hyme by,

In qwhome Rignith the flour of cheuelry ;

And told one what maner, and one what wyſ

He ſhuld his batelles ordand and dewys ;　784

who thought it would degrade him, to fight in proper person against so few.

[Fol. 10 b.]
The king of a hundred knights (Maleginis) undertakes the exploit;

who reconnoitres Arthur's host, and says it is 10,000 strong: whereon Galiot charges him to take the same number.

Galiot's host set out.

Arthur's host don their armour.

Arthur, hearing that Galiot is unarmed, will not arm himself;

but calls Gawane, and tells him how to order his battalions.

Befeching hyme, [hyme] willy to for-see
Aȝaine thei folk, wich was far mo than hee.
He knew the charg and paffith one his way
Furth to his horf, and makith no dulay ;   788
The clariounis blew and furth goth al onon,

And our ye watter and the furd ar gone.
Within o playne vpone that other fyd
Ther gawan gon his batellis to dewide,   792
As he wel couth, and set them in aray,
Syne with o manly contynans can fay,

" Ye falowis wich of the round table ben,
Through al this erth whois fam is hard and fen,   796
Remembrith now It ftondith one the poynt,
For why It lyith one your fperis poynt,[1]

The well-fare of the king and of our londe ;
And fen the fucour lyith in your honde,   800
And hardement is thing fhall moft awaill
Frome deth ther men of armys in bataill,
Lat now your manhed and your hie curage
The pryd of al thir multitude affuage ;   804
Deth or defence, non other thing we wot."

This frefch king, that maleginis was hot,
With al his oft he cummyne our the plan,
And gawan fend o batell hyme agan ;   808
In myde the borde,[2] and feftinit in the ftell
The fperithis poynt, that bitith fcharp and well ;

Bot al to few thei war, and mycht nocht left
This gret Rout that cummyth one fo faft.   812
Than haith fir gawan fend, them to fupport,
One othir batell with one knychtly forte ;

And fyne the thrid, and fyne the ferde alfo ;
And fyne hyme-felf one to the feld can go,   816
When that he fauch thar latter batell fteir,
And the ten thoufand cummyne al thei vejr ;

[1] At the bottom of this page appears for the first time a
catchword, which is—"The wel fare."   [2] Or "berde."

Qwhar that of armes prewit he so well,

His ennemys gane his mortall [ftrokis] fell. 820

He goith ymong them in his hie curage,

As he that had of knyghthed the wfage,

And couth hyme weill *conten in* to on hour ;

Aȝaine his ftrok refiftit uon armour ; 824

And mony kny*ch*t, that worth ware and bolde,

War thore with hyme of arthur*is* houfhold,

And knyghtly gan one to the feld them bere,

And mekil wroght of armys In to were ; 828

S*ir* gawan than vpone fuch wyfʒ hyme bure,

This othere goith al to difcu*m*fitoure ;

Sewyne thoufand fled, *and* of the feld thei go,

Whar-of this king in to his hart was wo, 832

For of hyme felf he was of hie curage.

To galiot than fend he in mefag,

That he fhuld help his folk for to defende ;

And he to hyme hath xxx^te thousand sende ; 836

Whar-of this king gladith in his hart,

And thinkith to Reweng all the fmart

That he to-for haith fuffirit and the payne.

And al his folk returnyt Is ayayne 840

Atour the feld, and cu*m*myne thilk as haill ;[1]

The fwyft horfʒ goith-firft to the affall.

This noble knyght that feith the g*re*te forfʒ

Of armyt men, that cu*m*myne vpone horfʒ, 844

To-giddir femblit al his falowfchip,

And thoght them at the fharp poynt to kep,

So that thar harm̄ fhal be ful deir yboght.

This vthere folk with ftraucht courfʒ hath focht 848

Out of aray atour the larg felld ;

Thar was the ftrok*is* feftnit i*n* the fhelde,

Thei war Refauit at the fper*is* end.

So arthur*is* folk can manfully defend ; 852

Side notes:

He goes among them in his courage,

and many other of Arthur's knights perform wonders.

Maleginis goeth to discomfiture, and 7,000 of his men flee.

836 Galiot sends him 30,000 more.

[Fol. 11 *b.*]

His folk return across the field as thick as hail.

Arthur's folk receive them manfully,

---

[1] MS. "thilk as (Raynè) haill," as if it were at first intended to find a rime to "ayayne."

The formeſt can thar lyues end conclude,
Whar ſone aſſemblit al the multitude.
Thar was defens, ther was gret aſſaill,
Richt wonderfull and ſtrong was yᵉ bataill,   856

but sustain mucn pain,

Whar arthuris folk ſuſtenit mekil payn,
And knychtly them defendit haith aȝaine.

and cannot en-dure against so many.

Bot endur thei mycht, apone no wyſ,
The multitude and ek the gret ſuppriſ;   860
But gawan, wich that ſetith al his payn
Vpone knyghthed, defendid ſo aȝaine,
That only in the manhede of this knyght
His folk reIoſit them of his gret myght,   864
And ek abaſit hath his ennemys;
For throw the feld he goith in ſuch wyſ,
And in the preſ ſo manfully them ſeruith,

Gawane carves helmets in two, and smites heads off shoulders;

His ſuerd atwo the helmys al to-kerwith,   868
The hedis of he be the ſhouderis ſmat;
The horſ goith, of the maiſter deſolat.
But what awaleth al his beſynes,
So ſtrong and ſo inſufferable vas the preſ?   872

but his men re-cross the ford to ȝo to their lodges.

His folk are paſſit atour the furdis ilkon,
Towart ther bretis and to ther luges gon;
Whar he and many worthy knyght alſo
Of arthuris houſ endurit mekill wo,   876
That neuer men mar in to armys vroght
Of manhed, ȝit was It al for noght.

[Fol. 12.]

Thar was the ſtrenth, ther was the paſing myght

Gawane fights alone till night,

Of gawan, wich that whill the dirk nyght   880
Befor the luges ſaucht al hyme aloñ,
When that his falowis entrit ware ilkoñ,
On arthuris half war mony tan and ſlan;

when Galiot's folk return home.

And galotis folk Is hame returnyd aȝaine,   884
For it was lait; away the oftis ridith,
And gawan ȝit apone his horſ abidith,
With ſuerd in hond, when thei away var gon,
And so for-wrocht hys lymmys ver ilkon,   888

And wondit ek his body vp and doune,
Vpone his horſ Right thore he fel in ſwoune ;

Gawane swoons
upon his horse.

And thei hyme tuk *and* to his lugyne bare,
Boith king and qwen of hyme vare i*n* diſpare ;   892

The king and
queen fear he has
brought himself
to confusion.

For thei ſuppoſit, throw marwellis that he vroght,
He had hyme-ſelf to his confuſiou*n* broght.

[T]his [1] was nere by of melyhalt, the hyll,
Whar lanſcclot ʒit was w*ith* thc lady ſtill:.   896
The knyc*htis* of the court [can] paſing home ;
This ladiis knyc*htis* to hir palice com,
And told to hir, how that the feld was vent,
A*n*d of gawan, and of his hardyme*nt*,   900

The lady of Mely-
halt hears of Ga-
wane's deeds;

That merwell was his manhed to bchold ;
And ſone thir tithing*is* to the knyc*ht* vas told,

and Lancelot
also,

That was with wo and hewyneſs oppreſt ;
So noyith hyme his ſuiorne and his reſt,   904
And but dulay one for o knyc*ht* he ſcnd,

who sends for a
knight to take a
message to the
lady ;

That was moſt ſpeciall with the lady kend.
He comyne, and the knyc*ht* vn to hyme ſaid,
" Diſpleſ yow not, ſi*r*, be ʒhe not ill paid,   908
So homly thus I yow exort to go,
To gare my lady ſpek o word or two
With me, that am a carful pr*e*ſonere." [2]
" S*ir*, your commande y ſhall, w*ith*outen were,   912
Fulfill ; " and to his lady paſſit hec
In lawly wyſ beſiching hir, that ſhe
Wald grant hyme to pas at his requeſt,
Vnto hir knyc*ht*, ſtood wnd*er* hir areſt ;   916
And ſhe, that knew al gentilleſ aright,
Furth to his chamber paſſit wight [3] the licht.

who comes to his
chamber.
[Fol. 12 b.]

A nd he aroſ and ſaluſt Curtaſly
The lady, and ſaid, " madem, her I,   920

Lancelot be-
seeches her to ap-
point his ransom,

Your preſoner, beſekith yow that ʒhe
Wold merſy and compaſſione have of me,

---

[1] See note to this line.
[2] MS. "presone*rere*."   [3] Read "with" (?).

And mak the ranfone wich that I may yeif ;

I waift my tyme in presoune thus to leife.   924

For why I her on be report be told,

That arthur, with the flour of his houfholde,

Is cummyne here, and in this cuntre lyis,

And ftant In danger of his ennemyis,   928

And haith affemblit ; and eft this fhalt bee

Within fhort tyme one new affemblee.

Thar-for, my lady, y youe grace befech,

That I mycht pas, my Ranfon for to fech ;   932

resuming that some of Arthur's knights will pay it. Fore I prefume thar longith to that fort

That louid me, and fhal my nede fupport."

" Shire knycht, It ftant nocht in fich dugree ;

She replies that she does not want a ransom, but has imprisoned him for his guilt.   It is no ranfone wich that caufith me   936

To holden yow, or don yow fich offens ;

It is your gilt, It is your wiolens,

Whar-of that I defir no thing but law,

Without report your awn trefpas to knaw."   940

" Madem, your plefance may ye wel fulfill

Of me, that am in prefone at your will.

He prays for pardon, Bot of that gilt, I was for til excuf,

For that I did of werrey nede behwf,   944

It tuechit to my honore and my fame ;

I mycht nocht lefe It but hurting of my nam,

And ek the knycht was mor to blam than I.

But ye, my lady, of your curtefly,   948

Wold ʒe deden my Ransoune to refauc,

and begs for liberty : Of prefone fo I my libertee myght haue,

Y ware ʒolde euermore [to be] your knyght,

Whill that I leif, with al my holl myght.   952

And if fo be ye lykith not to ma

or at least to be allowed to go to the next battle, My ranfone, [madem,] if me leif to ga

To the affemble, wich fal be of new ;

under a promise to return at night. And as that I am feithful knycht and trew,   956

At nycht to yow I enter fhall aʒaine,

But if that deth or other lat certañ,

Throw wich I [may] have fuch Impediment,
That I be hold,[1] magre myne entent."   960
" Sir knycht," quod fhe. " I grant yow leif, withthy   She consents, if
                                                        he will specify to
Your name to me that ʒe wil fpecify."   her his name.
" Madem, as ʒit, futly I ne may
Duclar my name, one be no maner way ;   964
But I promyt, als faft as I haue tyme   He refuses for the
                                                        present.
Conuenient, or may vith-outen cryme,
I fhall ;" and than the lady faith hyme tyll,
" And I, fchir knycht, one this condifcione will   968
Grant yow leve, fo that ye oblift bee   She grants him
                                                        leave, under the
For to Return, as ye haue faid to me."   proposed condi-
                                                        tion.
Thus thei accord, the lady goith to reft,
The fone difcending clofit in the veft ;   972
The ferd day was dewyfit for to bee
Betuex the oftis of the affemblee.

And galiot Richt arly by the day,
   Ayane the feld he can his folk aray ;   976
And fourty thoufand armyt men haith he,   Galiot assembles
                                                        40,000 freah men.
That war not at the othir affemble,
Commandit to the batell for to gon ;
" And I my-felf," quod he, " fhal me difpone   980
On to the feild aʒaine the thrid day ;
Whar of this were we fhal the end affay."

And arthuris folk that come one euery fyd,   Arthur also pro-
                                                        vides his men for
   He for the feld can them for to prouide,   984   the field.
Wich ware to few aʒaine the gret affere
Of galiot ʒit to fuften the were.
The knychtis al out of the cete roſ   The knights of
                                                        Melyhalt join
Of melyholt, and to the femble gois.   988   him.
And the lady haith, in to facret wyſ,   The lady secretly
                                                        provides Lance-
Gart for hir knycht and prefoner dewyſ   lot with a red
                                                        courser, and a
In red al thing, that ganith for the were ;   shield and spear,
                                                        both red also.
His curfeir red, fo was boith fcheld and fpere. 992

                        ¹ MS. " behoid."

And he, to qwham the prefone hath ben fmart,

With glaid defir apone his curfour ftart ;

He rides towards the field, and halts in a plain by the river-side.
Towart the feld anon he gan to ryd,

And in o plan houit one reu*er* syde.   996

This kny*cht*, the wich that long haith ben i*n* cag,

Lancelot is encouraged, seeing the blithe morn, the mead, the river, the green woods, and the knights and banners.
He grew in to o frefch *and* new curage,

Seing the morow bly*th*full and amen,

The med, the Reuer, and the vodis gren,   1000

The kny*cht*is in [ther] armys them arayinge,

[Fol. 13 b.]
The baner*is* ayaine the feld difplayng,

His ȝouth in ftrenth and in pr*o*fperytee,

And fyne of luft the gret aduerfytee.[1]   1004

Thus in his tho*cht* remembryng at the laft,

Casting his eyes aside, he sees the queen looking over a parapet.
Eft*er*ward one fyd he gan his Ey to caft,

Whar our a bertes[2] lying haith he sen

Out to the feld luking was the qwen ;   1008

Sudandly with that his goft aftart

Love catches him by the heart.
Of loue anone haith caucht hyme by the hart ;

Than faith he, "How long fhall It be so,

Loue, at yow fhall wirk me al this wo ?   1012

Apone this wyſ to be Infortunat,

Hir for to f*er*ue the wich thei no thing wate

What fufferance I in hir wo endure,

Nor of my wo, nor of myne aduenture ?   1016

And I wnworthy ame for to attane

To hir p*re*sens, nor dare I noght complane.

He counsels his heart to help itself at need,
Bot, hart, fen at yow knawith fhe is here,

That of thi lyue and of thi deith is ftere,   1020

Now is thi tyme, now help thi-felf at neid,

And the dewod of eu*er*y point of dred,

to forego cowardice,
That cowardy be none In to the feñ,

Fore and yow do, yow knowis thi peyne, I weyn ; 1024

Yow art wnable cu*er* to attane

To hir mercy, or cum be ony mayne.

---

[1] May we read "diuerfytee" ?   [2] MS. "abertes."

Tharfor y red hir thonk at yow diſſeruc,

Or in hir *presens* lyk o kny*ch*t to ſterf." 1028

and to deserve her thanks or die.

With that confuſit *with* an hewy tho*ch*t,

Confused with a heavy thought,

Wich ner his deith ful oft tyme haith hyme ſo*ch*t,

Deuoydit was his sprit*is* and his goſt,

He wiſt not of hyme-ſelf nor of his oſt ; 1032

Bot one his horſ, als ſtill as ony ſton.

he [sits] on his horse as still as stone.

When that the kny*ch*t*is* armyt war ilkon,

To warnnyng them vp goith the bludy ſown,

The bugles are blown, and the knights are ready on horseback, 20,000 in number.

And eue*r*y knyght vpone his horſ is bown ; 1036

Twenty thouſand armyt men of were.

The king that day he wold non armys bere ;

His batell*is* ware devyſit eue*r*ilkon,

And them forbad out our the furd*is* to gon. 1040

They are forbidden to cross the fords, but cannot be restrained.

Bot frome that thei ther ennemys haith ſen,

In to ſuch wys thei cout*h* them noght ſuſteñ ;

Bot ov*r* thei went vithouten more delay,

[Fol. 14.]

And can them one that oy*er* sid aſſay. 1044

The red kny*ch*t ſtill in to his hewy thoght

*The red knight still halting by the ford, a heral*c* seizes his bridle, and bids him awake.*

Was hufyng ʒit apone the furd, *and* noght

Wiſt of hime ſelf ; with that a harrold com,

And ſone the kny*ch*t he be the brydill nom, 1048

Saying, "awalk ! It is no tyme to ſlep ;

Your worſchip more expedient vare to kep."

No word he ſpak, ſo prikith hyme the ſmart

Of hevynes, that ſtood vnto his hart. 1052

Two ſcrewis cam with that, of quhich [that] oñ

Two shrews next approach ; one takes his shield off his neck,

The kny*ch*t*is* ſheld ry*ch*t frome his hals haith toñ ;

That vthir watt*er* takith atte laſt,

the other casts water at his ventayle, which causes him to wink, and arouse himself.

And in the kny*ch*t*is* wentail haith It caſt ; 1056

When that he felt the vatt*er* that vas cold,

He wonk, and gan about hyme to behold,

And thinkith how he ſum-quhat haith myſgoñ.

With that his ſpere In to his hand haith ton, 1060

Goith to the feild *with*outen vordis more ;

He goes to the field, and sees the first-conquest king.

So was he vare whare that there cam before,

O manly man he was in to al thing,

And clepit was the ferſt-conquest king.   1064

The Red knycht with [the] ſpuris ſmat the ſted,

The tother cam, that of hyme hath no drede;

They meet. With ferſ curag ben the knychtis met,

The king his ſpere apone the knycht hath set,   1068

That al in peciſ flaw in to the felde;

The red knight, though shield-less, overthrows his foe. His hawbrek helpit, ſuppos he had no ſcheld.

And he the king in to the ſcheld haith ton,

That horſ and man boith to the erd ar gon.   1072

The shrew restores his shield. Than to the knycht he cummyth, that haith tan

His ſheld, to hyme deliuerith It ayane,

Beſiching hyme that of his Ignorance,

That knew hyme nat, as takith no grewance.   1076

The knycht his ſche[l]d but mor delay haith tak,

And let hyme go, and no thing to hyme ſpak.

Than thei the [1] wich that ſo at erth haith ſen

The men of the first-conquest king come to the rescue. Ther lord, the ferſt-conqueſt king, y meñ,   1080

In haiſt thei cam, as that thei var agrevit,

And manfully thei haith ther king Releuit.

[A]nd Arthuris folk, that lykith not to byde,

In goith the spuris in the ſtedis syde;   1084

[Fol. 14 b.] To-giddir thar aſſemblit al the oſt :

At whois meting many o knycht was loſt.

The battle was right cruel to behold. The batell was richt crewell to behold,

Of knychtis wich that haith there lyvis ʒolde.   1088

One to the hart the ſpere goith throw the ſcheld,

The knychtis gaping lyith in the feld.

The red knycht, byrnyng in loues fyre,

Goith to o knycht, als ſwift as ony vyre,   1092

The wich he perſit throuch and throuch the hart;

The red knight loses his spear, but draws his sword, and roams the field like a lion. The ſpere is went; with that anon he ſtart,

And out o ſuerd in to his hond he tais;

Lyk to o lyone in to the feld he gais,   1096

---

[1] MS. "thei," altered to "thee," which is still wrong.

In to his Rag fmyting to and fro
Fro fum the arm, fro fum the nek in two,
Sum in the feild lying is in fwou*n*,
And sum his fuerd goith to the belt al douñe.　1100　Some he cleaves
to the belt.
For qwhen that he beholdith to the qwen,
Who had ben thore his manhed to haue sen,
His doing in to armys and his myght,
Shwld fay in world war not fuch o wight.　1104
His faloufchip siche comfort of his dede　　His fellows take
comfort from his
Haith ton, that thei ther ennemys ne dreid ;　deeds,
But can them-felf ay manfoly conten
In to the ftour, that hard was to fuften ;　1108
For galyot was O pafing multitude　　though Galiot's
host was a sur-
Of prewit men in armys that war gude,　passing multi-
The wich can w*ith* o frefch curag affaill　tude.
Ther ennemys that day In to batell ;　1112
That ne ware not the vorfchip *and* manhede　Had it not been
for the manhood
Of the red kny*cht*, in p*er*ell and in dreid　of the red knight,
Arthur*is* folk had ben, vith-outen vere ;　Arthur's folk had
been in peril.
Set thei var good, thei var of fmal powere.　1116
And gawan, wich gart bryng hyme-felf befor　Gawane is led to
the parapet,
To the bertes, set he was vondit sore,
Whar the qwen vas, and whar that he my*cht* see
The manere of the oft and affemble ;　1120
And when that he the gret manhed haith sen
Of the red kny*cht*, he faith one to the qwen,　and saith to the
queen, that none
" Madem, ȝone knyght in to the arnys Rede,　ever did better
than yon red
Nor neu*er* I hard nore faw in to no fted　1124　knight.
O kny*cht*, the wich that in to fchortar fpace
In armys haith mor forton nore mor grace ;
Nore bettir doith boith with fper and fcheild,
He is the hed and comfort of our feild."　1128　[Fol. 15.]
" Now, f*ir*, I traift that neu*er* more vas fen　The queen prays
for Lancelot.
No man in feild more knyghtly hyme *con*ten ;
I pray to hyme that eu*er*y thing hath cure,
Saif hyme fro deth or wykit aduenture."　1132

3

The field was
perilous on both
sides,
The feild It was rycht perellus and ftrong
On boith the fydis, and continewit long,

from early morn
till the sun had
gone down.
Ay from the fone the varldis face gan licht
Whill he was gone and cumyne vas the nycht ;   1136
And than o forß thei mycht It not afftart,
On euery fyd behouit them depart.

Every knight
then returns
home, and the red
knight privily
goes back to the
city.
The feild is don and ham goith euery knycht,
And prevaly, unwift of any wicht,   1140
The way the red knycht to the cete taiis,
As he had hecht, and in his chambre gais.
When arthure hard how the knycht Is gon,
He blamyt fore his lordis euerilk-one ;   1144
And oft he haith remembrit in his thoght,

Arthur, seeing
the multitude of
Galiot's men, re-
calls his dream,
saying,
What multitud that galiot had broght ;
Seing his folk that ware so ewil arayt,
In to his mynd he ftondith al affrayt,   1148
And faith, " I traift ful futh It fal be founde
My drem Richt as the clerkis gan expounde ;

" My men now
fail me at need."
For why my men failʒeis now at neid,
My-felf, my londe, in perell and in dreide."   1152

Galiot tells his
council
And galiot vpone hie worfchip set,
And his confell anon he gart be fet,
To them he faith, " with arthur weil ʒe see
How that It ftant, and to qwhat degre,   1156
Aʒanis ws that he is no poware ;

that there is no
honour in con-
quering Arthur,
Wharfor, me think, no worfchip to ws ware
In conqueryng of hyme, nor of his londe,
He haith no ftrenth, he may ws not vithftonde. 1160
Wharfor, me think It beft is to delay,

and proposes a
twelvemonth's
truce.
And refput hyme for a tuelmoñeth day,
Whill that he may affemble al his myght ;
Than is mor worfchip aʒanis hyme to ficht ;"   1164
And thus concludit thoght hyme for the beft.
The very knychtis paffing to there Reft ;
Of melyholt the ladeis knychtis ilkone
Went home, and to hir presens ar thei gon ;   ·1168

At qwhome ful fone than gan fcho to Inquere,

And al the maner of the oftis till spere :

How that It went, and in what maner wyſ,

Who haith moſt worſchip, *and* who is moſt to pryſ?

"Madem," q*uod* thei, "O kny*ch*t was In the feild,

Of Red was al his armour and his fheld,

Whois manhed can al otheris to exced,

May nan report in armys half his deid ; . 1176

Ne wor his worſchip, ſhortly to conclud,

Our folk of help had ben al deſtitud.

He haith the thonk, tho vorſchip in hyme lyis,

That we the feld defendit in fich wyſ." 1180

The lady thane one to hir-felf haith tho*ch*t,

"Whether Is ʒone my prefonar, ore noght?

The futhfaſtneſ that ſhal y wit onon."

When euery wight vn to ther Reſt war gon, 1184

She clepith one hir cwfynes ful nere

Wich was to hir moſt fpeciall and dere,

And faith to hir, "qwheyar if yone bee

Our prefoner, my confell Is we fee." 1188

With that the maden In hir hand hath ton

O torche, and to the ſtabille ar thei gon ;

And fond his ſted lying at the ground,

Wich wery was, ywet *with* mony wounde. 1192

The maden faith, "vpone this horſ is fen,

He in the place quhar strok*is* was hath beñ ;

And ʒhit the horſ It is no*ch*t wich that hee

Fur*th* *with* hyme hade ;"—the lady faid, "*per* dee,

He vſyt haith mo horſ than one or two ;

I red one to his armys at we go."

Tharwith one to his armys ar thei went ;

Thei fond his helm, thei fond his hawbrek rent, 1200

Thei fond his ſcheld was fruſchit al to no*ch*t ;

At ſchort, his armour In fich wyſ vas vro*ch*t

In eu*er*y place, that no thing was left haill,

Nore neu*er* eft accordith to bataill. 1204

The lady of Mely-holt aſks her knights who hath won moſt honour.

[Fol. 15 *b*.]

They reply, that a red knight had exceeded all others.

The lady wonders if her priſoner is meant.

She calls her cousin,

who takes a torch, and they go to the ſtable,

and find his ſteed wounded.

Next they view his armour,

and find his hauberk rent, and his shield fruſhed all to naught.

They think he has
well used his
armour.
Than faith the lady to hir cufyneß,

"What fal we fay, what of this mater geß?"

"Madem, I fay, thei have nocht ben abwsyt;

He that them bur fchortly he has them vfyt."   1208

"That may ʒe fay, fuppos the beft that lewis,

Or moft of worfchip in til armys prewis,

Or ʒhit haith ben in ony tyme beforñ,

Had them in feld in his maft curag borñ."   1212

They next visit
the knight him-
self,
"Now," quod the lady, "will we paß, and see

The knycht hyme-felf, and ther the futh may we

[Fol. 16.]
Knaw of this thing."   Incontynent them [1] boith

Thir ladeis vn to his chambre goith.   1216

who was now
asleep.
The knycht al wery fallyng was on flep;

This maden paffith In, and takith kep.

The lady's cousin
observes his
breast and shoul-
ders bloody, his
face hurt, and his
fists swollen.
Sche fauch his breft with al his fchowderis bare,

That bludy war and woundit her and thare;   1220

His face was al to-hurt and al to-fchent,

His newis fwellyng war and al to-Rent.

Sche fmylyt a lyt, and to hir lady faid,

"It femyth weill this knycht hath ben affaid."   1224

The lady next ob-
serves him,
The lady fauch, and rewit in hir thoght

The knychtis worfchip wich that he haith vroght.

and is smitten to
the heart by the
dart of love,
In hire Remembrance loues fyre dart

With hot defyre hir fmat one to the hart;   1228

And then a quhill, with-outen wordis mo,

In to hir mynd thinking to and fro,

She ftudeit fo, and at the laft abraid

and prays her
cousin to draw
aside, while she
kisses the knight.
Out of hir thocht, and fudandly thus faid,   1232

"With-draw," quod fhe, "one fyd a lyt [2] the lyght,

Or that I paß that I may kyß the knyght."

Her cousin re-
proves her,
"Madem," quod fche, "what is It at ʒe meñ?

Of hie worfchip our mekill have ʒe señ   1236

So sone to be fupprifit with o thoght.

lest the knight
should awake.
What is It at ʒhe think? prefwm ʒe noght

That if yon knycht wil walkin, and perfaif,

              [1] "then" (?).   [2] MS. "alyt."

He fhal yarof no thing bot ewill confaif ; 1240
In his entent Ruput yow therby
The ablare to al lychtneß and foly ?
And blam the more al vtheris in his mynd,
If your gret wit in fich defire he fynde ?" 1244

"Nay," quod the lady, "no thing may I do The lady replies.
For fich o knycht may be defam me to."

"Madem, I wot that for to loue yone knycht, Her cousin next argu** the point ;
Confidir his fame, his worfchip, and his mycht ; 1248
And to begyne as worfchip wil dewyß,
Syne he ayaine mycht lowe yow one fuch wyß,
And hold yow for his lady and his loue,
It war to yow no maner of Reprwe. 1252
But quhat if he appelit be and thret "What if he loves another?"
His hart to lowe, and ellis whar y-fet ?
And wel y wot, madem, if It be so,
His hart hyme sal not fuffir to loue two, 1256
For noble hart wil have no dowbilneß ; [Fol. 16 b.]
If It be fo, ʒhe tyne yowr low, I geß ;
Than is your-felf, than is your loue Refufit,
Your fam is hurt, your gladneß is conclufit. 1260
My confell is, therfore, you to abften
Whill that to yow the werray Rycht be fen
Of his entent, the wich ful fon ʒhe may
Have knawlag, If yow lykith to affay." 1264
So mokil to hir lady haith fhe vroght She persuades the lady to return to her chamber, without further delay.
That at that tyme fhe haith Returnyt hir thocht.
And to hir chambre went, withouten more,
Whar loue of new affaith hir ful sore. 1268
So well long thei fpeking of the knycht,
Hir cufynace hath don al at fhe mycht Her cousin labours to expel her love for Lancelot from her thoughts, but her labour is in vain.
For to expel that thing out of hir thocht ;
It wil not be, hir labour Is for nocht. 1272
Now leif we hir In to hir neweft pan,
And to arthur we wil retwrn agañ.

EXPLICIT PRIMUS LIBER, INCIPIT SECUNDUS.

[BOOK II.]

Night.

The clowdy nyght, wndir whois obſcure

    The reſt and quiet of euery criatur   1276

Lyith ſauf, quhare the goſt w*ith* beſyneß

Is occupiit, w*ith* thoghtfull hewynes;

And, for that thoc*h*t furth ſchewing vil h*is* myc*h*t,

Go ſare-wel reſt and quiet of the nyc*h*t.   1280

Artur, I meyne, to whome that reſt is noc*h*t,

But al the nyc*h*t ſuppriſit is with thoc*h*t;

In to his bed he turnyth to and fro,

Remembryng the apperans of his wo,   1284

That is to ſay, his deith, his confuſioune,

And of his realme the opin diſtruccioune.

That in h*i*s wit he can no thing prowide,

Bot tak his forton thar for to abyd.   1288

Vp goith the ſon, vp goith the hot morow;

The thoghtful king al the nyc*h*t to ſorow,

That ſauch the day, vpone his ſeit he ſtart,

And furth he goith, diſtrublit in his hart.   1292

A quhill he walkith in his penſyf goſt,

So was he ware thar cummyne to the oſt

O clerk, with whome he was aqwynt befor,

In to his tyme non bett*er* was y-bore;   1296

Of qwhois com he gretly vas Reioſit,

For in to hyme ſum comfort he ſuppoſit;   ﹚

Betuex them was one hartly affeccioune.

Non order*is* had he of Relegioune,   1300

Fam*us* he was, and of gret excellence,

And ryc*h*t exp*er*t in al the vij. ſcience;

Contemplatif and chaſt in gou*er*nance,

And clepit was the maiſt*er* amytans.   1304

Arthur cannot rest.

The sun goeth up.

[Fol. 17.]

Arthur goeth forth.

He hears that a clerk has arrived,

between whom and himself there was a hearty affection.

He was expert in the seven sciences,

and was named Amytans.

The king befor his palȝoune one the gren,
That knew hyme well, *and* haith his cummyn feñ,
Velcummyt hyme, and maid hyme rycht gud chere,
And he agan, agrewit as he were, 1308
Saith, "nothir of thi falofing, nor the,
Ne rak I nocht, ne charg I nocht," quod hee.
Than q*uod* the king, "maifter, *and* for what why
Ar ȝe agrewit? or quhat treffpas have I ·. 1312
Commytit, fo that I fhal yow difples?"
Quod he, "no thing It is ayane myn efß,
But only *contrare* of thi-felf alway;
So fare the courß yow paffith of the way. 1316
Thi fchip, that goth apone the ftormy vall,
Ney of thi careldis in the fwelf it fall,
Whar fhe almoft is in the perell drent;
That is to fay, yow art fo far myfwent 1320
Of wykitneß vpone the vrechit dans,
That yow art fallyng in the storng¹ vengans
Of goddis wreth, that fhal the fon deuour;
For of his ftrok approchit now the hour 1324
That boith thi Ringe, thi ceptre, *and* thi crovñ,
Frome hie eftat he fmyting fhal adoune.
And that accordith well, for in thi thocht
Yow knawith not hyme, the wich that haith the wrocht,
And fet the vp in to this hie eftat
From powert; for, as the-felwyne wat,
It cummyth al bot only of his myght,
And not of the, nor of thi elderis Richt 1332
To the difcending, as in heritage,
For yow was not byget in to spoufag.
Wharfor yow aucht his biding to obferf,
And at thy mycht yow fhuld hyme pleß *and* ferf; 1336
That dois yow nat, for yow art fo confuffit
With this fals warld, that thow haith hyme Refufit,

---

¹ So in MS. Is it necessary to alter it to "strong"?

Arthur welcomes him.

He recks nothing of Arthur's salutation.

The king inquires what trespass he has committed.

He replies, "It is not against me, but against thy-self.

Thy ship is al-most drowned in the whirlpool.

That is, God's wrath shall soon devour thee.

Because thou knowest Him not, who set thee up in this high estate,

though not begot-ten in spousage.
[Fol. 17 *b*.]

And brokine haith his reul and ordynans,

The wich to the he gave in gouernans.　　　1340

He made thee
king,

He maid the king, he maid the gouernour,

He maid the fo, and fet in hie honour

Of Realmys and of [diuerſ] peplis fere ;

Efter his loue thow ſhuld them Reul and ſtore,　　1344

And wnoppreſſit kep in to Iuſtice,

The wykit men and pwnyce for ther wice.

Yow dois no thing, bot al in the contrare,

and thou suffer-
est thy people to
fare ill.

And ſuffrith al thi puple to forfare ;　　　1348

Yow haith non Ey but one thyne awn delyt,

Or quhat that pleſing ſhall thyne appetyt.

In the defalt of law and of Iuſtice,

Wndir thi houd is fufferyt gret fuppriſ　　　1352

Of fadirleſ, and modirleſ alfo,

And wedwis ek fuſtenit mekill wo.

The poor are op-
pressed.

With gret myfchef oppreſſit ar the pure ;

And thow art cauſ of al this hol Iniure,　　　1356

Whar-of that god a raknyng fal craf

At the, and a fore Raknyng fal hafe ;

For thyne eſtat is gewyne to Redreſ

Thar ned, and kep them to rychtwyneſ ;　　　1360

And thar is non that ther complantis heris ;

The mychty folk, and ek the flattereris

Ar cheif with the, and doith this oppreſſioun ;

If they complain,
it is their confu-
sion.

If thai complen, It is ther confuſſioune.　　　1364

And daniell faith that who doith to the pure,

Or faderleſ, or modirleſ, EnIure,

Or to the puple, that ilke to god doth hee ;

And al this harme fuſtenit Is throw the.　　　1368

Yow fufferith them, oppreſſith and anoyith ;

So yow art cauſ, throw the thei ar diftroyth ;

Than, at thi mycht, god fo diſtroys yow.

What wilt thou
do, when God
destroys sinners
off the visage of
the earth ?

What ſhal he do aȝane ? quhat ſhal yow,　　　1372

When he diftroys by vengance of his fuerd

The fynaris fra the vysagis of the Erde ?

Than vtraly yow fhall diftroyt bee;
And that Richt weill apper*is* now of thee,   1376
For yow allon byleft art folitere;
And the wyſ salamon can duclar,
' Wo be to hyme that is byleft alone,
He haith no help ;' so Is thi forton goñe ;   1380
For he is callit, w*ith* quhom that god is no*ch*t,
Allone ; and fo thi wykitneſ haith wro*ch*t·.
That god hyme-felf he is bycu*m*myn thi fo,
Thi pupleis hart*is* haith thow tynt alfo ;   1384
Thi wykitneſ thus haith the maid alon,
That of this erth thi fortone Is y-goñ.
Yow mone thi lyf, yow mone thi vorfchip tyne,
And eft to deth that neu*er* fhal haf fyne."   1388
" **M**aist*er*," q*u*od he, " of yow*r*e beneuolens,
Y yow befech that tueching my*n* offens,
3he wald wichfaif your confell to me If
How I fal mend, and ek her-eftir leif."   1392
" Now," q*u*od the maifter, " and I have m*er*well qwhy
Yow afkith confail, and wil in non affy,
Nor wyrk thar-by; and 3hit yow may In tym,
If yow lykith to amend the cryme."   1396
" 3his," faith the king, " and futhfaftly I will
3our ordynans in eu*er*y thing fulfyll."
" And if the lift at confail to abide,
The remed of thi harme to prouyde—   1400
Firft, the begyning is of fapiens,
To dreid the lord and his mag*n*ificens ;
And what thow haith in contrar hyme ofendit,
Whill yow haith my*ch*t, of fre defir amend it ;¹   1404
Repent thi gilt, repent thi gret trefpaſ,
And remembir one goddis richwyfneſ ;
How for to hyme that wykitneſ anoyt,
And how the way of fynaris he diftroit ;   1408

Marginal notes:
Solomon faith, 'Wo to him who is left alone! He hath no help.'
[Fol. 18.]
Thou hast lost thy people's hearts,
and shalt come to death that hath no end."
Arthur asks how he shall amend,
and promises to fulfil his bidding.
The master replies, "Thou must first dread the Lord.
Repent thy guilt.

¹ MS. "amendit."

And if ye lyk to ryng wnd*er* his peſ,
Ye wengaus of his myc*h*ty hond yow feſ,
This fchalt yow do, if yow wil be p*er*fit.
Firſt, mone yow be penitent and contrit   1412
Of euery thing that tuechith thi confiens,
Done of fre will, or ȝhit of neglygens.

Thy need re-
quireth full con-
trition.
Thi neid requirith ful contretioune,
Princepaly with-out concluſioune ;   1416
With humble hart and goſtly byſyneſ,
Syne ſhalt yow go deuotly the confeſ

Confess to some
holy confessor.
Ther-of vnto ſum haly confeffour,
That the wil confail tueching thin arour ;   1420
And to fulfill his will and ordynans,

Do penance, and
amend all
wrong."
In ſatiffaccione and doing of penans,
And to amend al wrang and al Iniure,
By the ydone til euery Creature ;   1424

[Fol. 18 *b*.]
If yow can In to thi hart fynde,
Contretioune well degeſt In to thi mynd.
Now go thi weie, for if it leful were,
Confeſſioune to me, I ſhuld It here."   1428

Arthur tries to
remember every
sin done since his
years of inno-
cence,
Than arthur, Richt obedient *and* mek,
   In to his wit memoratyve can ſeik
Of euery gilt wich that he can pens,
Done frome he paſſith the ȝer*is* of Innocens ;   1432
And as his maiſter hyme commandit had.,

and made his con-
fession with la-
mentable cheer.
He goith and his confeſſione haith he maad
Richt deuotly with lementable chere ;
The man*er* wich quho lykith for to here   1436
He may It fynd In to the holl romans,
Of confeſſione o paſing c*er*cumſtans.
I can It not, I am no confeffour,
My wyt haith ewill confat of that labour,   1440
Quharof I wot I aucht repent me fore.
The king wich was confeſſit, what is more,
Goith and til his maiſt*er* tellith hee,
How euery fyne In to his awn degree   1444

He shew, that mycht occuryng to his mynde.
" Now," quod the maiftere, " left thow aght behynde
Of albenak the vorfchipful king ban,
The wich that vas in to my feruice flan, 1448
And of his wif difherift eft alfo?
Bot of ther fone, the wich was them fro,
Ne fpek ¹ y not;"—the king in his entent
Abafyt was, and furthwith is he went -. 1452
Azane, and to his confeffour declarith;
Syne to his maifter he ayane Reparith,
To quhome he faith, " I aftir my cunyng
Your ordinans fulfillit in al thing; 1456
And now right hartly y befeich and prey,
3he wald withfchaif fum thing to me fay,
That may me comfort in my gret dreid,
And how my men ar faljet in my Neid, 1460
And of my dreme, the wich that is fo dirk."
This maifter faith, " and thow art bound to virk
² A T my confail, and if yow has maad
  Thi confeffione, as yow before hath faid, 1464
And in thi conciens thinkith perfeuere,
As I prefume that thow onon fhalt here
That god hyme-felf fhal fo for yᵉ prouide,
Thow fhal Remayne and In thi Ring abyd. 1468
And why thi men ar faljet At this nede,
At fhort this is the cauſ, fhalt yow nocht dred,
Fore thow to gode was frawart and perwert;
Thi ryngne and the he thocht for to fubwart; 1472
And yow fal knaw na power may recift,
In contrar quhat god lykith to affi[f]t.
The vertw nore the ftrenth of victory
It cummyth not of man, bot anerly 1476

Marginal notes:
"Leftest thou aught behind," quoth the master, "about Ban, king of Albanak, and his disinherited wife?"

The king again confesses, and returns,

prays for comfort,

and inquires about his dream.

The master saith, "If thou art bound to work by my counsel,

thou shalt abide in thy kingdom. [Fol. 19.]

Strength of victory cometh from God only.

---

¹ MS. apparently has "srpek;" but a comparison with line 1543 shews that the apparent r is due to the meeting of two slight flourishes belonging to the s and p.

² This line (though it should not) begins with an illuminated letter.

Of hyme, the wich haith euery ftrinth ; *and* than,

If that the waiis pleffit hyme of man,

He fhal have forƥ aӡane his ennemys.

A-ryght agan apone the famyne vyƥ,   1480

Whoso displeases
Him shall be sub-
ject to his ene-
mies, as we read
in the Bible con-
cerning the Jews.

If he difpleƥ vn to the lord, he fhall

Be to his fais a fubiet or a thrall,

As that we may In to the bible red,

Tueching the folk he tuk hyme-felf to led   1484

In to the lond, the wich he them byhicht.

Ay when thei ӡhed in to his ways Richt,

Ther fois gon befor there fuerd to no*ch*t ;

When they
wrought against
Him, they were
so full of fear that
the sound of a
falling leaf made
a thousand flee.

And when that thei ayanis hyme hath vro*ch*t,   1488

Thei war fo full of radur and diffpare,

That of o leif fleing in the air,

The found of It haith gart o thoufand tak

At onys apone them-felf the bak,   1492

And al ther manhed vterly foryhet ;

Sich dreid the lord apone ther hart*is* fet.

So fhalt yow know no powar may wi*th*ftond,

Ther god hyme-felf hath ton the cauƥ on hond.   1496

Thine own of-
fence is the rea-
son why thy
people fail thee.

And ye quhy ftant in thyne awn offens,

That al thi puple falӡhet off defens.

And fum ar falӡeing magre ther entent ;

Thei ar to quhom thow yewyne hath thi rent,   1500

Thi gret Reuard, thi richeƥ and thi gold,

And cheriffith and held in thi houfhold.

Bot the moft *part* ar falӡheit the at wyll,

Thou hast shewn
some of them un-
kindness,

To quhome yow haith wnkyndneƥ fchawin till ; 1504

Wrong and inIure, and ek defalt of law,

And pwnyfing of qwhich that thei ftand aw ;

And makith feruice but reward or fee,

Syne haith no thonk bot fre*m*mytneƥ of the.   1508

Such folk to the cu*m*myth bot for dred,

Not of fre hart the for to help at nede.

And what awalith owthir fheld or fper,

Or horƥ or armoure according for ye were,   1512

Vith-outen man them for to ftere and led?

And man, yow wot, that vautith hart is ded,

That in to armys feruith he of noght ;

A cowart oft ful mekil harm haith vroght.   1516

In multitude nore зhit in confluens

Of fich, is nowther manhed nore defens.

And fo thow hath the rewlyt, that almoft

Of al thi puple the hartis ben ylost ;   ·.   1520

And tynt richt throw thyne awn myfgouernans

Of auerice and of thyne errogans.

What is o prince? quhat is o gouernoure

Withouten fame of worfchip and honour?   1524

What is his mycht, fuppos he be A lorde,

If that his folk fal nocht to hyme accorde?

May he his Rigne, may he his holl Empire

Suften al only of his owne defyre,   1528

In ferwyng of his wrechit appetit

Of awerice and of his awn delyt,

And hald his men, wncherift, in thraldome?

Nay ! that fhal fone his hie eftat confome.   1532

For many o knycht [1] therby is broght ydoune,

All vtraly to ther confufioune ;

For oft it makith vther kingis by

To wer on them In traft of victory ;   1536

And oft als throw his peple is diftroyth,

That fyndith them agrewit or anoyth ;

And god alfo oft with his awn fwerd,

Punyfith ther wyfis one this erd.   1540

Thus falith not o king but gouernans,

Boith realme and he goith one to myfchans."

AS thai war thus fpeking of this thinge,

Frome galiot cam two knychtis to the king ; 1544

That one the king of hundereth knychtis was ;

That other to nome the fyrft-conqueft king [2] has,

---

[1] "king" (?).

[2] MS. "kinghe," a spelling due to confusion with "knight."
See l. 1533.

Marginal notes:

[Fol. 19 b.]

and a man that wanteth heart is dead.

Thou hast so conducted thyself as to lose all thy people's hearts.

What is a prince without honour?

Can he by himself sustain his kingdom, by serving his own appetite?

His oppression of his people consumes his high estate, and makes other kings war on them.

God also punishes their vices."

Meanwhile, the king of a hundred knights and the first-conquest king come from Gallot,

At firft that galyot conquerit of one.

The nereft way one to the king thei gon,   1548

And vp he rofƷ. as he that wel couth do

Honor, to quhome that It afferith to ;

And Ʒhit he wift not at thei kingis were ;

So them [1] thei boith and vyth rycht knyghtly cher 1552

Reuerendly thei faluft hyme, and thane

and the former
delivers his mes-
sage, to the effect
that The king of hunder knyghtis he began

And faid hyme, " fir, to Ʒow my lord ws fende,

[Fol. 20.] Galiot, whilk bad ws fay he wende,   1556

That of this world the vorthieft king wor Ʒhe,

Greteft of men and of awtoritee.

Galiot wonders at
the feebleness of
Arthur's folk, Wharof he has gret wonder that Ʒhe ar

So feble cummyne In to his contrare,   1560

For to defend your cuntre and your londe,

And knowith well Ʒhe may hyme nocht withftonde.

Wharfor he thinkith no worfchip to conquere,

Nore in the weris more to perfynere ;   1564

Confiddir yowr waknefƷ and yowr Indegens,

AƷanis hyme as now to mak defens.

and is willing to
grant a year's
truce, Wharfore, my lord haith grantit by vs here

Trewis to yhow and refput for o Ʒhere,   1568

if Arthur will
return to fight
against him in a
year's time; If that yhow lykith by the Ʒheris fpace

For to retwrn ayane In to this place,

Her to manteine yhour cuntre and withftond

Hyme with the holl power of yhour lond.   1572

And for the tyme the trewis fhal endure,

Yhour cuntre and yhour lond he will affurre ;

And wit Ʒhe Ʒhit his powar is nocht here.

And als he bad ws fay yhow by the yhere,   1576

and desires to
have the red
knight in his
household. The gud knycht wich that the Red armys bure

And in the feild maid the difcumfiture,

The whilk the flour of knychthed may be cold,

He thinkith hyme to haue of his houfhold."   1580

[1] " then " (?).

"Well," quod the king, "I have hard quhat yhe fay,
But if god will, and ek if that I may,
In to fich wyß I think for to withftond,
Yhour lord fhall have no powar of my londe." 1584

Of this mefag the king Reiofing haß,
And of the trewis wich that grantit was,
Bot anoyt ʒhit of the knycht was he,
Wich thei awant to have in fuch dogre. 1588

Ther leif thei tuk ; and when at thei war gon,

¹This maifter faith, "how lykith god difpone !
  Now may yhow fe and futh is my recorde ;
For by hyme now is makith this accord ; 1592
And by non vthir worldly providens,
Sauf only grant of his bynewolans,
To fe if that the lykith to amend,
And to prouid thi cuntre to defend. 1596
Wharfor yow fhalt in to thi lond home fair,
And gowerne the as that I fhall declaire.
Firft, thi god with humble hart yow ferfe,
And his comand at al thi mycht obferf ; 1600
And fyne, lat paß the ilk bleffit wonde
Of lowe with mercy Iuftly throw thi londe ;
And y befeich—to quhome yow fal direke
The rewle vpone, the wrangis to correk— 1604
That yow be nocht in thi electioune blynde ;
For writin It Is and yow fal trew It fynde.
That, be thei for to thonk or ellis blame,
And towart god thi part fhal be the faɱ ; 1608
Of Ignorans fhalt yow nocht be excufit,
Bot in ther werkis forly be accufit,
For thow fhuld euer cheß apone fich wyß
The minifteris ² that rewll haith of Iuftice :— 1612
Firft, that he be defcret til wnderftond
And lowe and ek the mater of the londe ;

¹ The initial T is illuminated. ² MS. "mifteris."

And be of mycḧt and ek Autoritee,
(For puple ay contempnith low degre,)   1616
And that of trouth he folow furth the way ;
That is als mych as he louyth trewth alway,
And haitith al them the wich fal pas therfro.
Syne, that he god dreid and lowe al-so.   1620

Avoid avaricious and wrathful men.

Of auerice be-war with the defyre,
And of hyme full of haftynes and fyre ;
Be-war thar-for of malice and defire,
And hyme alfo that lowith no medyre ;   1624
For al this abhominable was hold,
When Iuftice was in to the tymis olde.
For qwho that is of an of thir by-know,
The left of them fubuertith all the low,   1628
And makith It w[n]Iustly [1] to procede ;

Eschew unfit men, for this shall be thy meed in the day of judgment.

Efchew tharfor, for this fal be thi meid
Apone the day when al thing goith aright,
Whar none excuß hidyng fchal ye lyght ;   1632
But he the Iug, that no man may fuffpek,
Euery thing ful Iuftly fal correk.
Be-war thar-with, as before have I told,
And cheß them wyfly that thi low fhal hold.   1636
And als I will that it well oft be sen,
Richt to thi-self how thei thi low conten ;

Be diligent to in-quire how judgment is given.

And how the Right, and how the dom is went,
For to Inquer that yow be delygent.   1640

[Fol. 21.]

And punyß for, for o thing fhal yow know,
The most trefpas is to fubuert the low,
So that yow be not in thar gilt accufit,
And frome the froit of bliffit folk refufit.   1644

Visit every chief town throughout the bounds of thy kingdom.

And pas yow fhalt to euery chef toune,
Throw-out the boundis of thi Regioune
Whar yow fall be, that Iuftice be Elyk
With-out diuifione baith to pur and ryk.   1648

[1] MS. " w Iustly."

And that thi puple have [ane] awdiens

W*ith* thar complant*is*, and alfo thi *presens* ;

For qwho his eris frome the puple ftekith,

And not his hond in ther fupport furth rekith,   1652

His dom fall be ful grewous & ful hard,

,When he fal cry and he fal noc*h*t be hard.

Wharfor thyne cris ifith to the pwre,   *Give thine ears to the poor.*

Bot in redreſ of ned, & not of in*I*ure ;   1656

Thus fall thei don of Reſſone & knawlag.

B ut king*is* when thei ben of tend*er* ag,   *Kings, while minors, may be excused;*

   Y wil not fay I traft thei ben excufit,

Bot fchortly thei fall be far accufit,   1660

When fo thei cum to yheris of Refone,   *but, when of age, they must punish those that have wrested justice.*

If thei tak not full contrifioune,

And pwnyſ them that hath ther low myfgyit.

That this is trouth it may not be denyit ;   1664

For vther ways thei fal them not difcharg,

[Excep thei pwnyſ them that have the charg][1]

One eftatis of ther realm, that fhold

W*ith*-in his ȝouth fe that his low be hold.[2]   1668

And thus thow the, w*ith* mercy, kep alway   *Temper Justice with mercy.*

Of Iuftice fur*th* the ilk bleffit way.

A nd of thi wordis beis trew and ftable,   *Be true and stable in thy words.*

   Spek not to mych, nore be not vareable.   1672

O king*is* word fhuld be o king*is* bonde,

And faid It is, a king*is* word fhuld ftond ;

O king*is* word, among our fad*er*is old,

Al-oùt more *precious* & more fur was hold   1676

Than was the oth or feel of any wight ;

O king of trouth fuld be the werray lyght,   *A king should be the very light of truth.*

So treuth and Iuftice to o king accordyth.

And als, as thir clerk*is* old recordith,   1680

[3] I n tyme is larges and humilitee

   Right well according vnto hie dugre,

[1] A blank space here occurs, just sufficient to contain one line.

[2] MS. " behold."

[3] The initial I is illuminated ; rather because there is here a change of subject than because it begins a new sentence.

4

And pleſſith boith to god and man al-so ;

[Fol. 21 b.] Wharfor I wil, incontinent thow go,   1684

And of thi lond in euery part abide,

Whar yow gar fet and clep one euery fid

Out of thi cuntreis, and ek out of thi tovnis,

Invite thy dukes, earls, great barons, thy poor knights, and thy bachelors, and welcome them severally.

Thi dukis, erlis, and thi gret baronis,   1688

Thi pur knychtis, and thi bach[e]leris,

And them refauf als hartly as afferis,

And be them-felf yow welcum them ilkon :

Syne, them to glaid and cheris, thee difpone   1692

With fefting and with humyll contynans.

Be not penfyve, nore proud in arrogans,

Keep company not with the rich man only, but with the poor worthy man also.

Bot with them hold in gladnes cumpany ;

Not with the Rich nor myghty anerly,   1696

Bot with the pure worthi man alfo,

With them thow fit, with them yow ryd and go.

I fay not to be our fameliar,

For, as the moft philofephur can duclar,   1700

Yet remember that familiarity breeds contempt.

To mych to oyſ familiaritee

Contempnyng bryngith one to hie dugre ;

Bot cherice them with wordis fair depaynt,

So with thi pupelle fal yow the aquaynt.   1704

Choose out of each district an aged knight to be thy counsellor.

Than of ilk cuntre wyfly yow enquere

An agit knycht to be thi confulere,

That haith ben hold in armys Richt famus,

Wyſ and difcret, & no thing Inwyus ;   1708

For there is non that knowith fo wel, I-wyſ

O worthy man as he that worthi Is.

When thou hast sojourned long in a place, then provide thee with plenty of horses, armour, gold, silver, and clothing;

When well long haith yow fwiornyt in a place,

And well acqueynt the vith thi puple has,   1712

Than fhalt thow ordand & prowid the

Of horſ and ek of armour gret plente ;

Of gold, and filuer, tressore, and cleithing,

And euery Riches that longith to o king ;   1716

and, before leaving, distribute gifts liberally.

And when the lykith for to tak thi leif,

By largeſ thus yow thi rew鸽rd geif,

First to the pure worthy honorable,

That is til armys and til manhed able ; 1720

(Set he be pur, ʒhit worfchip in hyme bidith) ;

If hyme the horſ one wich thi-felwyne Ridith, Give to the poor worthy man the horse thou thyself ridest.

And bid hyme that he Rid hyme for yhour fak ;

Syne til hyme gold and filuer yow betak ; 1724

The horſ to hyme for worfchip and prowes,

The trefor for his fredome and larges. -.

If moſt of Riches and of Cherifing ; [Fol. 22 a.]

Eftir this gud knycht berith vitnefing. 1728

Syne to thi tennandis & to thi wawafouris Give to thy tenants and vavasours easy hackneys, palfries, and coursers.

If eſſy haknays, palfrais, and curfouris,

And robis fich as plefand ben and fair ;

Syne to thi lordis, wich at mychty aire, 1732

As dukis, erlis, princis, and ek kingis, Give to thy lords things strange and uncouth.

Yow if them ſtrang, yow if them vncouth thingis,

As diuerſ iowellis, and ek preciouſ ſtonis,

Or halkis, hundis, ordinit for the nonis, 1736

Or wantone horſ that can nocht ſtand in ſtāble ;

Thar giftis mot be fair and delitable.

Thus, firſt vn to the vorthi pur yow if

Giftis, that may ther pouerte Releif ; 1740

And to the rich iftis of plefans,

That thei be fair, ſet nocht of gret fubftans ;

For riches afkith no thing bot delyt,

And powert haith ay ane appetyt 1744

For to support ther ned and Indigens :

Thus fhall yow if and makith thi difpens.

And ek the quen, my lady, fhalt alfo So, too, shall the queen give to maidens and ladies,

To madenis and to ladeis, quhar ʒhe go, 1748

If, and cheriſ one the famyne wyſ ;

For in to largeſ al thi welfar lyis. for all thy welfare lies in liberality.

And if thy giftis with fich continans

That thei be fen ay gifyne vith plefans ;. 1752

The wyſ man fais, and futh it is approuit,

Thar is no thonk, thar is no ift alowit,

Bot It be ifyne In to fich manere,

(That is to fay, als glaid in to his chere),   1756

As he the wich the ift of hyme Refauith ;

And do he not, the gifar is diffauith.

For who that iffis, as he not if wald,

Mor profit war his ift for to with-hald ;   1760

His thonk he tynith, and his ift alfo.

Bot that thow ifith, if with boith two,

That is to fay, vith hart and hand atonis ;

And fo the wyfman ay ye ift difponis.   1764

Beith larg and iffis frely of thi thing ;

For largeß is the trefour of o king,

And not this other Iowellis nor this gold

That is in to thi trefory with-holde.   1768

Who gladly iffith, be vertew of larges

His trefory encrefis of Richeßß,

And fal aȝañe the mor al-out refawe.

For he to quhome he ȝewith fall hawe,   1772

Firft his body, fyne his hart with two,

His gudis al for to difpone also

In his feruice ; and mor atour he fhall

Have O thing, and that is beft of all ;   1776

That is to fay, the worfchip and the loß

That vpone larges in this world furth goß.

And yow fhal knaw the lawbour & the preß

In to this erth about the gret Richeß.   1780

Is ony, bot[1] apone the cauß we see

Of met, of cloth, & of profperitee ?

All the remanant ffant apone the name

Of purches, furth apone this worldis fame.   1784

And well yow wot, in thyne allegians

Ful many Is, the wich haith fufficians

Of euery thing that longith to ther ned ;   1787

What haith yow more, qwich [haith] them al to lede,

---

[1] MS. "Is ony bout bot ;" "bout" being defaced.

For al thi Realmys and thi gret Riches,
If that yow lak of worſchip the encreſ?
Well leſ, al-out; for efter thar eſtate
Thei have vorſchip, and kepith It al-gat;   1792
And yow degradith al thyne hie dugree,
That ſo ſchuld ſhyne In to nobelitee,
Throuch wys and throw the wrechitneſ of hart.
And knowis yow not what fall be[1] thi part,   1796

Out of this world when yow ſal paſ the courſ?
Fair well, I-wyſ! yow neuer ſhall Recourſ
Whar no prince more ſhall the subiet[2] have,
But be als dep in to the erd y-grave,   1800
Sauf vertew only and worſchip wich abidith;
With them the world apone the laif dewidith;
And if he, wich ſhal eftir the ſucced,
By larges ſpend, of quhich that yhow had dreid,   1804
He of the world comendit is and priſit,
And yow ſtant furth of euery thing diſpiſit;
The puple faith and demyth thus of thee,
"Now is he gone, a werray vrech was hee,   1808
And he the wich that is our king and lord
Boith wertew haith & larges in accorde;
Welcum be he!" and ſo the puple foundith.
Thus through thi viſ his wertew mor aboundith, 1812
And his vertew the more thi wice furth ſchawith.
Wharfor ȝhe, wich that princes ben y-knawith,
Lat not yhour vrechit hart so yhow dant,
That he that cummyth next yhow may awant   1816
To be mor larg, nore more to be commendit;
Beſt kepit Is the Riches well diſpendit.
O ȝhe, the wich that kingis ben, fore ſham
Remembrith yhow, this world hath bot o naam 1820
Of good or ewill, efter ȝhe ar gone!
And wyſly tharfor cheſſith yhow the toñ

Side notes:
- Knowest thou not what shall be thy part, when thou passest away from this world?
- Virtue and honour will alone remain.
- And if thy successor be liberal, he will be commended of the world;
- [Fol. 23 a.]
- and his virtue will abound through thy vice.
- Riches well spent are the best kept.

---

[1] MS. has "by."   [2] MS. has "subei't."

Wich moſt accordith to nobilitee,

And knytith larges to yhour hic degre.   1824

For qwhar that fredome In O prince Ringnis,

It bryngith In the victory of kingis,

And makith realmys and puple boith to dout,

And ſubectis¹ of the cuntre al about.   1828

And qwho that thinkith ben o conquerour,

Suppos his largeſ ſumquhat pas myſour,   •

Ne rak he nat, bot frely iffith ay ;

And as he wynyth, beis var al-way   1832

To mych nor ȝhit to gredy that he hold,

Wich ſal the hartis of the puple colde.

And low and radour cummyth boith two

Of larges ; Reid and ȝhe ſal fynd It ſo.   1836

Alexander this lord the warld that wan,

Firſt with the ſuerd of larges he began,

And as he wynith ifith largely,

He rakith No thing bot of cheuelry ;   1840

Wharfor of hyme ſo paſſith the Renown,

That many o cetee, and many o ſtrang towñ

Of his worſchip that herith the Recorde,

Diſſirith ſo to haveing ſich o lorde ;   1844

And offerith them with-outen ſtrok of ſpere,

Suppos that thei war manly men of were,

But only for his gentilleſ that thei

Have hard ; and ſo he louit was al-way   1848

For his larges, humilitee, and manhed,

With his awn folk, that neuermore, we Reid,

For al his weris nor his gret trawell,

In al his tym that thei hyme onys faill ;   1852

Bot in his worſchip al thar befynes

Thei ſet, and lewith in to no diſtres ;

Whar-throw the ſuerd of victory he berith.

And many prince full oft the palm werith,   1856

¹ Or "ſubettis."

As has ben hard, by largeſ, of before,
victory, through
liberality;
In conqueringe of Rignis & of glore.

And wrechitnes Richt ſo, in the contrar,
while miserliness
hath made realms
Haith Realmys maid ful defolat & bare,   1860 desolate.

And king*is* broght doun from ful hie eſtat;

And who that Red ther old buk*is*, wat

The vicis lef, the wertew have in mynde,

And takith larges In his awn kynd;   1864

A-myd ſtanding of the vicis two,
Choose the mean
betweeu prodi-
gality and ava-
rice.
Prodegalitee and awerice alſo.

Wharfor her-of It nedith not to more,

So mych ther-of haith clerk*is* vrit to-fore.   1868

Bot who the wertw of larges & the law
Whoso chooses to
be liberal,
Sal cheſ, mot ned conſidir well & knaw

In to hyme-ſelf, and thir thre wnd*er*ſtande,
must understand
three things; the
The ſubſtans firſt, the powar of his land,   1872 *amount he has*, to
whom he giveth,
Whome to he iffith, and the cauſ wharfore,
and the *ſit time*
for giving.
The nedful tyme awatith eu*er*more.

Kepith thir thre; for qwho that ſal exced

His rent, he fallith ſodandly in nede.   1876

And ſo the king, that on to myſt*er* drowis,
(1) The king that
becomes *indigent*
overthrows his
subjects.
His subiett*is* and his puple he our-thrawis,

And them diſpolȝeith boith of lond and Rent;

So is the king, ſo is the puple ſchent.   1880

For-quhi the woice It ſcrik[i]th vp ful ewyne
For the voice of
the oppressed
shrieketh up
ceaselessly to
heaven;
W*ith*-out abaid, and paſſith to the hewyne,

Whar god hyme-ſelf refauith ther the crye

Of the oppreſioune and the teranny,   1884

And vith the ſuerd of wengans dou*n* y-ſmytith,
and God smiteth
down with the
sword of ven-
geance.
The wich that caruith al to for, and bitith,

And hyme diſtroyth, as has ben hard or this

Of euery king that wirkith ſich o mys.   1888

For ther is few eſchapith them, It ſall

Boith vpone hyme & his ſucceſſione fall;
For God hath
given the king
the wand of jus-
tice:
For he forſuth haith ifyne hyme the woꝰd

To Iuſtefy and Reull in pece his lond,   1892   [Fol. 24 a.]

The puple all fubmytit to his cure ;
And he aȝan one to no creatur
Save only fhall vn to his gode obey.
And if he paffith fo far out of the wey,   1896

and if he oppresses them whom he should rule,

Them to oppreſ, that he fhuld reul & gid,
Ther heritag, there gwdis to dewide,
Ye, wnder whome that he moft nedis ftond,

God shall stretch His mighty hand for correction.

At correccioune fal ftrek his mychty hond,   1900
Not euery day, bot fhal at onys fall
On hyme, mayhap, and his fuccefcione all.

Herein, alas! is the blindness of kings.

In this, allace ! the blyndis of the kingis,
And Is the fall of princis and of Rygnis.   1904
The moft wertew, the gret Intellegens,

The blessed token of a king's wisdom is for him to restrain his hand from his people's riches.

The bleſſit tokyne of wyfdom and prudens
Iſſ, in o king, for to reftren his honde
Frome his pupleis Riches & ther lond.   1908
Mot euery king have this wice in mynd
In tyme, and not when that he ned fynde !
And in thi larges beith war, I pray,

(2) Choose a fitting time.
(3) Take care to whom you give.

Of nedful tyme, for than is beft alway.   1912
Awyſ the ek quhome to that thow falt if,
Of there fam, and ek how that thei leif ;

Let not the virtuous and the vicious stand in the same degree.

And of the wertws and wicious folk alfo,
I the befeich dewidith well thir two,   1916
So that thei ftond nocht in[to] o degree ;
Difcreccioune fall mak the diuerfitee,
Wich clepith the moder of al vertewis.

Beware of flattery.

And beith war, I the befeich of this,   1920
That is to fay of flatry, wich that longith
To court, and al the kingis larges fongith.
The vertuouſ man no thing thar-of refauith,
The flattereris now fo the king diffauith   1924
And blyndith them that wot no thing, I-wyſ,
When thei do well, or quhen thei do o myſ ;
And latith kingis oft til wnderftonde
Thar vicis, and ek ye faltis of ther lond.   1928

In to the realme about o king Is holde
O flatterere were than is the ftormys cold,
Or peftelens, and mor the realme anoyith ;
For he the law and puple boith diftroyith. 1932

And in to principall ben ther three thing*is*,
That cauffith flattereris ftonding w*ith* tho king*is* ;
And on, It is the blyndit Ignorans
Of king*is*, wich that hath no gou*er*nans ·. 1936
To wnd*er*ftond who doith fich o myß ;
But who that fareft fchewith hym, I-wyß,
Moft fuffifith and beft to his plefans.
Wo to the realme that havith fich o chans ! 1940

And fecundly, quhar that o king Is
Weciuß hyme-felf, he cheriffith, ywys,
Al them the wich that one to vicis foundith,
Whar-throw that vicis and flattery ek aboundith. 1944

The thrid, is the ilk fchrewit harrmful wice,
Wich makith o king w*ith*in hyme-felf fo nyce,
That al thar flattry and ther gilt he knowith
In to his wit, and ʒhit he hyme w*ith*-drowith 1948
Them to repref, and of ther vicis he wot ;
And this It is wich that diffemblyng hot,
That in no way accordith for o king.
Is he not fet abuf apone his Ringnc, 1952
As fou*er*ane his puple for to lede ?
Whi fchuld he fpare, or quhom of fchuld he dred
To fay the treuth, as he of Right is hold ?
And if fo ware that al the king*is* wold, 1956
When that his leg*is* comytit ony wyce,
As beith not to fchamful, nore to nyce,
That thei prefume that he is negligent,
But als far as he thinkith that thei myß-went, 1960
But diffemblyng reprewith as afferis ;
And pwnice them quhar pwnyfing Requeris,
Sauf only m*er*cy in the tyme of ned.
And fo o king he fchuld his puple led, 1964

That no trefpaſ, that cummyth in his way,

Shuld paſ his hond wne-pwniſt away ;

Nore no good deid in to the famyn degree,

Nore no wertew, fuld wn-Reuardid bee.   1968

Then flattery,
that now is high,
should be low.
Than flattry fhuld, that now is he, be low,

And wice from the king*is* court *with*-drow ;

His miniſt*er*is that fhuld the Iuftice reull,

Shuld kep well furt*h* of quiet & reull,   1972

That now, god wat, as It conferwit Is,

The ſtere is loft, and al is gon amys ;

[Fol. 25 *a*.]   And vertew fhuld hame to the court hyme dreſ,

That exillith goith in to the wilder*n*es.   1976

If a king thus
stood like his own
degree, his people
would be virtu-
ous and wise.
Thus if o king ftud lyk his awn degree,

Wertwis and wyſ than fhuld his puple bee,

Only fet by vertew hyme to pleſ,

And fore adred his wifdom to difpleſ.   1980

And if that he towart the vicis draw,

His folk fall go on to that ilk law ;

What fhal hyme pleſ that wil noc*h*t ell*is* fynd,

Bot ther-apon fetith al ther mynde.   1984

Thus the rule of
his people and
kingdom stand-
eth only in the
king's virtue.
Thus only in the wertew of o king

The reull ftant of his puple & his ringne,

If he be wyſ and, but diffemblyng, fchewis,

As I have faid, the vicis one to fchrewis.   1988

And fo thus, ſir, It ftant apone thi will

For to omend thi puple, or to fpill ;

Or have thi court of vertewis folk, or fullis ;

Since thou art
wholly master of
the schools, teach
them, and they
shall gladly
learn."
Sen yow art holl maift*er* of the fcoullis   1992

Teichith them, and thei fal gladly leir,

That is to fay, that thei may no thing heir[1]

Sauf only wertew towart thyn eftat ;

And cheriſ them that wertews ben algait.   1996

And thinkith what that wertew is to thee ;

It pleſſith god, vphaldi*th* thi degree."

----

[1] Or, "leir." MS. apparently has "leir," corrected to
"heir."

"Maifter," quod he, "me think ry*ch*t profitable

Yow*r* confeell Is, and wond*er* honorable   2000

For me, and good ; ry*ch*t well I have *con*fauit,

And in myne hart*is* Inwartnefſ refauit.

I fhal fulfill and do yow*r* ordynans

Als far of wit as I have fuffifans ;   2004

Bot y befeich yow, in til hartly wyfſ,

That of my drem ȝhe fo to me dewyfſ,

The wich fo long haith occupeid my mynd,

How that I fhal no man*er* fucour fynd   2008

Bot only throw the wattir lyon, & fyne

The leich that is *with*outen medyfyne ;

And of the confell of the flour ; wich ayre

Wond*er*is lyk that no man can duclar."   2012

"Now, fir," q*uod* he, " and I of them al thre,
     What thei betakyne fhal I fchaw to the,

Such as the clerk*is* at them fpecifiit ;

Thei vfit no thing what thei fignefiit.   2016

The wattir lyone Is the god werray,

God to the lyone is lyknyt many way ;

But thei have hyme In to the wattir feñ,

Confufit were ther wittis al, y weñ ;   2020

The wattir was ther awn fragelitee,

And thar trefpas, and thar Inequitee

In to this world, the wich thei ftond y-clofit ;

That was the wattir wich thei have fuppofit,   2024

That haith there knowlag maad fo Inp*er*fyt ;

Thar fyne & ek ther worldis gret delyt,

As clowdy wattir, was eu*er*more betweñ,

That thei the lyone p*er*fitly hath no*ch*t feñ ;   2028

Bot as the wattir, wich was y*er* awn fynne,

That eu*er*mor thei ftond confufit In.

If thei haith ftond in to religioñ clen,

Thei had the lyone Not in watt*er* fen,   2032

Bot clerly vp in to the hewyne abuf,

Et*er*naly whar he fhal not remufe.

Side notes:

Arthur considers his counsel profitable.

He beseeches him to expound his dream,

how he shall only find help through the water-lion, the leech, and the flower.

The master's explanation. [Fol. 25 b.]

The water-lion is the very God.

The water is men's fragility;

whereby they see not the lion perfectly.

Had men been always religious, they had seen the lion not in water, but clearly.

And euermore in vatter of fyne vas hee.
For-quhi It is Impoffeble for to bee ; [1]   2036

The world is en-
closed in the
darkness of their
sin.
And thus the world, wich that thei ar In,
Y-clofit Is in dyrknes of ther fyne ;
And ek the thiknef of the air betwen
The lyone mad in vattir to be fen.   2040

For It was nocht bot ftrenth of ther clergy
Wich thei have here, and It is bot erthly,
That makith them there refouns dewyf,
And fe the lyone thus in erthly wyf.   2044

The lion is God's
Son, Jesu Christ.
This is the lyone, god, and goddis sone,
Ihesu crift, wich ay in hewyne fal wonne.
For as the lyone of euery beft is king,
So is he lord and maifter of al thing,   2048
That of the bleffit vyrgyne vas y-bore.
Ful many a natur the lyone haith, quhar-fore
That he to god refemblyt is, bot I
Lyk not mo at this tyme fpecify.   2052
This is the lyone, thar-of have yow no dred,
That fhal the help and comfort In thi ned.

The fentens here now woll I the defyne
The leech with-
out medicine is
also God.
  Of hyme, the lech withouten medyfyne,   2056
Wich is the god that euery thing hath vroght.

[Fol. 26 a.]
For yow may know that vther Is It noght,
Not as surgeons,
As furgynis and feficianis, wich that delith
With mortell thingis, and mortell thingis helyth, 2060
whose art is in
medicine,
And al thar art is in to medyfyne,
As it is ordanit be the mycht dewyne,
and in plaisters,
drinks, and vari-
ous anointments;
who know the
quality of the
year, and the dis-
position of the
planets.
As plafteris, drinkis, and anouyntmentis [2] feir,
And of the qualyte watyng of the yher ;   2064
And of the planetis difpoficioune,
And of the naturis of compleccyoune,
And in the diuerf changing of hwmowris.
Thus wnder reull lyith al there cwris ;   2068

---

[1] "see" (?).   [2] MS. "anonytmētis," or "anouytmētis."

And yhit thei far as blynd man In the way,
Oft quhen that deith thar craft lift to aſſay.
Bot god, the wich that is the foueran lech,
Nedith no maner medyfyne to fech ;   2072
For ther is no Infyrmyte, nore wound,
Bot as hyme lykith al is holl and found.
So can he heill Infyrmytee of thoght,   But God can heal
                                                      infirmity of
Wich that one erdly medefyne can noght ;   2076 thought,
And als the faul that to confuſioune goith,   and also the soul
                                                      that goeth to con-
And haith with hyme and vther parteis boith,   fusion.
His dedly wound god helyth frome the ground ;
On to his cure no medyfyne is found.   2080
This Is his mycht that neuer more ſhall fyne,
This is the leich withouten medyfyne ;
And If that yhow at confeſſioune hath ben
And makith the of al thi fynnis clen,   2084
Yow art than holl, and this ilk famyn is he   He shall be thy
                                                      leech in all neces-
Schall be thi leich In al neceſſitee.   sity.

Now of the flour y woll to the diſcern :
       This is the flour that haith[1] the froyt etern, 2088
This is the flour, this fadith for no ſchour,
This is the flour of euery flouris floure ;
This is the flour, of quhom the froyt vas born,   The flower is she
                                                      of whom the
This ws redemyt efter that we war lorn ;   2092 eternal fruit was
                                                      born,
This Is the flour that euer ſpryngith new,
This is the flour that changith neuer hew ;
This is the vyrgyne, this is the bleſſit flour   the virgin that
                                                      bore the Saviour,
That Iheſu bur that is our salweour,   2096
This flour wnwemmyt of hir wirginitee ;
This is the flour of our felicitee,
This is the flour to quhom ve ſhuld exort,
This is the flour not feſſith to ſupport   2100 that ceaseth not
                                                      to support us
In prayere, confeſſ, and in byſſynes,   caitiffis,
Vs catifis ay In to our wrechitnes   [Fol. 26 b.]

[1] The word, though indistinct, is almost certainly "haith."
Stevenson has "high ;" but this gives no sense.

On to hir sone, the quich hir confell herith ;
This is the flour that al our gladneß fterith,　　2104

Throuch whois prayer mony one is fawit,
That to the deth eternaly war refawit,
Ne war hir hartly fuplicatioune.
This is the flour of our faluatioune,　　2108
Next hir sone, the froyt of euery flour ;
This is the fam that fhal be thi fuccour,
If that the lykith hartly Reuerans
And feruice ȝeld one to hir excellens,　　2112
Syne worfchip hir with al thi byffyneß ;
Sche fal thi harm, fche fall thi ned redreß.

Sche fall fice confell if one to the two,
The lyone and the fouerane lech alfo,　　2116
Yow fall not Ned yi drem for to difpar,
Nor ȝhit no thing that is in thi contrare.
Now—quod the maifter—yow may well wnderftand
Tueching thi drem as I have born on hande ;　　2120
And planly haith the mater al declarith,
That yhow may **know of wich yow** was difparith.
The lech, the lyone, and the flour alfo,
Yow worfchip them, yow ferve them euermo ;　　2124
And ples the world as I have faid before ;
In gouernans thus ftondith al thi glore.

Do as yow lift, for al is in thi honde,
To tyne thi-felf, thi honore, and thi londe,　　2128
Or lyk o prince, o conquerour, or king,
In honore and in worfchip for to Ringe."

" Now," quod the king, " I fell that the fupport
Of yhour confell haith don me fich comfort,　　2132

Of euery raddour my hart is In to eß,
To ȝhour command, god will, y fal obeß.
Bot o thing is yneuch wn to me,

How galiot makith his awant that he　　2136
Shall have the knycht, that only by his honde
And manhed, was defendour of my londe ;

If that fhall fall y pray yhow tellith me,

And quhat he hecht, and of quhat lond is hee?" 2140

"What that he hecht yow fhall no foryer know,

His dedis fall her-efterwart hyme fchaw ;

Bot contrar the he fhall be found no way.

No more thar-of as now y will the fay." [1] 2144

With that the king haith at his maiftir tone

His leve, one to to his cuntre for to goñe ;

And al the oft makith none abyde,

To paffing home anone thei can prowid ; 2148

And to fir gawane thei haith o lytter maad,

Ful fore ywound, and hyme on with them haade.

[T]he king, as that the ftory can declar,

Paffith to o Cete that was Right fair, 2152

And clepit cardole, In to walis, was,

For that tyme than It was the nereft place,

And thar he foiornyt xxiiijti days

In ryall fefting, as the auttore fays. 2156

So difcretly his puple he haith cherit,

That he thar hartis holy haith conquerit.

And fir gawan, helyt holl and found

Be xv dais he was of euery wounde ; 2160

Right blyth therof in to the court war thei.

And fo befell, the xxiiij[2] day,

The king to fall in to o hewynes,

Right ate his table fiting at the meß ; 2164

And fir gawan cummyth hyme before,

And faid hyme, "fir, yhour thoght is al to fore,

Confidering the diuerß knychtis fere

Ar of wncouth and ftrang landis here." 2168

The king anfuert, as in to matalent,

"Sir, of my thocht, or ʒhit of myne entent,

Yhe have the wrang me to repref, for-quhy

Thar lewith none that fhuld me blam, for I 2172

The mafter evades reply.

[Fol. 27 a.]

The king and the hoft return home.

The king fojourns twenty-four days at Cardole, in Wales.

Sir Gawan is healed in fifteen days.

The king becomes mournful, as he fits at the mess.

Gawan rebukes him.

The king answers in "matalent,"

---

[1] At the bottom of the page is the catch-word, "With that the king." [2] MS. "xxviij," altered to "xxiiij."

that he was
thinking of the
worthiest knight
living;

Was thinkand one the worthieft that lewyt,

That al the worfchip In to armys prewyt;

And how the thonk of my defens he had,

And of the wow that galiot haith mad.　　　　2176

But I have fen, when that of my houfhold

Thar was, and of my falowfchip, that wold,

If that thei wift, quhat thing fhuld me pleß,

Thei wald nocht leif for trawell nor for eß.　　2180

And fum tyme It prefwmyt was & faid,

that he once had
the flower of
knighthood in his
household, but
now this flower
is away.

That in my houfhold of al this world I had

The flour of knychthed and of chevalry;

Bot now thar-of y fe the contrarye,　　　　2184

Sen that the flour of knychthed is away."

"Schir," quod he, "of Refone futh yhe fay;

[Fol. 27 b.]

And if god will, In al this warld fo Round

He fal be foght, if that he may be found."　　2188

Gawan departs to
seek Lancelot.

Than gawan goith with o knychtly chere,

At the hal·dure he faith In this maner:

" In this pafag who lykith for to wend ?

It is o Iorne moft for to comend　　　　2192

That In my tyme In to the court fallith,

To knyghtis wich that chewellry lowith

Or trawell In to armys for to hant;

And lat no knycht fra thyne-furth hyme awant　2196

All the knights
rise to go with
him.

That it denyith;"—with that onon thei roß,

Al the knychtis, and frome the burdis goß.

The king that fauch In to his hart was wo,

Arthur reproves
him.

And faid, "fir gawan, nece, why dois yow fo ?　2200

Knowis yow nocht I myne houfhold fuld encreß,

In knychthed, and in honore, and largeß ?

And now yow thinkith mak me diffolat

Of knychtis, and my houß tranfulat,　　　　2204

To fek o knycht, and It was neuer more

Hard fich o femble makith o before."

Gawan explains.

" Sir," quod he, "als few as may yhow pleßß;

For what I said was no thing for myne eß,　　2208

Nor for defir of faloufchip, for-why
To paſ alone, but cumpany, think I ;
And ilk knycht to paſ o fundry way ;
The mo thei paſ the fewar efchef thay,   2212
Bot thus fhal pas no mo bot as yhow left."
"Takith," quod he, " of quhom ȝhe lykith beſt,   Arthur aſſigns
                                                       him forty com-
Fourty in this pafag for to go ; "   panions.
At this command and gawan cheſit fo   .   2216
Fourty, quhich that he louit, & that was
Richt glaid in to his falowfchip to pas.

[A]nd furth thei go, and al anarmyt thei   These knights
                                                       arm themselves,
Come to the king, withouten more delay,   2220
The relykis brocht, as was the maner tho,   and bring the
                                                       relics, whereon
When any knyghtis frome the court fuld go.   to swear to shew
                                                       the truth.
Or when the paffit, or quhen thei com, thei fwor
The trouth to fchaw of euery aduentur.   2224
Sir gawan knelyng to his falowis fais,
" Yhe lordis, wich that in this feking gais,
So many noble and worthi knychtis ar ȝhe,
Me think in wayne yhour trauel fhuld nocht be,   2228
For aduentur is non so gret to pref,   [Fol. 28 a.]
As I fuppone, nor ȝhe fal It effchef,
And if ȝhe lyk as I that fhal dewyſ,
Yhour oth to fwer In to the famyne wyſ   2232
Myne oith to kep ; "—and that thei vndertak,
How euer fo that he his oith mak
It to conferf, and that thei have all fworñ.
Than gawan, wich that was the king beforn,   2236
On kneis fwore, " I fal the futh duclar   Gawane swears
                                                       not to return till
Of euery thing when I agan Repar,   he has found
                                                       Lancelot, or evi-
Nor neuer more aȝhane fal I returñ,   dence of him.
Nore in o place long for to fuiorñ   2240
Whill that the knycht or verray evydens
I have, that fhal be toknis of credens."
His faloufchip abafit of that thing,
And als therof anoyt was the king,   2244

5

Arthur reproves
him for forgetting
the coming day
of battle.
Sayng, " Nece, yow haith al foly vroght
And wilfulneß, that haith nocht in thi thoght
The day of batell of galot and me."

Gawane says it
must be so.
Quod gawan, " Now non other ways ma be."   2248

Gawane and his
fellows lace their
helms, and take
their leave.
Thar-with he and his falowfchip alfo
Thar halmys lafit, on to ther horß thei go,
Syne tuk ther lef, and frome the court the fare,
Thar names ware to long for to declar.   2252

Now fal we leif hyme and his cumpany,
That in thar feking paffith biffely ;

The story returns
to the lady of
Melyhalt.
And of the lady of melyhalt we tell,
With whome the knycht mot ned alway duell.   2256

¹[O] day fhe mayd hyme on to hir prefens fet,
And on o fege be-fid hir haith hyme fet,
" Sir, in keping I have yow halding long,"
And thus fche faid, " for gret trefpas & wrong,   2260
Magre my ftewart, in worfchip, and for-thi
3he fuld me thonk ;"—" madem," quod he, " and I
Thonk yhow fo that euer, at my mycht,
Whar-fo I paß that I fal be yhour knycht."   2264

She inquires
Lancelot's name.
" Grant mercy, fir, bot o thing I 30w pray,
What that 3he ar 3he wold wichfauf to fay."

He refuses to tell.
" Madem," quod he, " yhour mercy afk I, quhy
That for to fay apone no wyß may I."   2268

" No ! wil 3he not ? non oyer ways as now

She vows to keep
him in thrall till
the day of com-
bat ;
[Fol. 28 b.]
3he fal repent, and ek I mak avow
One to the thing the wich that I beft love,
Out frome my keping fal 3he not Remuf   2272
Befor the day of the affemblee,
Wich that, o 3her, is nereft for to bee ;
And if that 30w haith pleffit for to fay,
3he had fore me deliuerit ben this day ;   2276

and to go to the
court to try and
learn it.
And I fal knaw, quheyer 3he wil or no,
For I furth-with one to the court fal go,

¹ Room is here left in the MS. for an illuminated letter, and
a small " o " inserted as a note.

Whar that al thithing*is* goith & cumyth foñ."

"Madem," q*uod* he, " yhour plefance mot be doñe." 2280

W*ith* that the kny*ch*t one to his chalm*er* goith,

The knight retires.

And the lady hir makith to be wroith

A3anis hyme, but futhly vas fche not,

For he al-out was mor in to hir thoght. 2284

Than fchapith fhe a3ane the ferd day,

And richly fche gan hir-felf aray ;

Syne clepit haith apone her cufynes,

And faith, "y will one to the court me dreß ; 2288

Before going to the court,

And malice I have fchawin on to 3hon kny*ch*t,

For-quhy he wold no*ch*t fchew me quhat he hicht,

Bot fo, I-wyß, It is no*ch*t in my tho*ch*t,

For worthyar non In to this erth is wro*ch*t. 2292

Tharfor I pray, and hartly I requer

she prays her cousin to take care of him.

3he mak hyme al the cu*m*pany and chere,

And do hyme al the worfchip and the eß,

Excep his honore, wich that may hym pleß ; 2296

And quhen I cum deliu*er*ith hyme als fre

As he is now ;"—"ne have no dred," q*uod* f*ch*e.

[T]he lady p*ar*tit, and hir lef hath ton,

And by hir Iorne to the court Is gon. 2300

The king hapnit at logris for to bee,

The lady meets Arthur at Logris ;

Wich of his realme was than the chef cete ;

And haith hir met, and In til hartly wyß

Refauit her, and welcu*m*myt oft-fyß ; 2304

And haith hir home one to his palice bro*ch*t,

who brings her home to his palace ;

Whar that no dante nedith to be focht,

And maid hir cher w*ith* al his ful entent.

Eft fupir one to o chalm*er* ar thei went, 2308

The king and fche, and ek the quen al thre ;

Of hir tithand*is* at hir than afkit hee,

And what that hir one to the court had bro*ch*t?

and inquires what has brought her.

"S*ir*," q*uod* fche, "I come[1] not al for no*ch*t ; 2312

---

[1] MS. "conne."

She says she has
a friend who has
made a challenge,
[Fol. 29 a.]
I have o frend haith o dereyne ydoo,

And I can fynd none able knycht tharto ;

For he the wich that in the contrar Is

Is hardy, ftrong, and of gret kyne, I-wyß ;   2316

Bot, It is faid, If I mycht have with me

Зour knycht, quich in the last affemble

which the red
knight could best
maintain.
Was in the feld, and the red armys bur,

In his manhed y mycht my cauß affur ;   2320

And yhow, fir, richt hartly I exort

In to this ned my myfter to fupport."

"Madem, by faith one to the quen I aw

Arthur replies
that Gawane is
gone to seek him.
That I beft loue, the knycht I neuer faw   2324

In nerneß by which that I hyme knew ;

And ek gawane Is gan hyme for to few

With other fourty knychtis In to cumpany."

The lady fmylit at ther fanteffy ;   2328

The quen thar-with prefumyt wel that fche

The queen asks
the lady if she
knows where he
is.
Knew quhat he was, and faid, " madem, If зhe

Knowith of hyme what that he is, or quhar,

We зhow befech til ws for to declar."   2332

She replies no,
and proposes to
return.
"Madem," quod fche, " now be the faith that I

Aw to the king and yhow, as for no why

To court I cam, but of hyme to Inquere ;

And fen of hyme I can no tithingis here,   2336

Nedlyngis to-morn homwart mon I fair."

Arthur prays her
to stay.
"Na," quod the king, " madem, our fon It waire ;

зhe fal remayne her for the qwenys fak ;

Syne fhal зhe of our beft knychtis tak."   2340

"Sir," quod fche, " I pray зow me excuß,

For-quhy to paß nedis me behuß ;

Nor, fen I want the knycht which I have focht,

Wtheris with me to have defir I nocht,   2344

For I of otheris have that may fuffice."

Bot зhit the king hir prayt on fich wyß,

She remains till
the third day.
That fche remanit whill the thrid day ;

Syne tuk hir leif to pafing hom hir way.   2348

It nedis not the fefting to declar
Maid one to hir, nor company nor fare;
Sche had no knycht, fche had no damyfeill,
Nor thei richly rewardit war and well.   2352
Now goith the lady homwart, and fche
In her entent defyrus Is to fee
The flour of knychthed and of chevelry;
So was he pryfit and hold to euery wy. ·   2356
The lady, which one to hir palace come,
   Bot of fchort time remanith haith at home
When fche gart bryng, withouten Recidens,
With grete effere this knycht to hir prefens,   2360
And faid hyme; " fir, fo mekil have I focht
And knowith that be-for I knew nocht,
That If yhow lyk I wil yhour Ransone mak."
" Madem, gladly, wil зhe wichfauf to tak   2364
Efter that as my powar may atteñ,
Or that I may prowid be ony meñ."
"Now, fir," fho faid, " forfuth It fal be so,
Yhe fal have thre, and chefʒ yhow on of tho;   2368
And if yhow lykith them for to refuſ,
I can no mor, but зhe fal me excuſ,
Yhe nedis mot fuften yhour aduentur
Contynualy In ward for til endur."   2372
"Madem," quod he, "and I yhow hartly pray,
What that thei fay¹ зhe wald wichfauf to fay?"
" [T]he firft," quod fche, " who hath in to the cheñ
Of low yhour hart, and if зhe may dereñ?   2376
The next, yhour nam, the which зe fal not lye?
The thrid, if euer зhe think of cheualry
So mekil worfchip to atten in feild
Apone o day in armys wnder fcheld,   2380
As yat зhe dyd the famyne day, when зhe
In red armys was at the affemblee?"

¹ So MS. We should probably read "bee."

Marginal notes: She is sumptuously entertained, and returns home. [Fol. 29 b.] Soon after, she sends for Lancelot, and proposes to ransom him, on one of three conditions. Either he must tell whom he loves, or declare his name, or say if he expects again to equal his former exploits.

"Madem," q*uod* he, "is thar non vther way

Me to redem, but only thus to fay   2384

Of thing*is*, which that Rynyth me to blam,

Me to awant my lady or hir name ?

But If that I moft fchawin furth that one,

What su*er*te fchal I have for to gone   2388

At libertee out of this dang*er* free ?"

"Schir, for to dred no myft*er* is," q*uod* fhee ;

"As I am trew and fai*th*full woman hold,

3he fal go fre quhen one of thir is told."   2392

"Madem, yhour will non vther ways I may,

I mone obey ; and to the firft y fay,

¹[I]s, to declar the lady of myne hart,

My goft fal rather of my breft aftart"—   2396

Whar-by the lady fayndit al for noc*ht*

The lowe quhich long hath ben In to h*is* thoc*ht*—

"And of my nam, fchortly for to fay,

It ftondith fo that one no wyſ I may.   2400

Bot of the thrid, madem, I fe that I

Mon fay the thing that tuechith velany ;

For fut*h* it is I traft, and god before,

In feld that I fal do of armys more   2404

Than eu*er* I did, if I *com*mandit bee.

And now, madem, I have my libertee,

For I have faid I neu*er* thoc*ht* to fay."

"Now, fir,"q*uod* fche, "when-eu*er* 3he wil ye may; 2408

Bot o thing Is, I yhow hartly raquer,

Sen I have hold yhow apone fuch maner

Not as my fo, that 3he vald grant me till. ·

"Madem," q*uod* he, " It fal be as 3he will."   2412

" Now, fir," q*uod* fche, " it is no thing bot 3he

Remañ wi*th* ws wn to the affemble,

And euery thyng that In yhour myft*er* lyis

I fall gar ordan at yhour awn dewyſ ;   2416

¹ A space is here left for an illuminated letter.

And of the day I fhall yow certefy
Of the affemble ȝhe fal not pas therby."
" Madem," quod he, " It fal be as yhow lift."
" Now, fir," quod fche, "and than I hald It beft, 2420
That ȝhe remañ lyk to the famyne dogre
As that ȝhe war, yat non fal wit that ȝhe
Deliuerit war ; and in to facret wyf
Thus may ȝhe be ; and now yhe fal dewyf ·   2424
What armys that yhow lykyth I gar mak."
" Madem," quod he, " armys al of blak."
With this, this knycht is to his chalmer goñ ;
The lady gan ful prewaly diffpone   2428
For al that longith to the knycht, in feild ;
Al blak his horf, his armour, and his fcheld,
That nedful is, al thing fche well prewidith ;
And in hir keping thus with hir he bidith.   2432
Suppos of love fche takyne hath the charg,
Sche bur It clos, ther-of fche vas not larg,
Bot wyfly fche abftenit hir diffir,
For ellis quhat, fche knew, he was afyre ;   2436
Thar-for hir wit hir worfchip haith defendit,
For in this world thar was nan mor commendit,
Boith of difcreccioune and of womanhed,
Of gouernans, of nurtur, and of farhed.   2440
This knycht with hir thus al this whil mon duell,
And furth of arthur fumthing wil we tell—
   [T]hat walkyng vas furth in to his Regiounis,
And foiornyt in his ceteis and his townis,   2444
As he that had of vifdome fufficyans.
He kepit the lore of maifter amytans
In ryghtwyfnes, In fefting and larges,
In cherifing cumpany and hamlynes ;   2448
For he was biffy and was deligent,
And largly he iffith, and difpent
Rewardis, boith one to the pur & riche,
And holdith feft throw al the ȝher eliche.   2452

and inquires
what arms he
would like to
have made for
him. He chooses
black armour,

which is pro-
vided.

She keeps her
love close,

being commend-
ed for discretion.

The story returns
to Arthur—

[Fol. 30 b.]

who obeys the
counsel of Amy-
tans,

and gives away
largely ;

In al the warld pafiing gan his name,
He chargit not bot of encref and fame,
And how his puples hart*is* to emplef ;
Thar gladnes ay was to his hart moft ef.   2456
He rakith not of riches nor treffour,
Bot to difpend one worfchip & honour ;
He ifith riches, he ifith lond and rent,
He cheriffyth them w*ith* word*is* eloquent,   2460

and thus gains his
people's love. So that thei can them vtraly p*r*opone
In his fe*r*uice thar lyves to difpone :
So gladith theme his homely c*on*tynans,
His cherifyng, his wordis of plefans,   2464
His cumpany, and ek his mery chere,
His gret rewardis, and his ift*is* fere.
Thus hath the king non vthir befynes
Bot cherifing of kny*cht*is and largef,   2468
To mak hyme-felf of honour be c*om*mend ;
And thus the ʒher he drywith to the ende.

EXPLICIT SECUNDA P*AR*S, INCIPIT T*ER*CIA P*A*RS.

[BOOK III.]

The long dirk pafag[1] of the vinter, & the lycht
   Of phebus comprochit with his mycht;   2472

The sun ascends in his altitude.

The which, afcending In his altitud,
Awodith saturñ with his ftormys Rude ;
The foft dew one fra the hewyne doune valis[2]
Apone the erth, one hillis and on valis,   2476

The soft dew falls down from heaven.

And throw the fobir & the mwft hwmouris
Vp nurifit ar the erbis, and in the flouris
Natur the erth of many diuerſ hew
Our-fret, and cled with the tendir new.   2480

Nature decks the earth with various hues. The birds may hide

The birdis may them hiding in the grawis

[Fol. 31 a.]

Wel frome the halk, that oft ther lyf berevis ;
And scilla hie afcending in the ayre,

them from the hawk in the groves, and Scilla may ascend in

That euery vight may heryng hir declar   2484

the air.

Of the feffone the paffing luftynes.
This was the tyme that phebus gan hym dreſ
In to the rame, and haith his courſ bygown,
Or that the trewis and the ʒher vas Rown,   2488
Which was y-fet of galiot and the king
Of thar affemble, and of thar meting.

The time of com-bat between Galiot and the king drew near.

Arthur haith a xv dais before
Affemblit al his barnag and more   2492
That weryng wnder his fubieccioune,
Or louith hyme, or longith to his crown ;
And haith his Iornay tone, withouten let,
On to the place the wich that was y-fet,   2496

Arthur goes to the appointed place.

Whar he hath found befor hyme mony o knycht
That cummyng war with al thar holl mycht,

---

[1] So MS. Should we read "pasith" ?
[2] So MS. It should be "falis."

Al enarmyt both w*ith* fpere & fcheld,

And ful of lug*is* plantith haith the feld,   2500

Hyme In the wer for to fupport and ferf

At al ther my*ch*t, his thonk for to differf.

And gawan, which was in the feking ȝhit

Of the gud kny*ch*t, of hyme haith got no wit,   2504

Remembrith hyme apone the king*is* day,

And to his falowis one this wys can fay:

"To ȝhow is knowin the mate*r*, in what wyß

How that the king hath w*ith* his ennemys   2508

A ce*r*tan day, that now comprochit nere,

And one to ws war hewynes to here

That he var in to pe*r*ell or in to dreid,

And we away and he of ws haith neid;   2512

For we but hyme no thing may efchef,

And he but ws in honore well may lef;

For, be he loft, we may no thing w*ith*ftond,

Our-felf, our honore we tyne, & ek o*ur* lond.   2516

Tharfor, I red we pas on to the king,

Suppos our oth It hurt in to fum thing,

And in the feld w*ith* hyme for til endur,

Of lyf or deth and tak our aduentur."   2520

Thar-to thei ar confentit ene*r*ilkon,

And but dulay the have thar Iorney toñe.

When that the king them faw, in h*is* entent

Was of thar com Right wonde*r* well *content*;   2524

For he prefwmyt no thing that thei wold

Have cu*m*myne, but one furt*h* to ye*r* feking hold.

And thus the kinghis oft affemblit has

Aȝane the tyme, aȝaine the day that vas   2528

Y-ftatut and ordanit for to bee,

And euery thing hath fet in the dogre.

[A]nd galiot, that haith no thing forȝhet

The termys quhich that he befor had set,   2532

Affemblit has, apone his beft maner,

His folk, and al his other thing*is* fere,

That to o weryour longith to prouid,

And is y-come apone the tothir fyde. **2536**

Whar he befor was one than vas he two, doubling his army and artillery;

And al his vthir artilȝery also

He dowblith hath, that merwell was to feñ ;

And by the rewere lychtit one the greñ, **2540** and pitches on the green by the river.

And ftronghar thane ony wallit toune

His oft y-bout yclofit in Randoune.

Thus war thei cummyne apone ather fyd

Be-for the tyme, them-felf for to prowid. **2544** Before the truce is ended,

Or that the trewis was complet & rwn,

Men mycht have fen one euery fid begwn

Many a fair and knychtly Iuperty many combats are seen between lusty men;

Of lufty men, and of ȝong chevalry, **2548**

Difyrus In to armys for to pruf ;

Sum for wynyng, fum caufith vas for luf,

Sum In to worfchip to be exaltate,

Sum caufit was of wordis he & hate, **2552**

That lykit not ydill for to ben ;

A hundereth pair at onis one the gren. a hundred pair at once.

Thir lufty folk thus can thar tyme difpend,

Whill that the trewis goith to the ende. **2556**

The trewis paft, the day is cummyne onoñe, The truce past,

One euery fyd the can them to difpone ;

And thai that war moft facret & moft dere

To galiot, at hyme the can enquere, **2560** Galiot's friends inquire who shall fight on his side on the morrow.

" Who fal affemble one yhour fyd to-morñe ?

To-nycht the trewis to the end is worne."

He anfuerit, " As ȝhit one to this were

I ame awyfit I wil none armys bere, **2564**

Bot If It ftond of more Neceffitee ; [Fol. 32 a.]

Nor to the feld will pas, bot for to fee

Yhone knycht, the which that berith fich o fame."

Than clepit he the conqueft king be name, **2568** He commands the first-conquest king to take 30,000 men.

And hyme commandit xxx thoufand tak

Aȝaine the morne, and for the feld hyme mak.

And gawane haith, apone the toyer syde,
Confulit his Eme he fchuld for them prowid,   2572
And that he fchuld none armys to hyme tak
Whill[1] galiot will for the feld hyme mak.
"I grant," quod [he[2]], "wharfor зhe mone difpone

Gawane leads
Arthur's forces.

Yhow to the feld with al my folk to-mornc,   2576
And thinkith in yhour manhed and curage
For to recift зhone folkis gret owtrag."

The day comes.

[T]he nycht is gone, vp goith the morow gray,
The brycht fone fo cherith al the day :   2580
The knychtis gone to armys than, in haft ;
One goith the fcheildis and the helmys laft ;

Arthur's men
cross the ford.

Arthuris oft out our the furrde thai ryd.
And thai agane, apone the toyer syd,   2584

Galiot's men af-
femble in a vale.

Affemblit ar apone o lufty greyne,
In to o waill, whar fone thar mycht be feyne
Of knychtis to-gedder many o pair
In to the feld affemblyng her & thair,   2588
And ftedis which that haith thar mafter lorne ;[3]
The knychtis war done to the erth doune borne.

Sir Esquyris, a
manly knight,

Sir efquyris, which was o manly knycht
In to hyme-felf, and hardy vas & wycht ;   2592
And in till armys gretly for to pryf,
зhit he was pure, he prewit wel oft-fyf ;

at that time of
Galiot's com-
pany,

And that tyme was he of the cumpanee
Of galiot, bot efterwart was hee   2596
With arthur ; and that day In to the feild
He come, al armyt boith with fpere and fcheld,
With ferf defir, as he that had na dout,

attacks a band,

And is affemblit ewyne apone a rowt ;   2600
His fpere is gone, the knycht goith to the erd,
And out onon he pullith haith o fwerd ;

and proves his
manhood.

That day In armys prewit he rycht well
His ftrenth, his manhed ; arthuris folk thai fell. 2604

---

[1] MS. "Wihill."   [2] Omitted in MS.
[3] MS. has "borne." We should read "lorne," as in line 2092

Than galys gwynans, with o manly hart,

Which broꝛer was of ywane the baſtart,

He cummyne Is onone one to the ſtour

For conquering In armys of honour, 2608   [Fol. 32 b.]

And cownterit with eſquyris hath so

That [1] horſ and man, al four, to erth thai go ;

And ſtill o quhill lying at the ground.

With that o part of arthuris folk thei found 2612

Till gwyans, and haith hyme ſone reſkewit.

Aȝanis them til eſquyris thei ſewyt

Of galiotis well xxxᵗⁱ knychtis & mo ;

Gwyans goith done, and vthir vij alſo, 2616

The wich war tone & eſqwyris relewit.

Than ywane the anterus, aggrewit,

With kynnifmen one to the melle focht.

The hardy knychtis, that one thar worſchip thocht, 2620

Cownterit them In myddis of the fcheld,

Whar many o knycht was born doñ in the feld ;

Bot thei wich ware on galiotis part,

So wndertakand nor of fo hardy hart 2624

Ne ware thei not as was in ye contrare.

Sir galys gwyans was reſqwyt thare

With his falowis, and eſqwyris don bore.

Thar al the batellis cam, withouten more, 2628

On ather part, and is aſſemblit ſo

Whar fyfty thouſand war thei, & no mo.

In o plane befyd the gret Riwere

Xxx thouſand one galiotis half thei vare ; 2632

Of arthuris x thouſand and no mo

Thei ware, and ȝhit thai contenit them ſo

And in the feld ſo manly haith borñ,

That of thar fois haith the feld forſworñ. 2636

The conqueſt king, wich the perell knowith,

Ful manly one to the feld he drowith ;

The lord ſir gawan, couerit with his fcheld,

[1] MS. has "than."

Than Galys Gwynans, brother of Ywan,

encounters him, and horse and man go all four to earth.

Arthur's folk rescue Gwyans ;

thirty knights of Galiot's arrive, and rescue Esquyris.

Next Ywan comes to the mêlée.

Galiot's men give way.

Gwyans is again rescued.

50,000 men are assembled.

30,000 on Galiot's side approach the river,

and 10,000 on Arthur's.

Gawane puts the conquest-king to flight.

He rufchit in myddis of the feld,   2640
And haith them fo in to his com aſſayt,
That of his manhed ware thei al affrait ;
No langer mycht thei contrar hyme endur,
Bot fled, and goith one to difcumfiture.   2644

Galiot, full of an- And galiot, wich haith the difcumfit fen,
ger and grief,
sends out a new Fulfillit ful of anger and of ten,
band.
Incontinent he fend o new poware,
Whar-with the feldis al our-couerit ware   2648

[Fol. 33 a.]   Of armyt ftedis both in plait and maill,
With knychtis wich war reddy to affaill.

Gawane draws   Sir gawan, feing al the gret fuppris
his men together,
and shews them   Of fois cummyng In to fich o wys,   2652
comfortable
words.   Togiddir al his cumpany he drew,
And confortable wordis to them fchew ;
So at the cummyng of thar ennemys

They receive the Thei them refauf, in fo manly wyſ,   2656
foe in manly wise.
That many one felith deithis wound,
And wnder horſ lyith fobing one the ground.
This vther cummyth in to gret defir,
Fulfillit ful of matelent and Ire,   2660
So frefchly, with fo gret o confluens,
Thar ftrong aſſay hath don fich vyolens,
And at thar come arthuris folk fo led,
That thai war ay abayſit and adred.   2664
Bot gawan, wich that, by this vorldis fame,
Of manhed and of knychthed bur the name,
Haith prewit [hym] well be experiens ;
For only In til armys his defens   2668

Gawane encour- Haith maid his falowis tak fich hardyment,
ages his fellows,
That manfully thei biding one the bent.
Of his manhed war merwell to raherſ ;
The knychtis throw the fcheldis can he perſ,   2672
That many one thar dethis haith refauit ;
None armour frome his mychty hond them fauit,

though their foes Zhit ay for one ther ennemys wor thre.
are three to one ;

Long my*ch*t thei *noch*t endur in fuch dugree ; 2676
The pref it wos fo creuell & fo ftrong,
In gret anoy and haith *continewit* longe,
That, magre them, thei ned*is* moft abak
The way one to thar lug*is* for to tak. 2680

yet his men are forced to retreat to their tents.

S*ir* gawan thar fufferith gret myfchef,
And wonde*r*is in his kny*ch*thed can he pref ;
His faloufchip haith *mer*well that hym faw,
So haith his fois that of his fuerd ftud aw. 2684

King arthur, that al this whill beheld
The dange*r* and the *per*ell of the feld,
S*ir* ywan w*ith* o falowfchip he fende,
Them In that ned to help & to defend, 2688

Arthur behoids the peril of the field, and sends Sir Ywan to help them.

Qwich fond them In to danger and in were,
And ent*er*it nere In to thar tentis were.

[Fol. 33 *b*.]

S*ir* gawan fechtand was one fut At erde,
And no defend, but only in his fwerde, 2692
A3anis them bo*th* w*ith* fpere and fch*è*ld.
Of galowa the kny*ch*t goith to the erde.[1]

who finds Sir Gawane fighting on foot with only his sword.

Thar was the batell furyous and woud[2]
Of armyt kny*ch*t*is* ; to the grownde thai 3hud. 2696
S*ir* ywane, that was a noble knyght,
He fchew his ftrenth, he fchew thar h*is* gret my*ch*t,
In al his tyme that neu*er* of before
Off armys, nore of kny*ch*thed, did he more : 2700 .

The battle was furious and wood.

S*ir* gawan thar refkewit he of fors,
Magre his fois, and haith hyme fet one horf
That frome the firft *con*queft king he wan ;
Bot f*ir* gawan fo ewill was wondit than, 2704
And in the feld fupp*r*ifit was fo fore,
That he the werf thar-of was eue*r*more.

Sir Ywan rescues Sir Gawane,

Thar fchew the lord f*ir* ywan h*is* curage,
His manhed, & h*is* noble waffolage ; 2708
And gawan, in his doing, wald no*ch*t irk ;

who was so evilly wounded, that he was the worse thereof ever-more.

---

[1] Read "felde"? [2] MS. "woid," but the "*i*" is undotted, and is therefore perhaps meant for the first stroke of a "*u*."

Darkness parts the combatants.

So al the day enduring to the dyrk
Sal them, magre of thar defyre, conſtren
On ayar half fore [to] depart in twen.   2712
And when that gawan of his horſ vas toñ,
The blud out of his noiſ & mouth is goñ,
And largly ſo paſſith euery wounde,

Sir Gawane swoons,

In ſwonyng thore he fell one to the ground :   2716
Than of the puple petee was to here
The lemytable clamour, and the chere ;

so that the king despairs of his "niece's" life, and laments over him.

And of the king the forow and the care,
That of his necis lyf was in diſſpare.   2720
" Far well," he ſais, " my gladnes, & my delyt,
Apone knychthed far well myne appetit,
Fare well of manhed al the gret curage,
Yow flour of armys and of vaſſolage,   2724
Gif yow be loſt !"—thus til his tent hyme brocht

The surgeons are sought,

With wofull hart, and al the furryȝenis focht,
Wich for to cum was reddy at his neid ;
Thai fond the lord was of his lyf in dreid,   2728
For wondit was he, and ek wondit ſo,

who found he had two broken ribs, but no mortal wound.
[Fol. 34 a.]

And in his ſyd ware brokyne Ribys two.
Bot nocht for-thi the king thai maid beleif
That at that tyme he ſhuld the deith eſchef.   2732
[O]ff melyhalt the ladyis knychtis were
In to the feld, and can thir tithingis here,

The lady of Melyhalt's knights tell her how the battle went,

And home to thar lady ar thai went,
Til hir to ſchewing efter thar entent,   2736
In euery poynt, how that the batell ſtud
Of galiot, and of his multitud ;

and how Gawane bare him in the field, and of his wounds.

And how gawan hyme in the feld hath borñ,
Throw quhoys ſwerd ſo many o knycht vas lorñ,   2740
And of the knychtly wonderis that he wrocht,
Syne how that he one to his tent vas brocht.
The lady hard, that lowit gawan so,

She weeps for him.

She gan to wep, in to[1] hir hart vas wo.   2744

[1] MS. "in in " ; but "in to" is clearly meant.

Thir tythyng*is* one to lancelot ar goñ,

Whar-of that he was wond*er* wo-bygone,

And for the lady haftely he sent,

And fche til hyme, at his co*m*mand, Is went: 2748

He faluft hir, and faid, "madem, Is trew

Thir tithing*is* I her report of new

Of the affemble, and meting of the oft,

And of fir gawan, wich that fhuld be loft?.   2752

If that be fwth, adew the flour of armys,

Now neue*r*more recoue*r*yt be the harmys !

In hyme was manhed, curteffy, and trouth,

Befy trawell In knyc*h*thed, ey but fleuth,   2756

Humilyte, [and] gentrice, and cwrag ;

In hyme thar was no man*er* of outrage.

Allace ! knyc*h*t, allace ! what fhal yow fay ?

Yow may complen, yow may bewail the day   2760

As of his deith, an*d* gladfchip aucht to fes,

Baith menftrafy and fefting at the des ;

For of this lon*d* he was the holl comfort,

In tyme of ned al knyc*h*thed to fupport !   2764

Allace ! ma*d*em, and I durft fay at ʒhe

Al yhour beheft not kepit haith to me,

Whar-of that I was in to full belef

Aʒañe this day that I fchuld have my lef,   2768

And noc*h*t as cowart thus fchamfully to ly

Excludit in to cage frome chewalry,

Whar othir knyc*h*t*is* anarmyt on thar ftedis

Hawnt*is* ther ʒhouthhed in to knyc*h*tly dedis."   2772

"S*ir*," q*uo*d fche, "I red yhow not difpleß,

ʒhe may In tyme her-eft*er* cum at es ;

For the thrid day Is ordanit, & fhal be

Of the oft*is* a new affemble,   2776

And I have gart ordan al the gere

That longith to ʒour body for to were,

Boith horß and armour In the famyne wyß

Of fable, ewyne aftir ʒhour awn dewyß ;   2780

6

Lancelot requests to see the lady ;

and inquires if Gawane is really likely to die.

He laments over him,

first apostrophizing himself.

and next blaming the lady for not having allowed him to be present in the battle.

[Fol. 34 *b*.]

She promises he shall go to the next battle,

saying that his sable armour is ready.

And yhe ſal her remayne one to the day ;

Syne may ȝhe paſ, fore well ȝhe knaw the way."

"I will obey, madem, to yhour entent."

Wïth that ſche goith, and to hir reſt is went :   2784

In the morn she
takes her leave,
to go to the
court.
One the morn arly vp ſche roſ

Wïthout delay, and to the knycht ſche gois,

And twk hir lef, and ſaid that ſcho vald fare

On to the court, wïth-outen any mare.   2788

He kneels, and
thanks her often.
Than knelit he, and thankit hir oft-ſys;

That ſche ſo mych hath done hyme of gentriſ,

And hir byhecht euer, at his myght,

To be hir awn trew & ſtedfaſt knycht.   2792

She goes unto the
king,
Sche thonkith hyme, and ſyne ſche goith her way

On to the king, wïth-owten more delay,

Whar that in ¹ honour wïth king & qwen ſche ſall

Rycht thonkfully reſauit be wïth-all.   2796

Eft to ſir gawan thai hir led, & ſche

Ryght gladly hyme deſyrit for to ſee,

and finds Sir
Gawane quite dif-
ferent from what
had been told
her.
And ſche hyme fond, and ſche was glad tharfore,

All vthir ways than was hir told before.   2800

The knycht, the wich in to hir keping vas,

The lady's cousin
cherishes Lance-
lot in her best
manner.
Sche had commandit to hir cuſſynece,

Wich cheriſt hyme apone hir beſt manere,

And comfort hyme, and maid hym rycht gud chere. 2804

[T]he days goith, ſo paſſith als the nycht,

The third day,
the maiden goes
to his chamber,
and fastens on
his armour.
The thrid morow, as that the ſone vas lycht,

The knycht onon out of his bed aroſ,

The maden ſone one to his chalmer goſ,   2808

And ſacretly his armour one hyme ſpent.

He tuk his lef, and ſyne his way he went

He goes to the
same green, be-
side the river, as
before.
Ful prewaly, rycht to the ſamyne greñ

One the rewere, whar he befor had ben,   2812

Ewyne as the day [he] the firſt courſ hath maad.

Alone rycht thar he howit, and abaade,

---

¹ MS. "wïth ; " which is crossed out, and " in " inserted
above, rather minutely written.

Behalding to the bertes, whar the qweñ   [Fol. 35 *a.*]

Befor at the affemble he had feñ   2816   He abides there alone, looking towards the parapet where he saw the queen.

Ry*ch*t fo the fone fchewith fur*th* his ly*ch*t,

And to his armour went is euery wy*ch*t ;

One athir half the Iufting is bygon,   The jousting begins.

And many o fair and knych[t]ly courî is rown.   2820

The blak kny*ch*t ʒhit howyns on his fted,   The black knight still halts on his steed.

Of al thar doing takith he no hed,

Bot ay, apone the befynes of tho*ch*t,

In beholding his ey depa*r*tit nocht.   2824

To quhom the lady of melyhalt beheld,   The lady beholds him and knows him; but yet inquires who he is,

And knew hyme by h*is* armour & h*is* fcheld,

Qwhat that he was ; and thus fche faid one hy*ch*t :

"Who is he ʒone ? who may he be, ʒhone kny*ch*t,   2828

So ftill that hovith and fterith not his Ren,

And feith the kny*ch*t*is* rynyng one the greñ ?"

Than al beholdith, and in princypale   thus calling the attention of Gawane,

S*ir* gawan beholdith moft of all ;   2832

Of melyha[l]t the lady to hyme maid

Inc*on*tinent, his couche and gart be had

Be-fore o wyndew thore, as he my*ch*t se

The kny*ch*t, the oft, and al the affemble.   2836

He lukith fur*th*, and fone the kny*ch*t hath fen,

And, but delay, he faith one to the qwen,   who saith to the queen :

"Madem, if ʒhe remembir, fo it was   "Madam, remember that the red knight halted where yon knight halts."

The red kny*ch*t in to the famyne place   2840

That wencuft al [at] the firft affemble ;

Whar that ʒone kny*ch*t howis, howit hee."

"ʒha," q*uod* the qwen, " ry*ch*t well remembir I ;   "Why do you inquire ?" she replies.

Qwhat is the cauî at ʒhe inquere, & quhy ?"   2844

"Madem, of [al] this larg warld is he

The kny*ch*t the wich I moft defir to fee   "He is the knight, madam, whom I most desire to see."

His ftrenth, his manhed, his curag, and h*is* my*ch*t,

Or do in armys that longith to o kny*ch*t."   2848

[B]y thus, arthur, w*ith* confell well awyfit,

Haith ordanit his batell*is*, and devyfit :   Arthur arranges his lines of battle.

King Ydrus leads the first;
The firft of them led ydrus king, & he

O worthy man vas nemmyt for to bee.   2852

Harwy the Reweyll, an aged knight, the second.
The fecund led harwy the Reweyll,

That in this world was knycht that had moft feill

For to prowid that longith to the were,

One agit knycht, and well couth armys bere.   2856

[Fol. 35 b.]
[T]he thrid feld [he] deliuerit in the hond

King Angus, a cousin of Arthur, leads the third.
Of angus, king of ylys of fcotlande,

Wich cufing was one to king arthur nere,

One hardy knycht he was, withouten were.   2860

King Ywons the fourth.
The ferd batell led ywons the king,

O manly knycht he was In to al thing.

And thus dewyfit ware his batellis fere,

In every company are 15,000.
In euery feld xv thoufand were.   2864

[T]he fift [1] batell the lord fir ywan lede,

The lord Sir Ywan leads the rearguard.
Whois manhed was in euery cuntre dred,

Sone he was one to wryne the kyng,

Forwart, ftout, hardy, wyß, and 3hing ;   2868

Xx thoufand in his oft thai paft,

Wich ordanit was for to affemble laft.

Galiot's armies.
[A]nd galiot, apone the tothir fyde,

Rycht wyfly gan his batellis to dewid.   2872

Malenginys leads the first line ;
The firft of them led malenginys the king,

None hardyar In to this erth lewyng ;

He neuer more out of his cuntre Raid,

Nor he with hyme one hundereth knychtis hade.   2876

the first-conquest king the second ; Walydeyne the third ;
[T]he fecund the first-conqueft king led,

That for no perell of armys vas adred ;

The thrid, o king clepit walydeyne,

He led, and was o manly knycht, but weyne.   2880

Clamedeus the fourth ;
[T]he ferd, king clamedeus has,

Wich that lord of far ylys was.

and King Brandymagus the fifth.
The fift [2] batell, whar xl thoufand were,

King brandymagus had to led and ftere,   2884

---

[1] MS. "firft."   See l. 2870.   [2] MS. "firft."

O manly kny*ch*t, and prewit well oft-fyſ,
And in his confell wond*er* fcharp & wyſ.
Galiot non armys bur that day,

Galiot bore no arms;

Nor as o kny*ch*t he wald hyme-felf aray,   2888
But as o feruand in o habariowne,

but was arrayed as a servant in a habergeon with a "prekyne" hat, and a truncheon in his hand.

O prekyne hat, and ek o gret trownfciowñ
In til his hond, and one o curfour fet,
The beft that was in ony lond to get.   2892
Endlong the rewar men my*ch*t behold & fee,
Of kny*ch*t*is* weryne mony one affemble ;
And the blak kny*ch*t ftill he couth abyde,

The black knight still remains looking towards the parapet.

W*i*t*h*out remowyng, one the Riwer fyde,   2896
Bot to the bartes to behold and fee
Thar as his hart defyrit moft to bee :
And quhen the lady of melyhalt haith feñ

The lady says to the queen—
[Fol. 36 a.]

The kny*ch*t fo ftond, fche faid one to the qweñ,   2900
"Madem, It is my confell at ȝhe send

"Madam, pray commend yourself to yon knight."

One to ȝone kny*ch*t, ȝour-felf for to *com*mend,
Befeiching hyme that he wald wnd*er*tak
This day to do of armys, for ȝour fak."   2904
The quen anfuerit as that hir lykit no*ch*t,

The queen replies

For othir thing was more In to hir tho*ch*t,
" For well ȝhe fe the p*er*ell how disio[i]nt,
The adwentur now ftondith one the point   2908
Boith of my lord his honore, and h*is* lond,
And of his men, in[1] dang*er* how thai ftond :
Bot ȝhe, and ek thir vthere ladice may,

that the lady and the rest may send a message, but that she will not herself take part in it.

If that yhow lykith, to the kny*ch*t gar fay   2912
The mefag ; is none that wil yhow let,
For I tharof fal no*ch*t me ent*er*met."
On to the quen fcho faith, " her I,
If fo it pleſ thir vthir ladice by,   2916
Am for to fend one to the kny*ch*t content ; "
And al the ladice can thar-to affent,

---

[1] Stevenson reads "tᵗʰe"; but "the" is crossed out, and
"i*n*" written over it.

Befeching hir the mefag to dewyſ,

As fche that was moſt prudent & moſt wyſ.   2920

The lady sends a
discreet maiden,

Sche grantit, and o madeñ haith thai tone,

Difcret, apone this mefag for till gone ;

and Sir Gawane a
squire, with two
spears,

And ſir gawan a ſqwyar bad alſo,

With two ſperis one to the knycht to go.   2924

The lady than, withouten more dulay,

Haith chargit hir apone this wyſ to ſay:

to say that all the
ladies, the queen
alone excepted,
commend them to
the black knight,

"Schaw to the knycht, the ladice euer-ilkone

Ben In the court, excep the quen allon,   2928

Til hyme them haith recommandit oft-ſyſ,

Befeching hyme of knychthed and gentriſ,

(Or if It hapyne euermore that he fhall

Cum, quhar thai may, owther an or all,   2932

In ony thing awail hyme or ſupport,

Or do hyme ony plefans or comfort,)

and pray him to
essay some deed
of arms.

He wold wichfaif for loue of them this day

In armys ſum manhed to aſſay ;   2936

And ſay, ſir gawan hyme the ſperis ſent ;

Now go, this is the fek of our entent."

The damsel and
squire

The damyſell fche hath hir palfray tone,

The ſqwyar with the ſperis with hir goñ ;   2940

[Fol. 36 b.]

The nereſt way thai paſ one to ye knycht,

repeat the mes-
sage.

Whar fche repete hir mefag haith ful rycht :

Sir Lancelot, find-
ing the queen not
in the message,

And quhen he hard, and planly wnderſtude,

How that the quen not in the mefag ȝude,   2944

was not content,

He ſpak no word, bot he was not content ;

Bot, of ſir gawan, glaid in his entent,

He aſkit quhar he was, and of his fair ?

And thai to hyme the maner can duclair ;   2948

but asks the
squire to hold the
two spears ready
for him.

Than the ſqwyar he prayth that he wold

Paſ to the feld, the ſperis for to hold.

He faw the knychtis femblyng her and thare,

The ſtedis Rynyng with the ſadillis bare ;   2952

His ſpuris goith in to the ſtedis ſyde,

That was ful fwyft, and lykit not to byd ;

And he that was hardy, ferß, and ftout,

Furth by o fyd affemblyng on a rout   2956   He attacks a company of a hundred knights, slays the nearest,

Whar that one hundereth knychtis was, & mo ;

And with the firft has Recounterit so,

That frome the deth not helpith hym his fcheld,

Boith horß and man is lying in the feld ;   2960

The fpere is gone, and al in pecis brak,

And he the trunfcyoune in his hand hath tak   and with the stump of his

That two or thre he haith the fadillis reft,   spear bereaves two or three of

Whill in his hond fchortly no thing is left.   2964   their saddles.

Syne, to the fquyar, of the feld is goñ,

Fro hyme o fpere In to his hond haith ton,   He takes a new spear from the

And to the feld returnyt he aȝayne :   squire, and overthrows three

The firft he met, he goith one the plan,   2968   knights.

And ek the next, and fyne the thrid alfo ;

Nor in his hond, nore in his ftrak was ho.

His ennemys that veryng In affray

Befor his ftrok, and makith rovm alway ;   2972

And in fich wyß ay in the feld he vrocht,

Whill that his fperis gon var al to nocht ;

Whar-of fir gawan berith vitnefing

Throw al this world that thar vas non levyng,   2976

In fo fchort tyme fo mych of armys wrocht.

His fperis gone, out of the feld he focht,   His spears gone, he returns to his

And paffit is one to the Rewere syde,   first position.

Rycht thore as he was wont for to abyde ;   2980

And fo beholdyne In the famyne plañ,   [Fol. 37 a.]

As to the feld hyme lykit nocht aȝañ.

Sir gawan faw, and faith on to the quen,   Sir Gawane says to the queen :

" Madem, yhone knycht difponit [not],[1] I weyñ,   2984   " Madam, yon knight thinks

To help ws more, fore he fo is awyfit ;   himself despised, because you so

As I prefume, he thinkith hyme difpifit   specially excepted yourself in the

Of the mefag that we gart to hyme mak ;   message ;

Yhowre-felf yhe have fo fpecialy out-tak,   2988

---

[1] " not " seems required.

He thinkith ewill contempnit for to bee,

Confidering how that the neceffitee

Moft prinfpally to yhowr fupporting lyis.

Tharfor my confell is, yhow to dewyß,　　　　2992

And ek ʒhowre-felf in yhowr trefpas accuß,

ask him mercy, therefore, and ex-cuse your guilt.

And afk hyme mercy, and yhour gilt excuß.

For well it oucht o prince or o king

Til honore and til cheriß in al thing　　　　2996

O worthi man, that is in knychthed prewit.

For throw the body of o man efchevit

Mony o wondir, mony one aduenture,

That merwell war til any creature.　　　　3000

And als oft-tyme is boith hard & fen,

For often, by one knight's prowess, have 40,000 been worsted by 5,000.

Quhar xl thoufand haith difcumfit ben

Vith v thoufand, and only be o knycht;

For throw his ftreuth, his vorfchip, & his mycht, 3004

His falowfchip fich comfort of hym tais

That thai ne dreid the danger of thar fays.

And thus, madem, I wot, withouten were,

If yon knight will continue to help the king,

If that ʒhone knycht this day will perfywere　3008

With his manhed for helping of the king,

We fal have cauß to dred in to no thing.

Our folk of hyme thai fal fich comfort tak,

And fo adred thar ennemys fal mak,　　　　3012

That fur I am, onys or the nycht,

yon folk shall perforce take to flight."

Of forß ʒhone folk fal tak one them the flycht:

Wharffor, madem, that ʒhe have gilt to mend,

My confell is one to ʒhon knycht ʒe fend."　3016

She consents to send a message.

"Sir," quod fche, "quhat pleffith yhow to do

ʒhe may dewyß, and I confent thar-to."

Than was the lady of melyhalt content,

And to fir gawan in-to-contynent　　　　3020

[Fol. 37 b.]

Sche clepit the maid, wich that paffit ar;

A maiden is therefore sent to say,

And he hir bad the mefag thus duclar.

"Say [to]¹ the knycht, the quen hir recommendith,

¹ " to " seems required.

And fal correk in quhat that fche offendith   3024

At his awn will, how fo hyme lift dewyß;

And hyme exortith, in moft humyll wyß,   *that the queen humbly exhorts him*

As euer he will, whar that fche can or may,

Or powar haith hir charg, be ony way,   3028

And for his worfchip and his hie manhede,

And for hir luf, to helpen in that ned   *to help in that need to preserve the king's honour, and to deserve her thanks.*

The kingis honore, his land fore to preferf,·.

That he hir thonk for euer may deferf."   3032

And four fquyaris chargit he alfo

With thre horß and fperis x to go   *Sir Gawane also sends four squires with three horses and ten spears.*

Furth to the knycht, hyme prayng for his fak,

At his raqueft thame in his ned to tak.   3036

[T]he maden furth with the fqwyaris is went

One to the knycht, and fchawith yar entent.

Tho mefag hard, and ek ye prefent feñ,   *The message heard, he inquires about the queen,*

He anfwerit, and afkith of the qwen;   3040

"Sir," quod fche, ["sche"][1] in to ƺhone bartiis lyis,   *and is told that from yon parapet she can witness his deeds.*

Whar that this day yhour dedis fal dewyß,

Yhowr manhed, yhour worfchip, and affere,

How ƺhe conteñ, and how yhe armys bere;   3044

The quen hir-felf, and many o lady to,

Sal Iugis be, and vitnes how yhe do."

Than he, whois hart ftant in o new aray,

Saith, "damyceyll, on to my lady fay,   3048   *He returns a message that he is the queen's knight.*

How euer that hir lykith that it bee,

Als far as wit or powar is in me,

I am hir knycht, I fal at hir command

Do at I may, withouten more demand.   3052

And to fir gawan, for his gret gentriß,

Me recommend and thonk a thoufand fyß."

With that o fper he takith in his hond,

And fo in to his fterapis can he ftond   3056   *He stands in his stirrups; and seems to increase a foot in height.*

That to fir gawan femyth that the knycht

---

[1] A second "sche" is here required.

Encrefyng gon o larg fut one hycht;

And to the ladice faith he, and the qwen,

"Ʒhon is the knycht that euer I have fen   3060

In al my tyme moft knychtly of affere,

And in hyme-felf gon fareft armys bere."

[T]he knycht that haith Remembrit in his thocht

The qwenys chargis, & how fche hym befocht,   3064

Curag can encrefing to his hart;

His curfer lap, and gan onon to ftart;

And he the fqwaris haith reqwyrit fo,

That thai with hyme one to the feld wald go.   3068

without delay he
crosses over the
river to the field; Than goith he one, withouten mor abaid,

And our the reuar to the feld he raid;

Don goith his fpere onone In to the Reft,

and goes in
wherever he sees
most peril. And in he goith, withouten mor areft,   3072

Thar as he faw moft perell and moft dred

In al the feld, and moft of help [1] had ned,

Whar femblyt was the firft-conqueft king

With mony o knycht that was in his leding.   3076

The firft he met, doune goith boith horß & man;

The fper was holl, and to the next he Ran

That helpit hyme his hawbrek nor his fcheld,

Bot throuch and throuch haith perfit in the feld.   3080

Sir Kay, Sir
Sygramors, Sir
Gresown, Sir
Ywan, Sir Bran-
dellis, and Ga-
hers, all six in a
race spur across
the field with
stretched spears, Sir kay, the wich haith this encontyr fen,

His horß he ftrekith our the larg gren,

And fir fygramors ek the defyrand,

With fir grefown cummyth at yar honde,   3084

Son of the duk, and alfua fir ywan

The baftart, and fir brandellis onan,

And gaherß, wich that broyir was

To gawan; thir fex in a Raß   3088

Deliuerly com prekand our the feldis

With fperis ftraucht, and couerit with thar fcheldis;

Sum for love, fum honor to purcheß,

And aftir them one hundereth knychtis was,   3092

                    [1] MS. "held."

In famyne will, thar manhed to affay.

On his v falowis clepit than *fir* kay,

And faith them, " *firis*, thar has ȝhond*er* ben

A courſ that neu*er*-more farar was ſen   3096

Maid be o knyc*h*t, and we ar cu*m*myn ilkon

Only ws one [his] worfchip to difpone ;

And neu*er* we in al our dais myc*h*t

Have bet axampil than iffith ws ȝone knyc*h*t   3100

Of well doing ; and her I hecht for me

N*er* hyme al day, if that I may, to bee,

And folow hyme at al [my] myc*h*t I fall,

Bot deth or vthir adwentur me fall.   3104

W*ith* that thir fex, al in one affent,

W*ith* frefch curag In to the feld Is went.

The blak knyc*h*t*is* fpere in pec*is* goñe,   [Fol. 38 *b.*]

Frome o fqwyar oñe vthir haith he toñe,   3108

And to the feld onone he goith ful ryc*h*t ;

Thir fex w*ith* hyme ay holdith at y*ar* myc*h*t.

And than bygan his wond*er*is in the feld ;

Thar was no helme, no hawbryk, nore no fcheld,   3112

Nor yhit no knyc*h*t fo hardy, ferſ, nore ſtout,

No ȝhit no maner armour myc*h*t hald owt

His ſtrenth, nore was of powar to w*ith*ſtond ;

So mych of armys dyde he w*ith* his honde,   3116

That euery wight ferleit of h*is* deid,

And al his fois ſtondith ful of dreid.

So befely he can his tyme difpend,

That of the fperis wich *fir* gawan fend,   3120

Holl of them all thar was not lewit oñe ;

Throw wich but m*er*cy to the deyth is gon

Ful many o knyc*h*t, and many o weriour,

That cout*h* fuften ful hardely o ſtour.   3124

And of his horſ fupp*ri*ſit ded ar two,

One of his awn, of gawanis one alfo,

And he one fut was fechtand one the gren,

When that *fir* kay haith w*ith* his falowis feñ ;   3128

Sir Kay exhorts them

to keep near the black knight, and follow his guidance all day.

With a second spear, the black knight seeks the field, closely followed by the six.

No knight nor armour can withstand him.

Every wight wonders at his deeds.

He uses up all Gawane's spears.

Two horses of his are killed, and he fights on foot.

The squire brings
him a fresh horse;
The fqwyar with his horß than to hym brocht;

Magre his fois he to his courfeir focht

Deliuerly, as of o mychty hart,

he leaps into the
saddle without
stirrups.
Without fteropis in to his fadill ftart,   3132

That euery wycht beholding mervell has

Of his ftrenth and deliuer befynes.

Sir Kay asks who
he is,
Sir kay, feing his horß, and how that thai

War cled in to fir gawanis aray,   3136

Afkith at the fquyar if he knewith

What that he was, this knycht? & he hym fchewith

but the squire
cannot tell.
He wift no thing quhat that he was, nore hee

Befor that day hyme neuer faw with Ee.   3140

Than afkith he, how and one quhat wyß

On gawanis horß makith hyme fich feruice?

The fqw[y]ar faith, "forfuth y wot no more;

My lord ws bad, I not the cauß quharfore."   3144

The black knight
returns to the
field.
The blak knycht, horfit, to the feld can few

Als frefch as he was in the morow new;

The six comrades
follow him.
The fex falowis folowit hyme ilkone,

And al in front on to the feld ar goñ;   3148

[Fol. 39 a.]
Rycht frefchly one thar ennemys thai foght,

And many o fair poynt of armys vroght.

Malangin's host
is discomfited by
king Ydras; and
retreats to join
the second line,
commanded by
the Conquest-
king;
[T]han hapnyt to king malangins oft

By ydras king difcumfit was, & loft,   3152

And fled, and to the conqueft-king ar goñe,

Thar boith the batellis affemblit In to one;

King malengynis in to his hart was wo,

For of hyme-felf no better knycht mycht go;   3156

so that 40,000 are
now opposed to
15,000 of Arthur's.
Thar xl thoufand war thai for xv.

Than mycht the feld rycht perellus be fen

Of armyt knychtis gaping one the ground;

Sum deith, and fum with mony a grewous wond; 3160

For arthuris knychtis, that manly war and gud,

Suppos that vthir was o multitude,

Refauit tham well at the fperis end;

But one fuch wyß thai may not lang defend.   3164

The blak kny*ch*t faw the dang*er* of the feld,

And al his doing*is* knowith quho beheld,

And ek reme*m*brith in to his entent

Of the mefag that fche haith to hyme fent: 3168

Than curag, ftrenth encrefing w*ith* ma*n*hed,

Ful lyk o kny*ch*t one to the feld he raid,

Thinking to do his ladice love to have,

Or than his deth befor hir to refave.   ·.   3172

Thar he begynyth in his ferf curag

Of armys, as o lyoune in his rag ;

Than m*er*well was his doing to behold ;

Thar was no kny*ch*t fo ftrong, nor yhit fo bold, 3176

That in the feld befor his fuerd he met,

Nor he fo hard his ftrok apone hyme fet,

That ded or woudit to the erth he fo*ch*t ;

For thar was not bot wond*er*is that he wro*ch*t. 3180

And magre of his fois eu*er*ilkone,

In to the feld oft tymys hyme aloñ

Throuch and throuch he paffith to & fro ;

For in the ward[1] it was the man*er* tho   3184

That non o kny*ch*t fhuld be the brydill tak

Hyme to oreft, nore cum behynd h*is* bak,

Nor mo than on at onys one o kny*ch*t

Shuld ftrik, for that tyme worfchip ftud fo ry*ch*t. 3188

Ʒhit was the feld ry*ch*t p*er*ellus and ftrong

Till arthuris folk, fet thai *con*tenyt longe ;

Bot in fich wyf this blak kny*ch*t can *con*ten,

That thai, the wich that hath his manhed feñ,   3192

Sich hardyment haith takyne In his ded,

Them tho*ch*t thai had no man*er* cauf of dred,

Als long as he my*ch*t owthir ryd or go,

At euery ned he them recomfort fo.   3196

S*ir* kay haith w*ith* his falowis al the day

Folowit hyme al that he can or may,

The black knight, knowing who is beholding him,

thinks to have his lady's love, or die before her.

He works nothing but wonders ;

and often passes alone through the field.

[Fol. 39 b.]

He fights in such wise as to encourage all who see his deeds.

Sir Kay and his fellows follow him all day.

[1] Another spelling of *warld*, i. e. world, which occurs in the fuller form in l. 3212.

And woudir well thai have in armys prewit,

And with thar manhed oft thar folk relewit ;   3200

Bot well thai faucht in diuerſ placis fere,

But at last they are nearly all overpowered by numbers. With multitud yar folk confufit were,

That long in fich wyſ mycht thai nocht conteñ.

Sir Kay sends Gawane's squire with a message to Sir Harwy that he ought not to suffer the best knight that ever bore arms to be surprised, Sir kay, that hath fir gawans qſquyaris fen,   3204

He clepit hyme, and haith hyme prayt fo,

That to fir harwy the rewell wil he go,

And fay to hyme, "ws think hyme ewil awyfit ;

For her throuch hyme he fufferit be fupprifit   3208

The beft knycht that euer armys bur ;

And if it fo befell of adwentur,

In his defalt, that he be ded or lamyt,

This warld fal have hyme vtraly defamyt.   3212

nor six knights of the Round Table to be discomfited. And her ar of the round table alfo

A faloufchip, that fall in well and wo

Abid with hyme, and furth for to endur

Of lyf or deth, this day, thar adwentur ;   3216

And if fo fal difcumfyt at thai bee,

The king may fay that wonder ewill haith he

Contenit hyme, and kepit his honore,

Thus for to tyne of chevalry the flour !"   3220

The squire takes the message. The fqw[y]ar hard, and furth his way Raid,

In termys fchort he al his mefag faid.

Sir harwy faith, "y wytneſ god, that I

Neuer in my days comytit tratory,   3224

And if I now begyne In to myne eld,

In ewill tyme fyrſt com I to this feld ;

Sir Harwy says that Sir Kay shall have no cause to reprove him. Bot, if god will, I fal me fon difcharg.

Say to fir kay, I fal not ber the charg,   3228

He fal no mater have me to.rapref,

I fal amend this mys if that I lef."

The fqwyar went and tellit to fir kay ;

Sir Harwy comes to support them ; And fir harwy, in al the haft he may,   3232

Affemblyt hath his oftis, & onoñ

[Fol. 40 a.] In gret defyre on the feld is gon

Before his folk, and haldith fur*th* his way ;
Don goith his fper, and ewyne before f*ir* kay   3236
So hard o knyc*ht* he ftrykith in his ten
That hor*f* and he lay boith apone the gren.
S*ir* gawan faw the counte*r* that he maad,
And leuch for al the farues that he had :   3240

That day f*ir* harwy prewyt in the feld
Of armys more than longith to his eld,   and provee him-
                                                self a better war-
                                                rior than might
For he was more than fyfty yher of ag,   have been ex-
                                                pected of one so
Set he was fer*f* and ʒong in his curag ;   3244   old.
And fro that he affemblyt his bataill
Doune goith the folk of galot*is* al haill ;   Galiot's folk are
                                                beaten.
For to wi*th*ftond thai war of no poware,
And yhit of folk x thoufand mo thei vare.   3248

Kyng valydone, that fauch on fuch o wy*f*   King Valydone
     His falowis dang*er*it wi*th* thar ennemys,   comes to support
                                                them.
Wi*th* al his folk, being fre*f* and new,
Goith to the feld onon, them to reffkew ;   3252
Thar was the feld ryc*ht* p*er*ellus aʒañe,
Of arthuris folk ful many on var ilan.

Bot angus, quhich that lykith not to bid,   Angus comes to
     And faw the p*er*ell one the tother fid,   3256   aid Arthur's men.
His fted he ftrok, and wi*th* his oft is gon
Whar was moft ned, and thar the feld has ton.

Kyng clamedyus makith non abaid,   Clamedyus comes
     Bot wi*th* his oft one to the fid he raid.   3260   to aid Galiot's
                                                men.
And ywons king, that haith his cu*m*myn fen,   Ywons encoun-
                                                ters Clamedyus.
     Encounte*r*it hyme in myddis of the greñ.
The aucht batell*is* affemblyt one this wi*f* ;
On ather half the clamore and the cryi*f*   3264   Great clamour
                                                and lamentable
Was lametable and petws for til her,   cries on either
                                                side.
Of knyc*ht*is wich in diue*rf* placis fere
Wondit war, and fallyng to and fro,
ʒhit galyot*is* folk war xx thoufand mo.   3268

The blak knyc*ht* than on to hyme-felf he faid :   The black knight
                                                bids himself re-
     " Remembir the, how yhow haith ben araid,   member love's
                                                power over him ;

Ay ſen ye hour that yow was makid knycht,

With love, aȝane quhois powar & whois mycht   3272

Yow haith no ſtrenth, yow may It not endur,

Nor ȝhit non vthir erthly creatur ;

and that only his lady's mercy or his life's end can amend him.

And bot two thingis ar the to amend,

Thi ladice mercy, or thi lyvys end.   3276

And well yhow wot that on to hir preſens,

[Fol. 40 b.]

Til hir eſtat, nor til hir excellens,

Thi febilneſ neuermore is able

For to attan, ſche is ſo honorable.   3280

And ſen no way yow may ſo hie extend,

He counsels himself to strive for her thanks,

My verray confell is, that yow pretend

This day, (ſen yow becummyne art hir knycht

Of hir comand, and fechtit in hir ſycht),   3284

And well yow ſchaw, ſen yow may do no mor,

That of reſone ſche ſal the thank tharfore ;

and to be ashamed of every point of cowardice.

Of euery poynt of cowardy yow ſcham,

And in til armys purcheſ the ſum nam."   3288

With that of love in to o new deſir

Swift as a cross-bow-bolt he seeks the field.

His ſpere he ſtraucht, and ſwift as any wyre

With al his forſ the nereſt feld he ſoght ;

His ful ſtrenth in armys thar he vroght,   3292

In to the feld ruſching to and fro,

Doune goith the man, doune goith the horſ alſo ;

Sum throw the ſcheld is perſit to the hart,

Sum throw the hed, he may It not aftart.   3296

His sword carves the head from some, and cuts the arms of others in twain.

His bludy fuerd he dreuch, that carwit ſo

Fro ſum the hed, and ſum the arm in two ;

Sum in the feld fellit is in ſwoñ,

Throw ſum his ſuerd goith to the ſadill doune.   3300

His fois waren abaſit of his dedis,

His mortell ſtrok ſo gretly for to dred Is ;

When his foes see him, they leave the place for dread of death.

Whar thai hyme ſaw, within a lytall ſpace,

For dreid of ded, thai levyng hyme the place,   3304

That many o ſtrok ful oft he haith forloriñ ;

The ſpedy horſ away the knycht hath borñ.

In to his wyrking neuermore he feft,
Nor non abaid he makith, nor areft.   3308

His falowis, fo in his knychthed affuryd,
Thai ar recomfort, thar manhed is recoueryt,
And one thar fois ful ferfly thai foght,
Thar goith the lyf of many o knycht to nocht.   3312

So was the batell wonderful to tell,
Of knychtis to fe the multitud that fell,
That pety was til ony knycht to feñ
The knychtis lying gaping on the gren.   3316

The blak knycht ay continewit fo faft,
Whill¹ many one, difcumfit at the laft,
Are fled, and planly of the feld thei pas:
And galyot haith wondyr, for he was   3320
Of mor powar, and afkit at them qwhy
As cowartis thai fled fa fchamfully?

Than faith o knycht, for wondit in the brayne,
" Who lykith, he may Retwrn agayne   3324
Frome qwhens we come, merwalis for to fee,
That in his tyme neuer fich fauch hee."

" Marwell," quod he, " that dar I boldly fay
Thay may be callit, and quhat thai ar, I pray?"   3328
" Schir, in the feld forfuth thar is o knycht,
That only throw his body and his mycht
Wencuffith all, that thar may non fuften
His ftrokis, thai ar fo fureows and ken.   3332
He farith as o lyone or o beyre,
Wod in his rag, for fich is his affere.
Nor he the knycht in to the armys Red,
Wich at the first affemble in this fted   3336
Wencuffith all, and had the holl renown,
He may to this be no comparyfoune,
Fore neuer he fefith fen the day vas goñ,
Bot euermore continewit in to one."   3340

His knightly deeds assure his fellows.

It was pitiful to see the knights gaping upon the green.

[Fol. 41 a.]

Galiot asks his men why they flee.

A knight replies, that whoever likes may go and see marvels.

Galiot asks, what marvels; and the knight tells him there is a knight who vanquishes all;

who fares as a lion or a bear;

to whom the red knight bears no comparison.

¹ MS. "Whilk."

7

Galiot says he
will go and see.

Quod galiot, " in nome of god and we
Al, be tyme, the futhfaftneß fal see."

Galiot is armed,
rallies the flyers,
and encourages
his men.

[T]han he in armys that he had is gon,
And to the feld with hyme aȝane hath ton　　　3344
Al the flearis, and foundyne [in] [1] fich aray
His folk, that ner difcumfyt al war thay ;
Bot quhen thai faw cummyne our the plan
Thar lord, thai tuk fich hardement aȝaū,　　　3348

They shout their
war-cries.

That thar effenȝeis lowd thai gon to cry.
He chargit tham to go, that ware hyme by,
Straucht to the feld, with al thar holl forß ;
And thai, the wich that fparit not the horß,　　　3352
All redy war to fillyng his command,
And frefchly went, withowten more demand :
Throw qwich thar folk recoueryt haith thar place,

All think a new
host is coming.

For al the feld prefwmyt that thar was　　　3356
O new oft, one fuch o wyß thai foght ;

Arthur's folk de-
termine rather to
die than fly.

Whar arthuris folk had paffith al to nocht,
Ne war that thai the better war ilkoñe,
And at thai can them vtraly difpoñe　　　·　　　3360

[Fol. 41 b.]

Rathar to dee than flee, in thar entent,
And of the blak knycht haith fich hardyment ;
For at al perell, al harmys, and myfchef,
In tyme of ned he can tham al ralef.　　　3364

[T]har was the batell dangerus & ftrong,
Gret was the pres, bath perellus & throng ;

The black knight
is borne to the
ground.

The blak knycht is born on to the ground,
His horß hyme falyth, that fellith dethis wound. 3368

The six comrades
go to the earth.

The vi falowis, that falowit hyme al day,
Sich was the preß, that to the erth go thay ;
And thar in myd among his ennemys
He was about enclofit one fich wyß　　　3372

None know
where he is.

That quhare he was non of [his] falowis knew,
Nor mycht nocht cum to help hyme, nore refkew.

---

[1] The sense, but not the metre, requires "in."

And thus among his ennemys allon
His nakid fuerd out of his hond haith ton ;   3376   He defends him-
                                                                self with his
And thar he prewit his wertew & his ftrenth ;   sword.
For thar was none within the fuerdis lenth
That came, bot he goith to confufioune.
Thar was no helme, thar was no habirioune,   3380   No helm nor ha-
                                                                bergeon may re-
That may refift his fuerd, he fmytith so ;   sist his sword
One euery fyd he helpith to and fro,
That al about the compas thai mycht ken ;
The ded horß lyith virflyng with the men.   3384
Thai hyme affalзeing both with fcheld & fpere,
And he aзane ; as at the ftok the bere   He fares like a
                                                                bear at the stake,
Snybbith the hardy houndis that ar ken,   that snubs the
                                                                hardy hounds.
So farith he ; for neuer mycht be fen   3388
His fuerd to reft, that in the gret rout
He rowmyth all the compas hyme about.
   [A]nd galiot, beholding his manhed,
Within his-felf wonderith of his ded,   3392   Galiot wonders at
                                                                his deeds ;
How that the body only of o knycht
Haith lich o ftrenth, haith lich affere & mycht ;
Than faid he thus, " I wald not that throw me,
Or for my cauß, that fuch o knycht fuld dee,   3396   and says tnat
                                                                such a knight
To conquer all this world that is fo larg."   shall not die on
                                                                his account.
His horß than can he with his fpuris charg,
A gret trunfioune In to his hond hath ton,
And in the thikeft of the preß is goñ,   3400
And al his folk chargit he to feß.   He charges all his
                                                                folk to cease ;
At his command thai levyng al the preß ;
And quhen he had departit all the rout,   [Fol. 42 a.]
He faid, " fir knycht, havith now no dout."   3404
Wich anfwerit, " I have no cauß to dred."
" Зis," quod he, " fa euer god me fped,   and assures the
                                                                black knight that
Bot apone fut quhill зe ar fechtand here,   he will himself
                                                                warrant him from
And yhow defendith apone fich manere,   3408   all harm.
So hardely, and ek fo lyk o knycht,
I fal my-felf with al my holl mycht

Be yhour defens, and varand fra al harmys;

Bot had yhe left of worſchip In til armys,　　3412

What I have don I wold apone no wyſ;

Bot ſen yhe ar of knychthed ſo to prys,

Ʒhe ſal [1] no maner cauſ have for to dred:

He offers him as many horses as he needs; and proposes that they shall never again part.

And ſet yhour horſ be ſalit at this ned,　　3416

Diſpleſ yhow not, for-quhy ʒe ſal not want

Als many as yhow lykith for to hawnt;

And I my-ſelf, I ſal yhowr ſqwyar bee,

And, if god will, neuer more ſal wee　　3420

He 'lights from his horse, and gives him to Lancelot, who thanks him.

Depart;" with that, anon he can to lycht

Doune frome his horſ, and gaf hyme to ye knycht.

The lord he thonkit, and the horſ hath ton,

And als ſo freſch one to the feld is gon,　　3424

As at no ſtrokis he that day had ben.

His falowis glad, one horſ that hath hym ſen,

To galiot one vthir horſ thai broght;

And he goith one, and frome the feld he focht,　　3428

Galiot returns to his host, and chooses a band of 10,000 men.

And to the plan quhar that his oſtis were;

And brandymagus chargit he to ſtere

Efter hyme, within a lytill ſpace,

And x thouſand he takyne with hym haſ.　　3432

Towart the feld onon he can to Rid,

And chargit them befor ye oſt to byd.

The trumpets, clarions, horns, and bugles are sounded.

Wp goith the trumpetis, and the claryownis,

Hornys, bugillis blawing furth thar fownis,　　3436

That al the cuntre reſownit hath about;

Arthur's folk despair.

Than arthuris folk var in diſpar & dout,

That hard the noys, and ſaw the multitud

Of freſch folk; thai cam as thai war wod.　　3440

The sable knight, still fearless,

[B]ot he that was withowten any dred,

In ſabill cled, and ſaw the gret ned,

Aſſemblyt al his falowis, and arayd;

harangues his men, saying,

And thus to them in manly termes ſaid:　　3444

MS. "ſalt."

"What that ȝe ar I knaw not yhour eftat, [Fol. 42 b.]
Bot of manhed and worfchip, well I wat,
Out throuch this warld yhe aw to be commendit,
This day ȝe have fo knychtly yhow defendit. 3448
And now yhe fee how that, aȝanis the nycht,
Yhour ennemys pretendit with thar myght
Of multitud, and with thar new oft,
And with thar buglis and thar wyndis boft 3452
Frefchly cummyng In to fich aray,
To ifyne yhow one owtrag¹ or affray.
And now almoft cummyne Is the nycht,
Quharfor yhour ftrenth, yhour curag, & yhovr mycht
Yhe occupye in to fo manly wyfí,
That the worfchip of knychthed & empryfí
That yhe have wonyng, and ye gret renown
Be not yloft, be not ylaid doune. 3460
For one hour the fufferyng of diftrefí,
Gret harm It war yhe tyne the hie encrefí
Of vorfchip, feruit al this day before.
And to yhow al my confell is, tharfore, 3464
With manly curag, but radour, yhe pretend
To met tham fcharply at the fperis end,
So that thei feil the cold fperis poynt
Out-throw thar fcheldis, in thar hartis poynt. 3468
So fal thai fynd we ar no-thing affrayt;
Whar-throuch we fall the well lefí be affayt.
If that we met them fcharply in the berd,
The formeft fal mak al the laif afferd." 3472
And with o woyfí thai cry al, "fír knycht,
Apone yhour manhed, and yhour gret mycht,
We fal abid, for no man fhall efchef
Frome yhow this day, his manhed for to pref." 3476
And to his oft the lord fír yvane faid,
"Yhe comfort yow, yhe be no-thing affrayd,

Marginal glosses:
"I know not who ye are, but I know that ye ought to be commended.

Ye see how your enemies, as night approaches, are striving to give you an outrage or a fright.

Employ then your courage, so that the honour ye have won be not again lost.

Resolve then to meet them sharply, without fear, so that they may feel the cold spear in their hearts.

Perhaps then the foremost will make the rest afraid."

They promise to stand firm.

Sir Yvan also bids his men be comforted; for that they see all

¹ MS. "owtray." See Glossary.

Ws ned no more to dreding of fuppriſ ;

the strength of
their enemies.
We ſe the ſtrenth of al our ennemys."   3480

Thus he ſaid, for he wend thai var no mo,

Sir Gawane, how-
ever, knew
better.
Bot ſir gawan knew well It vas not ſo ;

For al the oftis mycht he ſe al day,

And the gret hoſt he ſaw quhar yat it lay.   3484

Gallot also ex-
horts his men.
[A]nd galiot he can his folk exort,

Befeching them to be of good comfort,

And ſich enconter

[The rest is wanting.]

NOTES.

[It may be observed, once for all, that the expression *in to* repeatedly occurs where we should simply use *in ;* and *one to* is in like manner put for *unto.* The ending *-ith* (for *-ed*) is frequent in the past tense, and *-it* (also for *-ed*) in the past participle, though this distinction is not always observed. A still more noticeable ending is *-ing* (for *-en*) in the infinitive. Observe further that the letters *v*, *u*, and *w* are perfectly convertible, and used quite indiscriminately ; so that *upone* means *upon ;* *vthir* means *uthir,* i. e, *other : our* is put for *over ; vounde* signifies *wound,* etc.]

Page 1, line 1. *The soft morow.* This nominative case has no verb. A similar construction occurs in the first lines of Books II. and III. 4. *Uprisith—his hot courss,* Upriseth in his hot course ; *chare,* chariot. 6. *sent,* sendeth ; so also *stant,* standeth, l. 326. 8. *valkyne,* waken. 10. *gyrss,* grass. 11. *assay,* assault. 13. *wox,* voice. 17. *frome I can,* from the time that I did. 18. *It deuit me,* it availed me. Jamieson gives " *Dow,* 1. to be able ; A.S. *dugan* (*valere*), to be able. 2. to avail ; Teut. *doogen.*"

P. 2, l. 23. *hewy ȝerys,* heavy years. 24. " Until that Phœbus had thrice gone through his full circuits " (lit. spheres). See the peculiar use of " pas " in other places. 26. " So, by such a manner, was my lot fated ;" see l. 41. 28. *carving can,* did cut. 30. *be the morow,* by the morn. 36. *neulyngis,* newly, anew. 43. *walkith,* walked. 50. *I-clede,* y-clad, clad. Ch. has *clede.* 54. " No one within thought he could be seen by any wight outside."

P. 3, l. 56. *clos it,* enclose it ; the MS. has *closit.* 57. *alphest.* This reading of the MS. is an error for *alcest.* See Chaucer, Prologue to Legend of good women, l. 511 :

> " The gret*e* goodnesse of the quene Alceste,
> That turned was into a dayesye,"

Alceste being the contracted form of Alcestis. 59. *Wnclosing gane,* did unclose. 60. " The bright sun had illumined the spray, and had updrawn (upwarped) into the lusty air the night's soft (sober) and moist showers; and had made the morning soft, pleasant, and fair." With this difficult passage we should compare 1. 2477. 66. *Quhill*, until. 67. *till ony richt*, to any wight. 69. *Bot gladness til the thochtful, euer mo*, etc., " But, as for gladness to the melancholy man, evermore the more he seeth of it, the more wo he hath." 73. *represent*, represented (accented on the second syllable). 74. *Al day gan be sor*, etc., "All the day, my spirit began to dwell in torment, through sorrow of thought ;" *be sor*, by sorrow (A.S. *sorh*). 77. *Ore· slep, or how I wot*, "Or sleep, ere I knew how." 83. *A-licht*, alighted. 84. *levis in to were*, livest in doubt.

P. 4, l. 91. *be morow*, by morrow ; at early morn. 99. *set*, although. 103. *weil accordinge*, very fitting. 105. *long ore he be sonde*, (It is) long ere he be sound. 108. *seith, for to consel*, saith, that as for concealing or shewing, etc. 109. *althir-best*, lit. best of all ; see Chaucer's use of *alderfirst, alderlast*.

P. 5, l. 127. *lat be thi nyss dispare*, let be thy nice (foolish) despair. 128. *erith*, earth. 134. *schall hyme hating*, shall hate him. The termination *-ing* is here the sign of the infinitive mood after the verb *shall*. 140. *Set*, although. 146. *tak one hand and mak*, undertake and compose ; *trety*, treatise ; *vnkouth*, unknown, new. 151. *belevis*, believe will please thy lady. 160. *yis*, this.

P. 6, l. 161. *troucht*, truth. 163. *discharge*, release. 170. *spir*, sphere. 171. "At command of a wise (god from) whose vision," etc. We sometimes find in old English the adjective "a wise" used absolutely for " a wise man." See "Le Morte Arthur," ed. F. J. Furnivall, l. 3318. 175. *tynt*, lost. 177. *be this worldis fame*. Here again, as in many other passages, "be " expresses with relation to, as regards. 185. *yaim*, them. 191. *demande*, demur.

P. 7, l. 198. *Quhill*, until. 200. *conten*, treat ; lit. contain. 202. Lancelot is here called the son of Ban, king of Albanak ; so again in l. 1447. 204. *redis*, read. 214. " I will not waste my efforts thereupon." 219. *unwyst*, unwist, unknown. 225. *nome*, name. 226. *Iwondit to the stak*, very deeply wounded ; but there is no doubt about the origin of the phrase. See Glossary. 228. *astart*, get rid of it, escape it.

P. 8, l. 240. *dedenyt to aras*, deigned to pluck out. 244. *hurtare*, hurter. 245. *Iwond*, wounded. 248. *ful wicht*, full nimble. 251. *of quhome*, by whom. 253. *send*, sent. 257. *pasing vassolag*, surpassing prowess. 260. " Passed down into the fell caves." 264. *tane*, taken. 266. *cure*, care.

P. 9, l. 267. *gart be maid*, caused to be made. 271. *awouc*, vow. 275. *in to that gret Revare*, in that great river. 284. *o gret confusione of pupil and knychtis, al enarmyt*, a great medley of people and knights, all fully armed. Stevenson actually reads *unarmyt!* 294. *I wil report ;* both here and in l. 320 we should almost expect to find " *I nil report ;*" i.e. I will not tell. It must mean, "I will tell you why I omit to mention these things." Compare lines 266, 320. 297. *thing*, think.

P. 10, l. 305. *veris*, wars. 306. *be the wais*, by the ways. 307. *Tuex*, betwixt; *accorde*, agreement. 314. *mot*, must. 316. *stek*, concluded. 319. *most conpilour*, very great composer. 320. "As to whose name I will only say, that it is unfit," etc. 326. *stant*, standeth. 328. *yroung*, rung. 330. *beith*, shall be; observe the *future* sense of *beith* in this place. 331. *suet*, sweet. 332. "His soul in bliss preserved be on that account." 334. *and this endit*. Whether *endit* here refers to *inditing* or *ending* is perhaps doubtful.

NOTES TO BOOK I.

P. 11, l. 336. If by *aryeit* is here meant the *sign*, not the *constellation* of Aries, the day referred to is April 1 or 2, according to Chaucer's "Astrolabie." 338. *bewis*, boughs. 340. *makyne gone*, did make. 341. *in ther chere*, after their fashion. (For *chere*, see Glossary.) 345. *auerding to*, belonging to. 351. *Anoit*, annoyed. 352. *For why*, wherefore; so also *for-thi*, therefore. 354. *can*, began. 355. *sende*, sent. 358. *heryng*, hear (infin. mood). In the next line it occurs as a present participle. 362. *to pas hyme*, to go, depart. 364. *meit*, to dream of; *aperans*, an appearance, apparition.

P. 12, l. 365. *hore*, hair. 375. *vombe*, womb; hence bowels. 377. *stert*, started. 384. *gert*, caused. 390. *traist*, trust. 397. *demande*, demur, delay. 398. *at*, that.

P. 13, l. 407. *whill*, until. 408. *the*, they. 410. *to viting*, to know. 412. *shawyth al hall*, sheweth all whole. 414. *chesith*, chooseth. 422. *shire*, sir. 424. *fore to awysing*, in order to take counsel. 432. All this about *astronomy* (i. e. astrology) should be compared with Gower; Conf. Amantis, lib. vii; ed. Pauli, vol. 3, pp. 133, 134. Arachell, Nembrote, Moises, Hermes are there mentioned as astrologers. 433. The MS. has "set" (*not* with a long *s*). Mr Stevenson has "fet," which would seem right.

P. 14, l. 435. *nembrot*, Nimrod; see *Genesis and Exodus* (E. E. T. S.), l. 659. 436. *herynes*, miswritten for *herymes*, i. e. Hermes. 439. "The which they found were wondrously evil set." 440. *his sweuen met*, dreamed his dream. 443. *waryng in to were*, were in doubt. 444. *danger*, power to punish; compare Shakspere's use of the word. 457. *but delay*, without delay. 459. *stondith heuy cherith*, stood heavy-cheered, was sad in his demeanour. 465. *fundyng*, found. 466. *depend to*, depend upon.

P. 15, l. 475. *tone*, taken. 478. *assey*, test. 481. *record*, to tell out, speak. 487. *preseruith It allan*, is preserved alone. 499. *affy in-tyll*, rely upon. 500. *failye*, fail. 504. *there clergy*, their science.

P. 16, l. 519. "Through the watery lion, who is also faithful,

and through the leech and eke the water also, and through the
counsel of the flower." It is very possible this passage is partly cor-
rupt; l. 520 should certainly be (as may be seen from lines 2010,
2056),   " And throuch the leich withouten medysyne."

The meanings of lion, leech, and flower are fully explained, however,
in lines 2013-2120.   524. *weyne*, vain.   527. *passid nat his thoght*,
left not his thoughts.   531. *rachis*, braches, dogs.   533. *grewhundis*,
grayhounds.   536. This purely conjectural line is merely inserted to
carry on the sense. It is imitated from line 3293. In the next
line we should read "grewhundis," rather than "grewhund."   538.
Befor ther hedis, before their heads.

P. 17, l. 545. "All armed, as was then the fashion."   546.
salust, saluted.   548. *kend*, known.   549. *lewyth*, liveth.   552. The
rime requires " land," as in l. 638.   553. *yald hyme our*, yield him
over.   554. *if tribut*, give tribute.   566. *recist*, resist ; *mone bee*,
must be.   568. *be*, by.   569. *day moneth day*, ere this day month ;
comp. l. 1162.

P. 18, l. 577. *fairhed*, fair-hood, beauty.   587. *magre myne en-*
tent, in spite of my intention.   591. *nome*, took.   593. *Inquere at*,
inquire of.   596. *wes*, was.   599. *rase*, rose.   605. *accordith*, agree
thereto.   606. *recordith*, belongith.   607. *visare*, wiser.

P. 19, l. 621. *This spek I lest*, this I list to speak.   622. *varnit*,
warned.   626. " Though the season of the year was contrary."   627.
atte, at the.   629. *the ilk*, that (Scotch *thilk*).   632. *Melyhalt*, the
name both of a hill, and of the town built upon it.   636. *affray*,
terror.   642. *wnconquest*, unconquered.   643. *cwre*, care.

P. 20, l. 649. *nemmyt*, named.   652. *were*, war.   654. *or than*
to morn, earlier than to-morrow.   660. *our few*, over few.   677.
northest, north-east.

P. 21, l. 686. *fechteris*, fighters.   688. *holde*, held.   691. *presone*,
prison.   697. *peite*, pity.   699. The metre of Lancelot's lament is
that of Chaucer's " Cuckoo and Nightingale," and was very possibly
copied from it.   *Qwhat haue y gilt*, what crime have I committed.
702. *ago*, gone.   703. *nat*, naught ; *me glaid*, gladden me.   706. *til*
haue, to have.   709. *Sen thelke tyme*, since that time.

P. 22, l. 718. *of remed*, for a remedy.   719. *sesith*, ceaseth.
723. *with this lady*, by this lady.   728. *laisere*, leisure.   731. *diuers*
wais sere, divers several ways.   733. *bur*, bore.   735. *cher*, car.
740. *dout*, to fear.   745. *but were*, without doubt.   This expression
often occurs.

P. 23, l. 751. *few menye*, small company ; an oddly sounding expression to modern ears.   753. *cold*, called.   754. *hot*, hight, was
named.   755. *but in his cumpany*, unless he had with him.   757.
He saith ; the speaker is the captain of the hundred knights, called
in l. 806 *Maleginis*.   768. *als fell*, just as many.   777. *hard*, heard.
781. *clepit*, called.

P. 24, l. 793, *as he wel couth*, as he well knew how. 796. *sen*, seen. 800. *sen*, since. 806. *was hot*, was hight, was named. 809. *In myde the borde and festinit in the stell*, In the midst they encounter, and fastened in the steel. See l. 850. 812. *Rout*, company. 815. *ferde*, fourth. 817. *sauch thar latter batell steir*, saw their last division stir.

P. 25, l. 820. *gane his mortall fell*. A word seems here omitted; if after *mortall* we insert *strokis*, the sense will be, " His enemies began his mortall strokes to feel." 825. *worth*, worthy. It would improve the metre to read *worthy* (l. 875). 828. *In to were*, in war, in the strife. 829. *hyme bure*, bore himself. 839. *to-for*, heretofore. 841. *Atour*, i. e. *at over*, across. 842. *assall*, assault. The rime shews we should read *assaill*, as in l. 855. 849. *socht atour*, made their way across. The use of *seke* in Early English is curious.

P. 26, l. 861. *setith his payn vpone*, devotes his endeavours to. 868. *al to-kerwith*, wholly cutteth in pieces. 880. *dirk*, dark. 883. *tan and slan*, taken and slain.

P. 27, l. 895. It frequently occurs in the MS. that a space is left at the beginning of a line, and the first letter of the line is omitted. It is evident that the intention was that the first letter should be illuminated, and that this, after all, was not done. Here, for instance, the T is omitted, as indicated by the square brackets. So also in l. 1083, etc. 897. *pasing home*, go home. 899. *was vent*, had gone. 905. *dulay*, delay. So also *duclar* for *declare*. 907. *comyne*, came. 908. *ill paid*, displeased. 909. *homly*, humbly. Stevenson reads *hourly*, but this is wrong; see l. 914. 911. *carful*, full of care, unhappy. 912. *withouten were*, without doubt. 914. *lawly*, lowly. 918. *wight*, with (unusual, and perhaps wrong).

P. 28, l. 924. *leife*, live. 929. *eft*, after. 933. *thar longith*, there belongeth. 943. *I was for til excuss*, I had some excuse. 944. " Because I did behove (to do it), out of very need." 946. *lefe it but*, leave it without. 953. *ma*, make. 954. *ga*, go. 955. *of new*, anew. 958. *But if that deth or other lat certan*, " Except it be owing to death or other sure hindrance."

P. 29, l. 960. *be hold*, be held. MS. *behold*. Stevenson suggested the alteration, which is certainly correct. 961. *withthy*, on the condition that. 965. *promyt*, promise; *als fast as*, as soon as. 973. *ferd*, fourth. 982. " Where we shall decide the end of this war."

P. 30, l. 997. *cag*, cage, prison. 999. *amen*, pleasant. 1000. *vodis*, woods. 1004. *lust*, pleasure (Ch.). But the line is obscure; unless we read " *diuersitee*." 1009. " His spirit started (owing to the) love (which) anon hath caught him," etc. 1012. *at*, that. 1014. " (As to) whom they know not at all." 1019. *sen at*, since that. 1022. *the dewod*, devoid thee. 1024. *and*, if. 1026. *be ony mayne*, by any mean.

P. 31, l. 1027. *y red*, I advise. 1035. *To warnnyng*, to warn.

1040. *our the furdis*, over the fords.   1044. *oyer.* So in MS.; the
y representing the old *th* (þ); other. 1046. *hufyng*, halting. 1050.
worschip, honour.   "It were more expedient to maintain your
honour." 1058. *wonk*, winked. 1062. *rare*, aware.

P. 32, 1. 1064. The meaning of "ferst-conquest" is "first-con-
quered" (*conquest* being Old Fr. for conquered). It is explained in
l. 1547 as having been a title given to the king whom Galiot first
subdued. 1067. *ferss*, fierce. 1070. *suppos*, although. 1073. *he ;*
viz. the shrew. 1077. The MS. has "fched." 1080. *ymen*, I mean.
1095. *tais*, takes.

P. 33, 1. 1109. *Galyo.*, put for *Galiotes*, the genitive case-ending
being often omitted, after a proper name especially. 1110. *prewit*,
proved, tried. 1129. *traist*, trust. 1131. *that euery thing hath
cure;* that (of) everything hath care.

P. 34, 1. 1135. "Aye from the time that the sun began to light
the world's face, until he was gone." 1137. *o forss*, perforce. 1141.
taiis, takes. 1142. *hecht*, promised. 1151. *failʒeis*, fail. 1154.
fet, fetched. 1156. *stant*, standeth. 1162. *resput*, respite. 1166.
very knychtis passing, weary knights go.

P. 35, 1. 1170. *till spere*, to inquire. 1177. *ne wor his worschip*,
had it not been for his valour. 1187. *qwheyar*, whether. 1191—4.
"And fond," etc. These four lines are now for the first time printed.
They were omitted by Stevenson, evidently by accident. 1196. *Per
dee.* Fr. *par Dieu :* an oath common in old ballads, generally in the
form *pardy.* 1197. *vsyt*, used. 1198. "I advise that we go unto
his arms" (armour). 1203. *haill*, whole.

P. 36, 1. 1207. *abwsyt*, abused, i. e. made an ill use of. 1208.
vsyt, used. 1209. *suppos the best that lewis*, even though (it were)
the best that lives. 1217. *on slep*, asleep. The prefix *a*- in English
is due to the Saxon *on*. 1221. *al to-hurt*, etc. See note in Glossary
on the word *To-kerwith*. 1225. *sauch*, saw ; *rewit*, rued, pitied.
1233. *one syd a lyt*, a little on one side. 1236. *our mekill*, over
much.

P. 37, 1. 1240. *yarof*, thereof. 1241. *ruput*, repute, think.
1242. *ablare*, abler, readier. 1253. Insert a comma after *thret*, and
destroy that after *lowe*. The meaning perhaps is, "But what if he
be appealed to and threatened, and (meanwhile) his heart be elsewhere set to love." Observe that *and* is often the third or fourth
word in the sentence it should begin. See l. 2833. 1258. *ʒhe tyne
yowr low*, you lose your love. 1260. *conclusit*, ended. 1265. *mokil*,
much. 1268. *of new*, anew, again. 1273. *pan*, pain.

NOTES TO BOOK II.

P. 38, 1. 1279. *thocht*, anxiety. 1284. *apperans*, i. e. vision, as
in l. 364. 1295. *aqwynt*, acquainted ; Burns uses *acquent.* 1297.
com, coming.

P. 39, l. 1316. "So far out of the way you go in your course."
Compare l. 1797. 1317. "Thy ship, that goeth upon the stormy
surge, nigh of thy revels (i. e. because of thy revels) in the gulf it
falls, where it is almost drowned in the peril." 1321. "In the
wretched dance of wickedness." See the curious uses of the word
"daunce" in Chaucer. 1323. *the son*, thee soon. 1330. *powert*,
poverty; *as the-selwyne wat*, as thyself knows. 1334. *in to spousag*,
in wedlock.

P. 40, l. 1343. The word *diuerss* is required to complete the line;
cf. l. 731. 1352. *suppriss*, oppression. 1354. *wedwis*, widows.
1367. *that ilke*, that same. 1369. *sufferith*, makest to suffer.

P. 41, l. 1379. Eccles. iv. 9, 10. 1387. *yow mone*, thou must.
1392. *her-efter leif*, hereafter live. 1401. A comma is scarcely needed
after "*sapiens*." It means "The fear of the Lord is the beginning
of wisdom." Prov. ix. 10.

P. 42, l. 1409. *to ryng under his pess*, to reign under His peace,
by His permission. Roquefort gives *pais*, licence, permission. 1420.
arour, error. 1427. *leful*, lawful.

P. 43, l. 1447. Ban, king of Albanak, was Lancelot's father.
See l. 202, 1450. 1474. The MS. has "affit."

P. 44, l. 1491. *tak the bak apone themself*, turn their backs.
1500. *yewyne*, given. 1504. *till*, to; redundant. 1506. *stand aw*,
stand in awe. So also in l. 2684. The same expression occurs in
The Bruce, iii. 62, ed. Pinkerton, p. 42, ed. Jamieson; and also in
Havelok, l. 277, where the word *in*, supplied from conjecture, should
be struck out.

P. 45, l. 1537. *throw his peple*, by his people. 1541. *Thus falith
not*, etc., "Except wise conduct falleth to a king." 1546. It may
be right to retain the spelling of the MS.—"kinghe;" for, though
strange and unusual, it occurs again in l. 2527.

P. 46, l. 1556. *wende*, weened. 1560. *in to his contrare*, against
him. 1568. *trewis*, truce. 1575. *his powar*, his chief army. 1576.
by the yhere, by the ear, privately. 1579. *cold*, called; as in l. 753.

P. 47, l. 1597. *home fair*, go home. 1608. *And;* redundant in
modern English. For many of the precepts given by Amytans the
author must have been indebted to Gower, or, at any rate, to the
author of the *Secreta Secretorum*. See Gower; Conf. Amantis; ed.
Pauli, lib. vii; vol. 3, pp. 152—159. And cf. Tyrwhitt's note to
the Canterbury Tales, l. 16915; and Warton's Hist. Eng. Poetry.

P. 48, l. 1628. *lest*, least; *low*, law. It requires care to dis-
tinguish the two meanings of *low*, viz. *love* and *law*. 1633. *Iug*,
judge.

P. 49, l. 1660. *sar*, sorely. 1666. A line omitted. The inserted
line is purely conjectural.

P. 50, l. 1704. *pupelle*, people. 1708. *Inwyus*, envious. 1716.
longith, belongeth. 1717. *the lykith*, it likes thee, thou art pleased.

P. 51, l. 1724. *betak til hyme*, confer upon him. 1730. *essy*,

easy. 1736. *for the nonis*, for the occasion. See White's Ormulum.
1739. *vn to the vorthi pur yow if*, unto the worthy poor thou give.
1742. *set nocht of gret substans*, though not of great value. 1754.
alowit, approved of.

P. 52, l. 1761. *tynith*, loseth. 1763. *atonis*, at once. 1771. *re-sawe*, receive. 1773. *with two*, also.

P. 53, l. 1791. *well less, al-out*, much less, altogether. The
punctuation hereabouts in Stevenson's edition is very wild. 1795.
wys, vice ; *the wrechitness*, thy miserliness. 1797. *pass the courss*,
go thy way. 1808. *vrech*, wretch ; but here used instead of *miser*.
1812. *viss*, vice. 1814. *ben y-knawith*, are known (to be) (?). 1815.
dant, daunt. 1822. *the ton*, the one.

P. 54, l. 1832. *beis var*, beware. 1834. *colde*, cool. 1852. *onys*,
once. 1855. *whar-throw*, through which, whereby.

P. 55, l. 1864. *awn*, own. The metre requires the more usual
form *awin*. 1879. *dispolȝeith*, despoileth. 1881. *For-quhi*, where-fore. In this line the MS. has "scrikth."

P. 56, l. 1899. *most nedis*, must needs. *Ye = the ;* i. e. The
one, He. 1909. *Mot*, might. 1917. *in* should be *into*, as elsewhere.

P. 57, l. 1940. *havith*, hath. 1950. *hot*, hight, is called.

P. 58, l. 1966. *wnepwnist*, unpunished. 1990. *omend*, amend ;
spill, destroy.

P. 59, l. 2011. *ayre*, are. 2012. *duclar*, declare ; so also *dulay*
for delay. 2017. *the god werray*, the Very God.

P. 60, l. 2036. *For-quhi*, wherefore. 2040. *mad*, made. 2041.
clergy, science. 2062. *be the mycht dewyne*, by the might divine.

P. 61, l. 2069. *far*, fare. 2079. *helyth frome the ground*, heals
from the bottom ; i. e. effectually. 2100. *not sessith*, who ceaseth not.

P. 62, l. 2107. *Ne war*, were it not for ; *hartly*, hearty ; it
occurs again four lines below. 2135. *yneuch*, enough. He means
he will ask but one question more.

P. 63, l. 2148. *To passing home*, to go home. 2162. *the* xxiiij
day. The first *i* in the MS. is like a "v" smudged over ; we should
read "xxiiij," as in l. 2155. The contraction is to be read *four and
twentieth*, not *twenty-fourth ;* so also in l. 610.

P. 64, l. 2190. *hal dure*, hall door. 2192. *o iorne most for to
comend*, a journey most to be commended. 2194. *lowith*, love.

P. 65, l. 2212. *the fewar eschef thay*, the less they achieve.
2229. "For no adventure will prove so great, that ye shall not
achieve it." 2241. *whill*, until.

P. 66, l. 2247. *galot ;* so in MS. 2265. *grant mercy*, great
thanks ; Fr. *grand merci*. 2267. *quhy*, because.

P. 67, l. 2279. *thithingis*, tidings ; probably an error of the
scribe for *tithingis*. Stevenson has *chichingis!* 2284. *al-out*, alto-gether. 2304. *oft syss*, oft-times. See Glossary (*Syss*). 2306. *dante*,
dainty. 2310. *tithandis*, tidings ; compare l. 2279.

P. 68, l. 2323. *aw*, owe. 2328. *fantessy*, fancy, notion. 2334.

for no why, for no reason. 2337. *'mon I fair*, must I go. 2338. *our son It waire*, over soon it were. 2342. *For-quhy*, because.

P. 69, l. 2352. *nor* has the force of *but*. 2366. *be ony men*, by any means. 2368. *on of tho*, one of them. 2375. *chen of low*, chain of love. 2376. *and if ʒhe may deren*, an if you may declare.

P. 70, l. 2409. *hartly raquer*, heartily require. 2416. *gar ordan*, cause to be provided.

P. 71, l. 2428. *prewaly disspone*, privily dispose. 2436. *ellisquhat;* I suppose this means, "he was on fire *elsewhere*." 2448. *hamlynes*, homeliness. 2452. *fest throw al the ʒher cliche*, feast through all the year alike.

P. 72, l. 2469. *commend*, commended. 2470. *he drywith*, he driveth, pursueth. The reading is not *drawith*, as in Stevenson.

NOTES TO BOOK III.

P. 73, l. 2471. This line is too long, and the sense imperfect; but there is no doubt about the reading of the MS. 2474. *Awodith*, expels. 2475. *doune valis*, falls down; for it is evident that *valis* is an error for *falis*, the mistake having arisen from confusion with the succeeding line. 2480. *cled*, clad. 2487. *bygown*, begun. In the next line Stevenson has *sown;* but the true reading is *Rown*, run; as in l. 2820. 2492. *barnag*, baronage, nobility.

P. 74, l. 2522. *but dulay*, without delay; *the*, they. 2524. *thar com*, their coming. 2530. *in the dogre*, in its (due) degree.

P. 75, l. 2545. *Or that*, ere that. 2552. *he and hate*, high and hot. 2558. *the can*, they began.

P. 76, l. 2574. *hyme mak*, prepare himself; or perhaps simply, make (for the field), go. 2582. *helmys last; last* clearly means *laced ;* see l. 2250. 2594. *ʒhit*, although. 2599. *dout*, fear. 2600. *is assemblit*, made an attack. The peculiar use of *assemble* must always be borne in mind. 2601. *erd*, earth.

P. 77, l. 2612. *found till gwyans*, go to Gwyans. 2614. *til esquyris thei sewyt*, after Esquyris they followed. 2619. *one to the melle socht*, made their way to the mêlée. 2627. *don bore*, borne down. 2630. Fifty thousand. It would appear that Galiot had 40,000, of whom 10,000 were held *in reserve ;* so that in l. 2632 only 30,000 are mentioned. See l. 2569, 2647.

P. 78, l. 2646. *ten*, sorrow, vexation. 2656. *resauf*, receive. 2663. *at thar come*, at their coming ; *led*, put down. 2670. *biding one the bent*, abide on the grassy plain.

P. 79, l. 2679. "That, despite their efforts, they must needs retire." 2684. *stud aw*, stood in awe ; see note to l. 1506. 2693, 4. These lines do not rime. But we should certainly read *felde, erde* having slipped in from confusion with l. 2691. The knight of Galloway goes *to the field*, i. e. joins battle.

P. 80, 1. 2712. *On ayar half*, on either side. The MS. omits *to*.
2713. *of*, off. 2714. *noiss*, nose. 2731. *Bot nocht forthi*, But not
on that account.

P. 81, 1. 2754. *harmys*, loss. 2761. *aucht to ses*, ought to
cease. 2765. *at*, that. 2768. *my lef*, my leave, permission. 2770.
in to cage, in prison.

P. 82, 1. 2802. *commandit*, commended.

P. 83, 1. 2819. *one athir half*, on either side. 2820. *rown*, run.
2821. *howyns;* an ungrammatical form; perhaps *howyng* is meant.
2827. *one hycht*, on height; i. e. aloud. 2829. *sterith*, stirreth.
2833. "The lady of Melyhalt made (her way) to him, and immediately caused his couch to be placed before a window." Mr
Stevenson reads,

> "Of Melyhalt the lady to hyme maid
> Incontinent his couche, and gart he [1] had," etc.

i. e. "The lady immediately made his bed for him," etc. 2841. *wencust*, vanquished. After this word we should perhaps insert "at," as
in 1. 3336.

P. 84, 11. 2877-2880. These lines were printed by me for the first
time, four lines having been here again omitted by Mr Stevenson.
2880. *but weyne*, without doubt. 2884. *to led and stere* to lead and
direct.

P. 85, 1. 2893. *Endlong*, along. 2894. *weryne*, were. 2913. *let*,
hinder.

P. 86, 1. 2925. *dulay*, delay; as in several other places. 2938.
fek, effect. 2944. *ʒude*, went. 2947. *fair*, welfare.

P. 87, 1. 2964. *Whill*, until. 2970. *ho*, stop, pause. 2971. *veryng In affray*, were in terror. 2972. *rovm*, room. 2978. *socht*,
made his way. 2984. *disponit*, intends; but we must insert "not,"
to complete the sense and the metre.

P. 88, 1. 2998. *eschevit* (used passively), is achieved. 3003. *o
knycht*, a single knight. 3005. *tais*, takes. 3006. *fays*, foes. 3013.
onys or the nycht, once ere the night. 3015. *that ʒhe have gilt to
mend*, to amend that in which ye have trespassed.

P. 89, 1. 3052. *Do at I may*, Do that which I can.

P. 90, 1. 3065. This line is printed by Mr Stevenson,

> "Curag can [   ] encresing in [1] his hart";

but it is not clear that a word is wanting, for the metre is as complete as in many other lines; whilst, as regards the sense, "the
knycht" is probably a nominative without a verb, and 1. 3065 means,
"Courage did increase in his heart." Or the reader may, if he
pleases, insert "fele." Compare 1. 3058. 3066. *lap*, leaped. 3079.
Observe the omission of the word "neither" in this line. 3080.
persit, pierced. 3086. *onan*, anon. A.S. *on-án*.

---

[1] But the MS. has "be;" also "melyhat" instead of "Melyhalt."
[2] MS. has "to."

P. 91, l. 3093. *In samyne will*, with like intent. 3100. *bet ax-ampil*, better example. 3104. *bot*, unless; *me fall*, befall me. 3108. *one vthir*, another. 3120. *send*, sent. 3121. *lewit one*, left one. 3122. *but mercy*, without mercy.

P. 92, l. 3134. *deliuer besynes*, clever readiness. 3136. *aray*, livery. 3140. *Ee*, eye. 3146. *the morow new*, the early morning. 3160. *deith*, dead. 3162. *Suppos*, although.

P. 93, l. 3178. *Nor;* we now use *but.* 3184. *ward;* see Glossary. *tho*, then.

P. 94, l. 3200. *relewit*, relieved. 3201. *diuerss placis sere;* as *sere = diuerss*, one of these words is redundant. So in l. 3266. 3207. *ewil awysit*, ill advised. 3217. "And if it so happen, that they be discomfited."

P. 95, l. 3240. *leuch*, laughed; *sarues*, service. 3246. *al haill*, all whole. 3248. *x thousand mo*, ten thousand, and more. 3259. *abaid*, delay. 3263. *aucht*, eight. 3265. *petws for til her*, piteous to hear.

P. 96, l. 3297. *dreuch*, drew. 3299. *fellit*, fallen. 3304. *lev-yng*, leave.

P. 97, l. 3307. *sest*, ceased. 3321. *askit at*, asked of. 3331. *Wencussith*, vanquisheth. 3340. *in to one*, continually; which is sometimes the sense of A.S. *on-án*.

P. 98, l. 3353. *to fillyng*, to fulfil. 3357. *soght*, came on; see Glossary. 3359. *Ne war*, etc., "Had it not been that they were, individually, the better men." 3364. *ralef*, relieve. 3368. *fellith*, feeleth.

P. 99, l. 3384. *virslyng*, wrestling, *i. e.* entangled with; a strong expression! 3385. *assalʒeing*, assail. 3390. *rowmyth*, roometh, emptieth. 3403. *departit*, parted. 3404. *dout*, fear.

P. 100, l. 3412. *left*, failed. 3423. *The lord*, i. e. Galiot, as I suppose; Mr Stevenson has, "The Lord." 3430. *stere*, to stir, move, come.

P. 101, l. 3450. *pretendit*, endeavour. 3457. *occupye*, employ. 3461. *For one hour*, etc., "On account of suffering distress for one hour." 3470. *the well less*, much less; see l. 1791. 3471. *berd*, beard. 3473. *o woyss*, one voice. 3475. *eschef frome yhow*, not, *win* from you; but, *withdraw* himself from you. See Glossary.

P. 102, l. 3481. *wend thai var no mo*, thought they were no more. 3487. *And sich enconter*, and such encounter. These three words are written at the bottom of the page as a catchword. The rest of the MS. is wanting.

GLOSSARIAL INDEX.

[As many of the words occurring in " Lancelot " are well explained either in Jamieson's Scottish Dictionary or in Roquefort's " Glossaire de la langue Romane," I have frequently referred to these works by means of the letters J. and R. Other abbreviations, as O.N. for Old Norse; Goth. for Mœso-Gothic; Su.-G. for Suio-Gothic, etc., will be readily understood. Ch. has also been used as an abbreviation for Chaucer. The various French, Danish, German, and other words referred to in the Glossary are merely added by way of illustration, to indicate in what direction a word may be most easily traced up. To ensure accuracy as far as possible, I have verified every foreign word by the aid of dictionaries, referring for Gothic words to my own Glossary, edited for the Philological Society; for Suio-Gothic words, to Ihre's Glossarium; for Icelandic words, to Egilsson; and for Old French words, to Roquefort and Burguy. Whatever errors occur below may thus, I hope, be readily traced.]

Abaid,) delay, tarrying, 1882,
Abyde,) 2147, 3069, 3308.
   A.S. *abídan*, J.
Abasit,) abashed, humbled, di-
Abasyt, } spirited, cast down,
Abaysit,) 378, 1452, 2664.
   Abasit of, dispirited by, 3301.
   R. *abaiser*.
Abasit of (used passively), were
   dispirited by, 2243.
Abraid, awoke, 1231 ; (Ch.) A.S.
   on-bredan.
Abwsyt (abused), made an ill use
   of, 1207.
Access, a fever ; or better, a fit of
   the ague ; Lat. *accessus febris*,
   (Wright's Glossary), 31.
Accorde, to agree with, 1526.
   Fr. *s'accorder*.
Accordith, is suitable for, becomes,
   1679, 1951 ; agree therewith,
   605; is useful for, is fit for, 1204.

According for, suitable for, 1512.
   R. *accordant*.
Adred, terrified, 378, 2664. A.S.
   on-drœdan, to dread.
Affek, effect, 382. Cf. *Fek*.
Afferd, afraid, 3472. A.S. *afered,
   afœran*.
Affere, warlike preparation, 985 ;
   aspect, bearing, 3043, 3334,
   3394. See J., who makes it
   of Teutonic origin ; but it may
   be no more than the O.Fr.
   afeire, afaire=state, condition;
   as explained by Burguy.
Afferith, belongs to, suits, 1550.
Afferis, is suitable, 1690, 1961.
   R. *aferer*.
Affrait, terrified, from the verb
   Affray (Ch.), 2462, 3469. R.
   effraer.
Affray, terror, fright, 636, 3454.
   Fr. *effroi*.

Affy in till, trust to, rely upon, 499, 1394. R. *affier.*

Afyre, on fire, 30, 251; hence, used allegorically, in love, 2436.

Agrewit, ⎫ aggrieved, vexed,
Aggrewit, ⎭ 1308, 1538; angry, enraged, 2618. R. *agrever.*

Ago, gone, 159. A.S. *of-gán.*

Aire, are, 1732.

Algait, Algat, always, 1996, 1792. .Gothic *gatwô*, a street, way.

Al magre thine, in spite of thee, 115. An expression compounded of A.S. *al*, wholly; *maugre* (Fr. *mal grè*), ill-will, and *thine* (A.S. *thin*, the gen. case of *thú*, thou).

Al-out, altogether, 1676,1791, etc.

Alowit, approved, 1754. Fr. *al-louer.*

Als, (1) as; (2) also.

Amen, ⎫ pleasant, 64, 999. Lat.
Ameyne, ⎭ *amœnus.*

Anarmyt, fully armed, 545, 620, 2219, 2771. See *Enarmyt.*

And, if, 1024, 1591; and if (= an if), if, 2376.

Anerly, only, 1476, 1696. A.S. *án-líc.*

Anoit, ⎫ annoyed, vexed, 351,
Anoyt, ⎭ 2244.

Anoyt, annoyeth, 1407.

Anterous, (for Aunterous, the shortened form of Áventurous), adventurous, 2618. Fr. *aventure.*

Aparalit, apparelled, 338.

Aperans, an appearance, a vision, 364. *So also* Apperans, 1284.

Apone, upon, 765, etc.

Appetit, desire, 2722. Ch. has *appetite* as a verb, to desire.

Aqwynt, acquainted, 1295. Burns uses *acquent.*

Aras, to pluck out, 240. Fr. *arracher.*

Araid, disordered, afflicted, 3270.

See *Araye* in Halliwell. The examples there given shew that to *araye* sometimes actually signifies to *disorder.*

Arest, stop, delay, 678, 3072, 3308. Fr. *arrêt.*

Arly, early, 4, 384, 975. A.S. *árlíce.*

Artilȝery, implements of warfare, 2538. See R. *artillerie.* Compare 1 Samuel, xx. 40.

Assay, (1) assault, trial, 11, 35, 112, 712; attack, 537, 2662. As a verb, to assault, attack, assail, 570, 1044. Fr. *assaillir.* (2) to essay, attempt, 2936; to test, 478, 982. Fr. *essaier.*

Assaid, ⎫ assaulted, 1224, 2641.
Assayt, ⎭

Assall, assault, attack, 842. We should perhaps read "assaill," as in l. 855.

Assalȝeing, assail (3 *pers. plural*), 3385.

Assemblay, an assembling of knights for a combat, a tournament, 267.

Assemble, a hostile meeting, combat, battle, 978, 3336. See J.

Assemblyng, encountering, 2588.

Assemblyng on, attacking, 2956.

Assey, to test, 478. *See* Assay.

Astart, to start away from; hence to escape from, avoid, 228, 3296. Ch. has *asterte.*

At, that, 1019, etc. Compare Dan. *at;* O.N. *at.*

Atour, at over, i. e. across, 841, 849, 873; in excess, in addition, besides, 1775.

Ather, either, 2629, 2819, 3264. A.S. *ægther.*

Atte, at the, 627, 1055.

Aucht, eight, 3263. Compare Ger. *acht.*

Auentur, adventure, 601.

Auer, ever, 273, etc.

Auerding to, belonging to (?), 345. The sense seems to point to the A.S. *and-weardian*, to be present, Goth. *and-wairths*, present.

Aventur, Auentoure, adventure, 80, 222.

Aw, owe, deserve; the present tense of the verb of which *ought* is the past tense; 3447. A.S. *áh, áhte.*

Awalk, awake, 1049. Goth. *wakan.* The form *awalk* occurs in Dunbar,

"*Awalk*, luvaris, out of your slomering."
            (The Thistle and the Rose.)

Awant, boast, 2136. As a verb, 1588; and as a reflective verb, 2196, 2386. Fr. *se vanter.* Ch. has *avante.*

Awin, own, 89. A.S. *ágen.*

Awodith, maketh to depart, 2474. See *Avoid* in Nares' Glossary, edited by Halliwell and Wright.

Awow, } vow, 234, 242, 246.
Awoue, } Ch. has *avowe.*

Awys, consideration, advisement, 558.

Awyſ the, advise thee, consider, 1913.

Awyſ, } to consider, 424, 429.
Awyſing, } Fr. *s'aviser.*

Awysment, advisement, consideration, 360, 680.

Ay, ever, continually, 1135, 1486. A.S. *á.*

Ayar (*written instead of* Athar), either, 2712.

Ayre, are, 2011.

Ayanis, 744, } against.
Aȝanis, 1164, 2283, } A.S. *ongean.*

Aȝane, Aȝeine, again, 3253, 380.

Bachleris, bachelors; a name given to novices in arms or arts, 1689. See *bacheler* in R.

Banaris, banners, 770.

Bartes, 2897. } *See* Bertes.
Bartiis, 3041. }

Barnag, baronage, nobility, 2492. See *barniez* in R.

Batell, a battalion, division of an army, 784, 808, etc.

Be, by. A.S. *be.*

Behest, promise, 2766. A.S. *behæs.*

Behufis, behoves, 579. A.S. *behófan*, often used impersonally.

Behuſ, } it behoves, it is neces-
Behwſ, } sary (to do), 944, 2342; apparently contracted from *behufis.*

Beleif, *in phr.* ore belief = beyond belief, 112.

Bent, a grassy plain (properly a coarse grass; in German, *binse*), 2670. J.

Bertes, a parapet, a tower, 1007, 1118, 2815. R. *bretesche*, from Low Latin *brestachia.*

Betak til, to confer upon, 1724. A.S. *be-tǽcan*, in the sense, to assign.

Betakyne, betoken, 2014. A.S. *be-tǽcan*, in the sense, to shew.

Bewis, boughs, 338. A.S. *boh.*

Billis, letters, 142. Fr. *billet.*

Blindis, blindness (?), 1903.

Borde, to meet in a hostile manner, encounter, 809. We find in R. *border*, to joust, fight with lances. Compare Fr. *aborder*, and Spenser's use of *bord.* See *horde* in Burguy.

Bot, (1) but; (2) without. In general, *without* is expressed by *but*, and the conjunction by *bot;* but this distinction is occasionally violated.

Bown, ready, prepared, 1036. O.N. *búinn*, past part. of *búa*, to prepare. Su.-G. *boa*, to prepare. J.

Bretis, fortifications, forts, 874;

"properly wooden towers or castles : *Bretachiæ*, castella lignea, quibus castra et oppida muniebantur, Gallis *Bretesque.* Du Cange." Jamieson. See *Bertes.*

Bukis, books, 434, 1862.

Burdis, boards, i. e. tables, 2198. A.S. *bórd*, which means—1. a plank ; 2. a table, etc.

Bur, bore, 733, 778.

But, without ; common in the phrase *but were*, without doubt.

But if, unless, except, 958.

Byhecht,) promised, 1485, 2791.
Byhicht,) A.S. *be-hǽtan.*

Byknow, notorious for, known to be guilty of, 1627. Compare "I *know* nothing *by* myself" (1 Cor. iv. 4). Compare also Dan. *bekiende*, to make known.

By, near at hand, 1535, 2916.

Cag,) cage, prison, 997, 2770.
Cage,)

Can, an auxiliary verb, used nearly as we now use *did.*

Careldis, plural of Careld, a merry-making, revel (?), 1318. "*Caraude*, réjouissance ;" and "*Caroler*, danser, se divertir, mener une vie joyeuse." Roquefort.

Catifis, wretches, 2102. R. *caitif, captif.* Compare Ital. *cattivo.*

Chalmer, chamber, 2281, 2308, 2427, 2808. J.

Chare,) chariot, 4, 735. R. *cher.*
Cher,)

Charge, load, 693. Fr. *charge ;* see *discharge* in the line following (694), meaning to shake off a load.

Chargit, gave attention to, 710, 2454. Fr. *se charger de.*

Chen, chain, 2375.

Cher, car, chariot, 735. See *Chare.*

Chere, cheer, demeanour, 83, 341,

695 ; sad demeanour, outward grief, 2718. Fr. *chère ;* compare Ital. *ciera*, the face, look. "*Wepinge* was hyr mosté *chere.*" (Le Morte Arthur, l. 726.)

Chefl, choose, 1611, 1636, 2368. A. S. *ceósan ;* Ger. *kiesen ;* Dutch *kiezen.*

Clariouns, clarions, 771, 789.

Clepe, to call, 90, 99. A.S. *clepan.*

Clepit, callest, 93 ; called, 781.

Clepith, is called, 1919.

Clergy, science, knowledge, 504, 511, 2041. R. *clergie.*

Closine, closed, concluded, 316.

Closith, enclosed, shut up, 427.

Cold, called, 753, 1579.

Commandit, commended, 2802.

Comprochit, approached, 2472, 2509.

Conpilour, compiler, poet, 319.

Conquest, conquered, 574 ; Fyrst-conquest, first conquered, 1545, etc.

Conseruyt, preserved, 332.

Conten (used as a reflective verb), to demean oneself valorously, to maintain one's ground, 823, 1107, 1130. See R. "*contenement*, contenance, conduite, maintien, posture."

Contenit hyme, behaved himself, 3219 ; Contenit them, 2634.

Contenyt, endured, 3190.

Contretioun, contrition, 1415, 1426.

Contynans, demeanour, 1693, 1747.

Counter, encounter, attack, charge, 3239.

Couth, could, 793. A.S. *cunnan ;* past tense, *ic cúðe.*

Cowardy, cowardice, 1023, 3287.

Cownterit, encountered, 2609, 2621. J.

Crownel, coronal, corolla of a flower, 59. J.

Cummyne, ⎱ came, 807, 907.
Comyne, ⎰

Cumyne, 650, 1136, ⎱ come (past
Cumyng, 447, ⎱ part.).
Cummyng, 2498, ⎰

Cunyng, knowledge, 1455.

Cusynace, 1270, ⎱
Cusynece, 2802, ⎱ kinswoman.
Cusynes, 2287, ⎱
Cwsynes, 1185, ⎰

Cwre, care, 98, 266, 643. Lat. *cura*. (N.B. Though *Cwre* = *cura*, yet *cura* should be distinguished from A.S. *cearu*.)

Danger, power to punish; "the power of a feudal lord over his vassals," (Wright), 444. Also, power to injure, 3006. See R. *dangier*.

Dans, (dance), in the phrase "wrechit dans," evil mode of life, 1321. See Chaucer's use of *daunce;* and compare—

"I sai ʒow lely how thai lye Dongen doun alle in a *daunce*."

Lawrence Minot ; quoted in Specimens of Early English, by R. Morris ; p. 194.

Dede, 90, ⎱ death. Dan. *död*.
Ded, 3304, ⎰ A.S. *deáð*. O.N. *dauði*.

Deden, deign, 949. J.

Dedenyt, deigned, 240.

Deid, died, 215.

Deith, dead (past part.), 3160.

Delitable, delightful, 1738. R. *delitable*.

Deliuer, nimble, clever, 3134.

Deliuerly, (cleverly), nimbly, lightly, 3089, 3131. R. *delivre*.

Demande, demur, 191, 397, 3052, 3354. See R. " *demander*, contremander, changer, revoquer l'ordre donné."

Depart, to part, 3421. R. *departir*.

Departit, parted, 3403.

Depaynt, painted, 46, 1703. Fr. *dépeint*. Ch. *depeint*.

Depend me, waste or consume (my powers), 214 ; possibly miswritten for *despend*. Cf. *Dispendit*. Depend to, to concern, appertain to, 466.

Deren, to speak out, tell, 2376. R. *derainier*.

Dereyne, a plea, 2313 ; " haith o dereyne ydoo," hath appealed to trial by combat. R. *derainier*.

Des, daïs, high table, 2762. R. *deis;* Lat. *discus*.

Deuit, availed, 18. See note.

Devith, ⎱ deafen, 92, 94. " Su.-
Dewith, ⎰ G. *deofwa ;* Icel. *deyfa*," J. Compare Dan. *döve*. Burns has *deave*.

Dewod the, devoid thyself, 1022.

Deuoydit was = departed, 1031. Compare *Awodith*.

Dewyſ, to tell, narrate, 373.

Discharg, to put aside one's liability, 163, 1665.

Diseſ, lack of ease, misery, 707.

Disiont (Disioint?), disjointed, out of joint ; hence uncertain, hazardous, 2907. " Disjoint, A difficult situation." Halliwell.

Dispendit, spent, 1808. R. *despendre*.

Dispens, expenditure, 1746. Fr. *dépense*.

Dispolʒeith, despoileth, 1879

Dispone, to dispose, provide ; or, as a reflective verb, to be disposed to do, to intend, 54, 446, 980, 1590, 2428, 2462.

Disponit, declines (?) ; but much more probably, intends ; and we must read "disponit not," 2984.

Dout, fear, 2599, 3404, 3438 ; (as a verb), to fear, 740, 1827. Ch. *doute*. R. *doubtance*.

Drent, drowned, 1319. A.S. *drencan*.

Dreß (as a reflective verb), to direct oneself, proceed, go, 1975, 2288, 2486. Lat. *dirigere*.

Drywith, drives ; "he drywith to the end," i.e. concludes, 2470.

Duclar, declare, 3022.

Dulay, delay, 681, 788, 2925.

Effere, shew, pomp, 2360. Compare *Affere*.

Efter, after, 217. A.S. *efter*.

Eld, old age, 3225, 3242. A.S. *yldo*. Gothic *alds*.

Elyk, Eliche, alike, 182, 2452.

Eme, uncle, 2572. A.S. *edm*.

Empit, emptied, empty, 180. A.S. *æmtian*.

Empleß, to please, 2455. J.

Empriß, worth, honour, 129, 269, 3458 ; *cf*. Romans of Partenay, l. 2013. Anxiety, oppression, 393. R. *emprindre*.

Enarmyt, fully armed, 285, 751, 2499. J.

Endit, indited, 138 ; indite, 206 ; inditing, poem (?), 334. If the meaning were, "this ends," the form "endis" would be required ; besides which, the rime shews that the *i* is long ; cf. ll. 138, 206.

Endlong, along, 2893. A.S. *andlang* ; Ger. *entlang*.

Entent, intention, will, meaning, thoughts, 448, 1451, 1499, 2938. R. *entente*. Used by Chaucer.

Entermet, to intermeddle with, to have do with, 2914. R. *entremetre*.

Enweronyt, environed, 53.

Erde, earth, 1072, 1540, 2601. Compare Ger. *erde*.

Erdly, earthly, 498.

Erith, earth, 128. A.S. *eorð*.

Eschef (1. eschew), to shun, withdraw himself, 3475. R. *eschever;*

(2. achieve), to accomplish, 2212, 2513. R. *eschavir*. Eschef deith, to die, 2732.

Escheuit, achieved, 258.

Eschevit, is achieved, 2998.

Eß, 174, Eeß, 706, } ease.

Essenȝeis (ensigns), warcries, 3349, J. See also R. *enseigne*.

Euerilkon, every one, 1039, etc.

Exasy, extasy, 76. (Possibly miswritten.)

Exortith, beseecheth, 3026.

Extend, attain, 3281.

Failȝeis, fail, (3 pers. plu. indicative), 1151.

Fairhed (fairhood), beauty, 577. In A.S. *fægernes*, but in Dan. *förhed*.

Fall, to happen, befall, 493, 2139. A.S. *feallan ;* Dan. *falde*.

Fallyng, fallen, 1217, 1322.

Falowschip, used as we now use company, 1105, 2687, etc.

Falȝeing, failing, 1499.

Falȝet, Falȝheit, failed, 1460, 1469, 1498, 1503.

Farhed, beauty, 2440. See *Fairhed*.

Fayndit (feigned), dissembled, 2397.

Fays, foes, 3006. A.S. *fáh*.

Fechtand, fighting, 2691, 3127, 3407. Ger. *fechten*.

Fechteris, fighters, 686.

Feill, knowledge, skill, 2854. J. A.S. *félian*.

Fek (effect), sum, amount, result, drift, 2938. Fr. *effet*.

Fell, to feel, 820, 2131.

Fellith, feeleth, 3368.

Fell, many ; als fell, as many, 768. A.S. *féala ;* Gothic *filu*.

Fell, horrible, 260. A.S. *fell*, cruel, fierce.

Ferde, fourth, 815, 973, 2285. Compare Dan. *fierde*.

Ferleit, wondered, 3117. A.S. *fǽr-líc*, sudden, fearful. Burns has *ferlie*.

Fet, fetched, 433, 1154. A.S. *feccan*, past tense, *ic feahte*.

Fongith, catcheth, seizeth, 1922. A.S. *fangan;* Goth. *fahan*.

Forfare, to fare amiss, to perish, 1348. A.S. *for-faran*.

Forlorn, lost, 3305. A.S. *forloren;* cf. Goth. *fra-liusan*.

For-quhy ; see *For-why*.

For-thi,) (there-fore), on that ac-
For-thy,) count, 332, 2261, 2731. A.S. *forthý;* where *thý* (Gothic *thê*) is the instrumental case of *se*, that.

For-wrocht (for-wrought), over-worked, wearied out, 888. A.S. *forwyrcan*.

For-why, 798, 925, 2209,) for
For-quhy, 2171, 2342, 2290,) the reason that, because that.

Found, to advance, go, 2612. J. A.S. *fundian*, to try to find, go forward.

Franchis, generosity, 230. R. *franchise*.

Fremmytneſ, strangeness, aliena-tion, 1508. A.S. *fremdnes*.

Froit, enjoyment, 1644 ; fruit, 2088, 2109. R. *fruit*.

Frome, from the time that, 17, 1432. Goth. *frums*, a beginning.

Fruschit, broken, dashed in pieces, 1201. R. *frois*, broken ; from the verb *froier*.

Fundyne, 497,) found (past
Fundyng, 465,) part.).

Fyne, faithful, true, 519. See R. "*fine*, fidéle ;" and "*fine*, foi."

Fyne, end, 1388, 2081. Fr. *fin*.

Ganith, is suitable for, 991. Icel. *gegna*. J. Compare Dan. *gavne*.

Ganyth, it ; it profits ; *used impersonally*, 121. R. *gaagner*.

Gare, to cause, 910, 2416. Dan. *giöre ;* Icel. *göra*.

Gart, caused, 267, 2777.

Gentilleſ, 917, 1847. See *Gentrice*.

Gentrice, 13ŏ 2757,) courtesy,
Gentriſ, 2790.) nobleness. R. *gentilesse·*

Gere, gear, eqüipment, armour, 2777. A.S. *gearwa*.

Gert, 384. See *Gart*.

Giffis, give thou, (lit. give *ye*, the plural being used in addressing the king), 463. A.S. *gifan*.

Gifyne, given, 1752.

Gilt, offended, done wrong, 699, 3015. A.S. *gyltan*.

Grewhundis, greyhounds, 533, 537. "O.N. *grey, grey-hundr*, a bitch." Wedgwood.

Gowerne the, conduct thyself, 1598.

Grawis, groves, 2481. Ch. *greves*.

Gyrſ, grass, 10. A.S. *gœrs*.

Gyſ, guise, fashion, custom, 545. Ch. *gise*.

Haade, had, 2150.

Habariowne, habergeon, 2889. From *haubergeon*, the French form of Ger. *halsberge*. See *Hawbrek*.

Habirioune, habergeon, 3380.

Heill, whole, 3246. A.S. *hœl*.

Haknay, an ambling horse for a lady, 1730. R. *hacquenée*.

Half ; *in the phrase* on arthuris *half*, i. e. on Arthur's *side*, 883. Compare use of Germ. *halb*.

Halk, a hawk, 1736, 2482. A.S. *hafoc*.

Hall,)
Hoil, (various spellings of Haill,
Holl, (whole.
Hail,)

Hals, neck, 1054. A.S. *hals*. Goth. *hals*.

Hant, to exercise, practise, 2191. Fr. *hanter*, lit. to frequent.

Hardement, 801, 2669,) hardi-
Hardyment, 900, 3362,) hood, boldness. R. *hardement*.

Harrold, herald, 1047.

Hate, hot, 2552.

Havith, hath, 1940; have, 3404.

Hawbrek, 1070, 1200,) hauberk,
Hawbryk, 3112,) neck-defence; Ger. *hals-berge*, armour for the neck.

Hawnt, to use, 3418. See *Hant.*

Hawntis, exercise, 2772.

He, high, 1969, 2552. A.S. *háh.*

Hecht, hight, is called, 2140; was called, 2290.

Hecht, to promise, 3101; promised (*past part.*), 1142. A.S. *hátan.*

Hedis, heads, 538, 869.

Hewy, 442,) heavy. A.S. *hefig.*
Heuy, 459,)

Hie, 550,) high. See *He.*
Hye, 297,)

Hienes, highness, 126.

Ho, pause, stop, cessation, 2970. According to J. radically the same with the verb *Houe*, or *How* (see *Houit*). The Dutch, however, use *hou*, hold! from *houden*, to hold.

Holl, whole, 106, 745.

Hore, hair, 365.

"Holʒe were his yʒen and vnder campe hores." (Early English Alliterative Poems; *ed.* Morris. See Poem B. l. 1695.) The meaning of the line quoted is, "Hollow were his eyes, and under bent hairs."

Hot, hight, was called, 754, 806; is called, 1950. A.S. *hátan* (neuter).

Houit, delayed, tarried, halted, 996. "W. *hofian, hofio*, to

fluctuate, hover, suspend," Morris.

Hovith, stays, halts, 2829.

Howit, halted, 2814, 2842.

Howyns, halts, tarries, 2821. Probably miswritten for "howyng."

Hufyng, halting, delaying, 1046.

Hundyre, a hundred, 756, 1554.

I, in, 332: Dan. *i·;* Icel. *í.*

Iclosit, y-closed; i. e. enclosed, shut in, 53.

If, to give, 554. In lines 1718-1910 the word occurs repeatedly in several forms; as *iffis, iffith*, giveth; *iffis*, give ye (put for give thou); *ifyne*, given, etc.

Ifyne, to give, 3454.

Iftis, gifts, 1741. In the line preceding we have *giftis.*

Ilk; the ilk (= thilk) that, 629, 1601. Literally, the ilk = the same. A.S. *ylc.* See 1367.

Ilk, each, 2211, etc. A.S. *ælc.*

Illumynare, luminary, 3.

Incontinent,) immediately, 253,
Incontynent,) 1215, 2647, 2834. Still used in French.

In-to-contynent (= Incontinent), 3020.

In to, used for " in ;" *passim.*

Iornaye, journey, 680.

Irk, to become slothful, grow weary, tire, 2709. A.S. *eargian.*

Iuperty, combat, 2547. Fr. *jeu parti*, a thing left undecided; hence the meanings, 1. strife, conflict; 2. jeopardy, as in Ch. See J.; and Tyrwhitt's note to C.T. 16211.

Iwond, 245,) wounded. We
Iwondit, 226,) find in A.S. both *wúnd* and *wúnded.*

I-wyſ, certainly, of a surety, 1709, 1925, 1938. A.S. *gewís;* Ger. *gewiss.* Often *wrongly* in-

terpreted to mean, *I know.* See
Wit.

Kend, known, 548, 906.

Laif, the remainder (lit. what is
left), 1802, 3472. A.S. *láf.*
Burns has "the *lave.*"
Lametable, lamentable, 3265. The
omission of the *n* occurs again
in l. 2718, where we have
lemytable.
Larges, liberality, 608, 1681, 1750.
Fr. *largesse.*
Larg, prodigal, profuse, 2434.
Lat, impediment, 958. A.S. *lǽtan,*
means (1) to suffer, (2) to hinder.
Lat, to let, permit (used as an
auxiliary verb), 803.
Latith, preventeth, 1927.
Lawrare, a laurel, 82. Ch. *laurer.*
Learis, liars, 493.
Led, put down, beat down, de-
pressed, overpowered, 2663.
It is the past tense of A.S.
lecgan, to lay, to cause to sub-
mit, to kill.
Lef, to live, 564, 3230.
Leful, lawful, 1427.
Legis, lieges, subjects, 1957. R.
lige; Lat. *ligatus.*
Leich, leech, physician, 106. A.S.
lǽce; Dan. *læge.* See 520, 2056.
Leif, to live, 952, 1392. A.S.
lybban; Goth. *liban.*
Leir, to learn, 1993. Comp. D.
leeren.
Lest, to list, to please, 555, 621.
A.S. *lystan.*
Lest, to last out against, sustain,
811. A.S. *lǽstan.*
Lest, least, 1628.
Let, hindrance, 2495.
Leuch, laughed, 3240. A.S. *hlihan,*
past tense *ic hloh.*
Lewis, liveth, 1209.
Lewith, left, deserted, 1854.

Liging, 376. The sense requires
lay, i. e. the 3rd *p. s. pt. t. in-
dic.,* but properly the word is
the present participle, *lying.*
Longith, belongeth, 738, 1921,
2429, 2778. Compare Dan.
lange, to reach.
Longith, belonged, 3242.
Longyne, belonging, 433.
Lorn, lost, 2092; destroyed, 2740.
See *For-lorn.*
Loſ, praise, 1777. Lat. *laus.*
Ch. has *losed,* praised.
Low, ⎱ (1) law, 1602, 1628, 1636,
Lowe, ⎰ etc. (2) love, 29, 1620.
It is sometimes hard to say
which is meant. Compare Dan.
lov, law; A.S. *luf,* love.
Luges, tents, 874, 881, 2500,
2680. Fr. *loge, logis;* Ger.
laube, a bower, from *laub,* foli-
age; Gothic *laúf,* a leaf.
Lugyne, a lodging, tent, 891.
Lyt, a little, 1233. At lyte, in
little, used as an expletive, 143.

Ma; short form of Make, 953.
Maad, made, 697.
Magre of, in spite of, 500, 960,
2679, 2702, 2711. Sometimes
"magre" is found without
"of." Fr. *mal gré.*
Matalent, ⎱ displeasure, anger,
Matelent, ⎰ 2169, 2660. In both
cases Mr Stevenson wrongly
has *maltalent.* R. *maltalent,*
mautalent.
Mayne, 1026. See *Men.*
Medyre, mediator (?), 1624. I am
not at all sure of this word,
but we find in R. many strange
forms of "mediator," such as
méener, méeisneres, etc. In the
Supplement to the "Diction-
naire de l'Academie" we find
mediaire, qui occupe le milieu,
from Low Lat. *mediarius.* N.B.

In the MS. the "d" is indistinct. See *mediare* in Ducange.

Meit, to dream, 363. A.S. *mœtan*.

Mekill, much, 876, 1236. Mokil, 1265.

Melle, contest, battle, 2619. Fr. *melée*, J.

Memoratyve, mindful, bearing in remembrance, 1430. Fr. *mémoratif*.

Men, mean, way; "be ony men" = by any means, 2366; so, too, "be ony mayne," 1026. Fr. *moyen*.

Men, to tell, declare, 510. A.S. *mœnan*.

Menye, a company, multitude (without special reference to number); whence ' "a few menye," a small company, 751. Apparently from A.S. *menigu;* Ger. *menge;* but it may have nothing to do with the modern word *many*, and is more probably from the O.F. *maisnée*, a household.

Met, dreamt, 440. See *Meit*.

Meyne, 41. See *Men*.

Misgyit, misguided, 1663. R. *guier*.

Mo, more, 3187, etc. A.S. *má*.

Mon, man, 96.

Moneth, month, 569. A.S. *mónáδ;* Goth. *menoth*.

Morow, morning, 1, 30, 64, 341. Goth. *maúrgins*.

Mot, must, 195. A.S. *ic mót*.

Mys, a fault, 1888, 1937, 3230. A.S. *mis*. Do o myδ, to commit a fault, 1926.

Mysour, measure, 1830.

Myster, need, 1877, 2322. Ch. *mistere;* R. *mester;* Lat. *ministerium*. Cf. Ital. *mestiere*.

Nat, naught, 703. Shortened from A.S. *ná wuht*, i.e. *no whit*.

Nece, nephew, 2200, 2245, 2720. R. *niez*.

Nedlyngis, of necessity, 2337, J. A.S. *neádinga*.

Nemmyt, considered, estimated, 649, 2852. A.S. *nemnan*, to name, call.

Ner, near, 441.

Neulyngis, newly, again, 36, J. A.S. *niwĕ-líce* (?).

Newis, for Nevis, nieves, fists, 1222. Icel. *hnefi*. Dan. *nœve*. Burns has *nieve;* Shakspeare *neif*.

Noght, not, 1182.

Noiδ, nose, 2714. R. *néis*.

Nome, name, 226, 320, 1546, 3341. Fr. *nomme*.

Nome, took, 591, 1048. A.S. *niman*, past tense, ic *nám*.

Northest, north-east, 677.

Not (shortened from Ne wot), know not, 522, 3144. A.S. *nát*, from *nitan = ne witan*.

Not, naught, 720. See *Nat*.

Noyith, annoyeth, 904. Fr. *nuire*. Lat. *nocere*.

Noyt, annoyed, offended, 471.

Nys, } (nice), foolish, 127, 1946.
Nyce, } Fr. *niais*.

O, a, an, *passim;* one, a single, 2998, 3003, 3393, etc.

Obeisand, obedient, 641.

Obeδ, obey, 2134.

Oblist, obliged, 969.

Occupye, to use, employ, 3457; to dwell, 75. Lat. *occupare*.

Of, with, 66.

Oft-syδ, oft-times, 2304, 2594, 2789, 2885, 2929. See *Syδ*.

On, and, 519. Possibly a mistake.

One, on, often used for In; One to = unto.

Onan, } anon, 158, 1466, 2602,
Onone, } etc. The form "onan,"
Onon, } l. 3086, suggests the

derivation of *anon;* viz. from A.S. *on-án,* in one; hence, forthwith, immediately.

Onys, once, at some time or other, 3013; at onys, at once, 3187.

Opin, 1286, } open.
Opine, 13, }

Or, ere, before, 77, 1887, 2545. A.S. *ćr.*

Ordand, to set in array, 784; to prepare, procure, 1713. R. *ordener;* Lat. *ordinare.*

Ordan, to provide, 2416, 2777.

Ordynat, ordained, 490. See l. 507.

Orest (=Arest), to arrest, stop, 3186.

Orient, east, 5.

Oucht, it; it is the duty of (= Lat. *debet*), 2995. Strictly, we should here have had " it owes" (*debet*), not "it ought" (*debuit*). See *Aw.*

Ourfret, over-adorned, decked out, 71, 2480. A.S. *frætwian,* to trim, adorn.

Out-throng (= Lat. *expressit*), expressed, uttered, 65. A.S. *út,* out, and *þringan,* to press.

Owtrag, outrage, 3454. R. *outrage;* Ital. *oltraggio,* from Lat. *ultra.* The MS. has *outray,* probably owing to confusion with *affray* in the same line. We find "owtrag" in l. 2578.

Oyſ, to use, 1701, J.

Paid, pleased; ill paid, displeased, 908. Low Lat. *pagare,* to pay, satisfy.

Palȝonis, pavilions, tents, 734; *plural of*

Palȝoune, a pavilion, a tent, 1305. R. gives *pavillon,* a tent; cf. Low Lat. *papilio,* a tent.

Pan, pain, 1273.

Pas hyme, to pace, go, 362.

Paſ, to go, 1213.

Pasing, pacing, departing, 371; surpassing, 303, 346, 689, etc.

Pens, to think of, 1431. Fr. *penser.*

Planly, at once, 3319. J. gives "Playn, out of hand, like Fr. *de plain.*" In the same line "of" = off.

Plant, plaint, complaint, 137. Fr. *plainte.*

Plesance, Plesans, pleasure, 941, 1939.

Plessith, pleases, 68.

Possede, to possess, 578. Fr. *posseder.*

Poware, a power, a strong band of men, 2647. We now say *force.*

Powert, poverty, 1330, 1744.

Pref, to prove, 2229, 3476.

Prekand, pricking, spurring, 3089. See the very first l. of Spenser's *Faerie Queene.*

Prekyne, 2890, showy (?), gaudy (?). J. gives "Preek, to be spruce; to crest; as 'A bit *preekin* bodie,' one attached to dress; *to prick,* to dress oneself." Compare D. *prijcken.*

Pretend, to attempt, aspire to, 3282, 3465. Fr. *prétendre.* So, too, in lines 559, 583.

Pretendit, endeavour, attempt, 3442.

Process, narration, 316. Wright gives "Proces, a story or relation, a process." The writer is referring to his prologue or introduction.

Promyt, to promise, 965.

Proponit, proposed, 361, 445.

Pupil, people, 285.

Puple, people, 1367, 1498, 1520.

Pur, 1648, }
Pure, 1697, } poor.
Pwre, 1655, }

Quh-. Words beginning thus begin in modern English with Wh. Thus, Quhen = when, etc.

Quhilk (whilk), which, 184. A.S. *hwylc* = Lat. *qualis* rather than *qui.*

Quhill, while, *used as a noun,* 1229, 1293. A.S. *hwíl,* a period of time.

Quhill, until, 24, 198. See *Whill.*

Quhy; the quhy = the why, the reason, 123, 1497.

Qwhelis, wheels, 736. A.S. *hweol.*

Qwheyar, whether, 1187.

Quhois, } whose, 171, 1297.
Qwhois, }

Rachis, hounds, 531. Su-G. *racka,* a bitch, which from the v. *racka,* to race, course. Perhaps connected with *brach.*

Radur, fear, 1489, J. From Su-G. *rædd,* fearful; Dan. *ræd.*

Raddour, 2133, } fear.
Radour, 1835, 3465, }

Raid, rode, 3070, 3260, etc.

Ralef, relieve, 3364.

Ramed, remedy, 117. See *Remed.*

Randoune, in, 2542. The corresponding line (l. 739) suggests that *in Randoune = al about,* i.e. in a circuit. But if we translate it by " in haste," or "in great force," we keep nearer to the true etymology. In Ogilvie's Imperial Dictionary, *s.v.* Random, we find the Nor. Fr. *randonnée* explained to mean the "sweeping circuit made by a wounded and frightened animal;" but the true meaning of *randonnée* is certainly *force, impetuosity;* see R., Cotgrave, etc. In Danish, *rand* is a surrounding edge or margin; while in Dutch we find *rondom* round about.

Raquer, require, 2409.

Raß, race, swift course, 3088. A.S. *ræs.* Compare Eng. *mill-race,* and D. *ras.*

Recidens, delay, 2359. R. *residier,* to defer.

Recist, resist, 566, 660, 2578.

Recounterit, met (in a hostile manner), encountered, 2958. Fr. *rencontrer.*

Record, witness, testimony; hence value, 388. R. *record.*

Recorde, to speak of, mention; hard recorde, heard say, 121, 595.

Recorde, speak out, 454, 481. See R. *recorder.*

Recordith, is suitable, belongs, 606.

Recourse, to return, 1798. Lat. *recurrere.*

Red, to advise, 1027, 1198. A.S. *rǽdan;* Goth. *rêdan.*

Relewit (relieved), lifted up again, rescued, 2617. Fr. *relever.* J.

Remede, 89, } remedy.
Remed, 718, }

Remuß, remove, 655.

Report, to narrate, 266; to explain, 294; to state, 320.

Reprefe, reproof, defeat, 764.

Reput, he reputed, i.e. thought, considered, 743.

Resauit, received, 2796.

Resawit, received, kept, 2106. We should have expected to find " reseruit."

Resonite, resounded, 66.

Resydens, delay 670. See *Recidens.*

Revare, 275, }
Rewar, 2893, } river.
Rewere, 2812, }

Reweyll, proud, haughty, 2853. R. *revelé,* fier, hautain, orgueilleux. Compare Lat. *rebellare.*

Richwysneß, righteousness, 1406. A.S. *rihtwísnes.*

Rigne, 94, 1527, ⎫ a kingdom. Fr.
Ring, 1468,   ⎬ *régne.* Ch.
Ringe, 1325,   ⎭ *regne.*
Rignis, kingdoms, 1858.
Rignis, Rignith, reigneth, 1825, 782.
Ringne, a kingdom, 1952.
Rout, a company, a band, 812, 2956, 3403. Rowt, 2600.
Rowmyth, roometh, i.e. makes void, empties, 3390. A.S. *rúmian.*
Rown, run; *past part.* 2488, 2820.
Rwn, run, 2545.
Rygnis, kingdoms, 1904.
Ryne, to run, 113. See 2952.
Ryng, to reign, 1409, 2130.

Sa, so, 3322, 3406. Dan. *saa.*
Saade, said, 698.
Salust, saluted, 546, 919, 1553, 2749. Ch. *salewe.*
Salosing, salutation, 1309.
Sar, sorely, 1660.
Sauch, saw, 817, 1219, 1225. A.S. *ic seáh,* from *seón.*
Schawin, shewn, 2387.
Schent, disgraced, ruined, 1880. A.S. *scendan;* Dan. *skiænde.*
Schrewit, accursed, 1945.
Scilla, the name of a bird, also called Ciris, 2483.

—— "plumis in avem mutata vocatur Ciris, et a tonso est hoc nomen adepta capillo."—(Ovid, Met. viii. 150.)

Screwis, shrews, ill-natured persons, 1053. More often used of males than females in old authors.
Sedulis, letters, 142. R. *cedule.*
Sege, a seat, 2258. Fr. *siége.*
Semble, a warlike assembly, hostile gathering, 988, 2206.
Semblit, assembled, 845. G. *sammeln;* from Goth. *sama, samana.*
Semblyng, encountering, 2951. See *Assemble.*

Sen, since, 709, 800, etc. Sen at, since that. In Piers Plowman we find *syn.*
Septure, sceptre, 666.
Sere, several, various, 594, 731, 746. "Su-G. *sær,* adv. denoting separation." J. Cf. Lat. *se-.*
Sess, to cease, 14, etc. Fr. *cesser.*
Set, although.
Sew, to follow up, seek, 2326. R. *suir;* Fr. *suivre.*
Sew, to follow up, go, proceed, 3145. Sewyt, 2614.
Shauyth, shewith, 412.
Sice, such, 2115. Scotch, *sic.*
Snybbyth, snubs, checks, 3387. Comp. D. *sneb,* a beak; *snebbig,* snappish.
Sobing, sobbing, moaning, 2658.
Socht, ⎫ sought to go ; and hence,
Soght, ⎭ made his (or their) way, proceeded, went, 2619, 3179, 3357, 3428. Sought one, advanced upon, attacked, 3149, 3311. Sought to, made his way to, 3130. A.S. *sécan,* past tense *ic sóhte,* to seek, approach, go towards.
Sor, sorrow, anxiety, 74. A.S. *sorh;* Goth. *saúrga.*
Sort, lot, fate, 26. Fr. *sort.*
Sound, to be consonant with, 149. See Gloss. to Tyrwhitt's Chaucer. Lat. *sonare.*
Soundith, 1811. " So the puple soundith," so the opinion of the people tends.

" As fer as *souneth* into honestee."
(Chaucer: *Monkes Prologue.*)

Soundith, tend, 1943 ; tends, 149.
Sown, sound, 1035. Fr. *son.*
Sownis, sounds, 772, 3436.
Spent, fastened, clasped, 2809. A.S. *spannan,* to clasp, join. Comp. Dan. *spænde,* to stretch, span, buckle together.

Spere, } sphere, 6, 170 ; speris,
Spir, } spheres, circuits, 24.
Spere, to inquire, 1170. A.S.
spirian, to track. Cf. G.
spur.
Sperithis, spear's, 810.
Spill, to destroy, ruin, 1990.
A.S. *spillan*.
Spreit, spirit, 81, 364.
Stak, 226. J. gives " to the
steeks, *completely ;* " and this
is the sense here. See Jamieson : s.v. " Steik." Halliwell
gives *stake*, to block up ; also
steck, a stopping place (cf.
Shakespeare's *sticking-place*,
Macb. i. vii. l. 60). In the N.
of France it is said of one killed
or severely wounded, *il a eu
son estoque*, he has had his
belly-ful ; from *estoquer*, to
cram, satiate, "stodge." Compare Ital. *stucco*, cloyed. It
has also been suggested that
to the stak may mean to the
stock, i.e. up to the hilt, very
deeply.
Start, started up, leapt, 994,
1094.
Stede, stead, place, 218, 1124.
A.S. *stede*.
Steir, to stir, 817. A.S. *stirian*.
Stekith, shuts, 1651. Ger. *stecken*.
Burns has *steek*.
Stek, shut, concluded, 316.
Stell, steel, 809. Stell commonly
means a stall, or fixed place ;
but the form *stell* for *steel*
occurs ; e.g. " Brounstelle was
heuy and also kene." *Arthur*,
l. 97.
Sterapis, 3056, } stirrups. A.S.
Steropis, 3132, } *sti-rap* or *stige-
ráp*, from *stigan*, to mount, and
ráp, rope.
Stere, ruler, arbiter, 1020 ; con-
trol, guidance, 1974.

Stere, to rule, control, 1344, 2884,
A.S. *stýran*.
Stere, to stir, move, go, 3430.
See *Steir*.
Sterith, stirreth, 2829.
Sterf, to die, 1028. A.S. *steorfan*.
Sterit, governed, 612. A.S. *stýran*.
Stert, started, 377.
Stok, the stake to which a baited
bear is chained, 3386.
Stour, conflict, 1108, 2607, 3124.
R. *estour*.
Straucht, stretched out, 3090. A.S.
streccan, past part. *gestreht*.
Strekith, stretcheth, i.e. exciteth
to his full stride, 3082.
Subiet, 1799, }
Subeitis, 1828, } subject ; sub-
Subiettis, 1878, } jects.
Sudandly, Sodandly, suddenly,
1009, 1876.
Suet, sweet, 331.
Suppris, (surprise), overwhelming
power, 691, 860, 2651 ; oppres-
sion, 1352. Fr. *surprendre*, to
catch unawares.
Supprisit, overwhelmed, 1237,
1282 ; overpowered, 2705,
3208. Supprisit ded, suddenly
killed, 3125.
Surryʒenis, surgeons, 2726.
Suth, sooth, true, 110. A.S. *sóð*.
Suthfastnes, truth, 1183. A.S.
sóðfœstnes.
Sutly, soothly, truly, 963.
Swelf, a gulf such as is in the
centre of a whirlpool, a vortex,
1318, J. A.S. *swelgan*, to swal-
low up.
Sweuen, a dream, 440. A.S. *swefn*.
Swth, sooth, true, 2753. See
Suth.
Syne, 2026, }
Synne, 2029, } sin.
Syne, afterwards, next. J. 45,
794, etc.
Syþ, times, 3054. A.S. *síð*.

Tais, 1095, 3005,) takes. Abbre-
Taiis, 1141.   ) viated, as
"ma" is from "make." See *Ma.*
Tane, taken, 264.
Ten, grief, vexation, 2646, 3237.
A.S. *teonan*, to vex.
Tennandis, tennants, vassals hold-
ing fiefs, 1729. R. *tenancier.*
Than, then, 3111.
The, (1) they, (2) thee, (3) thy.
Thelke, that, 709. See l. 629,
where *the ilk* occurs; and see
Ilk.
Thir, these, those, 2734, 2745,
2911, 3110, etc.
Thithingis, tidings, 2279. A.S.
tidan, to happen.
Tho, then, 545,2221; them, 2368.
Thoore, there, 628. Thore, 1102.
Thrid, third, 370, 2347, 2401.
A.S. *þridda.*
Throng, closely pressed, crowded,
3366. A.S. *þringan.*
Til, to; til have, to have, 706.
Tint, lost, 1384. See *Tyne.*
Tithandis, tidings, 2310.
Tithingis, tidings, 902, 2336.
To, too, besides, 3045.
Togidder, together, 254.
To-kerwith, carves or cuts to
pieces; al to-kerwith, cuts all
to pieces, 868. A.S. *to-ceorfian.*
The prefix *to-* is intensive, and
forms a part of the verb. See
Judges ix. 53: "All to-brake
his skull;" i.e. utterly brake;
sometimes misprinted "all to
break" (!).
Ton, taken, 1054, 1071.
Ton, one; the ton, the one, 1822.
The tone = A.S. *þæt áne.*
To-schent, disfigured, 1221. The
intensive form of the A.S. verb
scendan, to shame, destroy. In
the same line we have *to-hurt*,
and in the next line *to-rent*,
words modelled on the same

form. We find, e.g., in Spenser,
the forms *all to-rent, all to-
brus'd.* (See the note on the
prefix *To-* in the Glossary to
William of Palerne.)
Tothir, the other, 2536. The tothir
= A.S. *þæt opere*, where *þæt* is
the neuter gender of the definite
article. Burns has *the tither.*
Toyer (= tother), the other; *y* be-
ing written for the A.S. *þ (th)*,
2571, 2584.
Traist, to trust, to be confident,
390, 1129, 1149, J. Trast,
1659.
Traisting of (trusting), reliance
upon, or expectation of, 25, J.
Translat, 508,) to transfer, re
Transulat, 2204,) move.
Tratory, treachery, 3224. See R.
traïtor.
Trety, treatise, 145. Fr. *traité.*
Trewis, truce, 1568, 2488, 2545.
Tronsione, 239,   ) a   trun-
Trunscyoune, 2962,) cheon, a
Trownsciown, 2890,) stump of
a spear. Fr. *tronçon;* from
Lat. *truncus.* In the last pas-
sage it means a sceptre, *bâton.*
"One hytte hym vpon the oldé wounde
Wyth A tronchon of an ore;" (oar.)
(Le Morte Arthur, l. 3071.)
Troucht, truth, 161.
Tueching, 403,) touching.
Tweching, 386,)
Tyne, to lose, 1258, 1387. Icel.
týna.
Tynith, loseth, 1761.
Tynt, lost, 175, 1384, 1521.

Unwist, unknown, 1140.

Valis, falls; we should read
"falis," 2475.
Valkyne, to waken, 8. See *Awalk*
Vall, billow, wave, 1317. Ger.
welle, a wave; *quelle*, a spring;

Icel. *vella*, to *well* up, boil. Cf. also A.S. *wœl;* Du. *wiel;* Lancashire *weele*, an eddy, whirlpool. So, too, in Burns:—

"Whyles owre a linn the burnie plays,
As thro' the glen it wimpl't ;
Whyles round a rocky scaur it stays,
Whyles in a *wiel* it dimpl't."

Varand, to warrant, protect, 3411. R. *warandir.*

Varnit, warned, 622.

Vassolag, a deed of prowess. Pasing vassolag, surpassing valour, 257. R. has *vasselage*, courage, valour, valourous deeds, as indicative of the fulfilment of the duties of a *vassal*. We now speak of rendering *good service.*

Vassolage, valour, 2724.

Veir, were, 818.

Veris, wars, 305. See *Were.*

Veryng, were, 2971. A.S. *wǽron.*

Vicht, a wight, a person, 10, 55, 67. A.S. *wiht.*

Virslyng, wrestling, struggling, 3384. J. gives the forms *warsell, wersill.*

Visare, wiser, 607.

Viting, to know, 410. A.S. *witan.*

Vncouth, lit. *unknown;* hence little known, rare, valuable, 1734. A.S. *uncúð.*

Vodis, woods, 1000.

Vombe, womb, bowels, 375. Goth. *wamba.*

Vondit, wounded, 700.

Ypwarpith, warped up, i.e. drawn up, 63. See Note to this line. It occurs in Gawain Douglas's prologue, to his translation of the 12th Book of the Æneid. Du. *opwerpen*, from Goth. *wairpan*, to cast.

Vsyt, used, 1197, 1208.

Vyre, a cross-bow bolt, 1092. R. *vire :* cf. Lat. *vertere.*

Wald, would, 419, 470, etc.

Walkin, to waken, wake, 1239. See *Awalk.*

Wapnis, weapons, 241. A.S. *wǽpen*, or *wǽpn.*

Ward, world, 3184. Grose's Provincial Dictionary gives *Ward =* world ; and the omission of the *l* is not uncommon ; see *Genesis and Exodus* (E.E. T.S.), ll. 32, 1315.

Wassolage, valour, 2708. See *Vassolag.*

Wat, know, 512.

Wawasouris, vavasours, 1729. A *Vavasour* was a sub-vassal, holding a small fief dependent on a larger fief; a sort of esquire. R. *vavaseur.*

Weil, very. Weil long, a very long time, 79. Comp. Ger. *viel*, J.

Wencussith, vanquisheth, 3331 ; vanquished, 3337.

Wencust, vanquished, 2841.

Wend, (1) to go, 2191 ; (2) weened, thought, 3481.

Wentail, ventaile, a part of the helmet which opened to admit air, 1056. R. *ventaile;* from Lat. *ventus.*

Were, (1) war. Fr. *guerre.* R. *werre*, 308, etc. (2) doubt, 84, etc. "But were," without doubt. A.S. *wǽr*, cautious, *wary.* (3) worse, 1930. Burns has *waur.*

Wering, weary, 58. A.S. *wérig.*

Werray, very, true, 1262, 2017.

Werroure, warrior, 248.

Weriour, warrior, 663.

Wers, worse, 515.

Weryng, were, 2493.

Wex, to be grieved, be vexed, 156.

Weyn, vain, 382, 524.

Weyne, *in phr.* but weyne, without doubt, 2880. A.S. *wénan*, to ween, to suppose.

9

Whill, until, 1136, J. Formed from A.S. *hwíl*, a period of time.

Wice, advice, counsel, 1909. Shortened from Awys.

Wichsaif, vouchsafe, 355, 1391.

Wichsauf, *id.* 2364.

Wicht, wight, person, 131.

Wicht, strong, nimble, 248. "Su-G. *wig*," J. Sw. *vig*.

Wight, with, 918. Possibly mis-written.

Wist, knew, 225, 1047. See *Wit*.

Wit, to know, 268. A.S. *witan*; pres. *ic wát*, past tense, *ic wiste*.

Wit, knowledge, 2504.

With, by, 723.

Withschaif, vouchsafe, 1458.

With-thy, on this condition, 961. See *For-thy*.

Wnkouth, little known, 146. See *Vncouth*.

Wnwemmyt, undefiled, 2097. A.S. *wam, wem*, a spot.

Wnwyst, unknown, secretly, 219, 269.

Wod (wood), mad, 3334, 3440. A.S. *wód*. Goth. *wóds*.

Woid, mad, 2695. Perhaps we should read *woud*.

Wonde, wand, rod, or sceptre of justice, 1601, 1891. J.

Wonk, winked, 1058.

Wonne, to dwell, 2046. A.S. *wunian*.

Worschip, honour, 1158, 1164. A.S. *weorð-scipe*.

Wot, know, 192, etc. See *Wit*.

Wox, voice, 13. Lat. *vox*.

Woyſ, voice, 3473.

Wrechitnes, misery, 2102; miser-liness, niggardliness, 1795, 1859.

Wy, reason; "to euery wy," for every reason, on all accounts, 2356. Compare *Quhy*.

Wycht, strong, nimble, 2592. See *Wicht*.

Wynyth, getteth, acquireth, 1832.

Wyre, a cross-bow bolt, 3290. See *Vyre*.

Wys, vice, 1795. Wysis, 1540.

Y, written for "th." Thus we find "oyer" for "other," etc. The error arose with scribes who did not understand either the true form or force of the old symbol þ.

Yaf, gave, 387.

Yald, yield, 553; yielded, 558. A.S. *gildan*.

Yclepit, called, 414.

Yef, give, 563.

Yeif, give, 923.

Yer, year, 610. Used instead of the plural "yeris," as in l. 3243.

Yewyne, given, 1500.

Ygrave, buried, 1800. Comp. Ger. *begraben*.

Yhere, ear, 1576.

Yher, year, 2064. Used instead of "yheris," 3243.

Yhis, yes, 1397.

Yis, yes, 514; this, 160.

Ylys, isles, 2858, 2882.

Ymoug, among, 821.

Yneuch, enough, 2135. A.S. *genog*.

Yolde, yielded (to be), 951, 1088.

Ystatut, appointed, 2529. Fr. *statuer*.

Ywyſ, certainly, 1798, 1942. See *Iwyſ*.

Ʒeme, to take of, regard, have respect to, 665. A.S. *géman*.

Ʒere, year, 342.

Ʒerys, years, 23, 1432.

Ʒewith, giveth, 1772.

Ʒha, yes, 2843. Ger. *ja*.

Ʒhe, ye, 921. Observe that, as in this line, *ye* (A.S. *ge*) is the *nominative*, and *you* (A.S. *eów*) the *objective* case.

Ʒhed, went, 1486. Ch. has *yede*.

A.S. *ic eóde*, past tense of *gán*,
to go. Goth. *ik iddja*, past
tense of *gaggan*, to go.

Ʒher, year, 2064, 2274.

Ʒhing, young, 2868.

Ʒhis, yes, 1397.

Ʒhouth-hed, youth-hood, youth, 2772.

Ʒhud, went, 2696. See Ʒhed.

Ʒis, yes, 3406.

Ʒolde, yielded, 291, 380, 951.
A.S. *ic geald*, past tense of
gyldan, to pay, to yield.

Ʒude, went, 2944. See Ʒhed.

INDEX OF NAMES, ETC.

Albanak, 202, 1447.
Alexander, 1837.
Alphest, 57.
Amytans, 1304, 2446.
Angus, 2858.
April, 1.
Arachell, 434.
Ari s, 336.
Arthur (*passim*).
Ban, 202, 1447.
Bible, the, 1483.
Brandellis, 3086.
Brandymagus, 2884, 3430.
Camelot, 275, 280, 357, 407.
Cardole, 2153.
Carlisle, 347.
Christ, 2046.
Clamedeus, 2881, 3259.
Dagenet, 278.
Daniel, 1365.
Danȝelome, 435.
Esquyris, 2591, 2609, etc.
First-conquest king, 1064, etc. ; 2568, etc.
Gahers, 3087.
Galiot (*passim*).
Galys Gwyans, 2605, 2613, etc.
Galygantynis, 599.
Galloway, 2690.
Gawane (*passim*).
Gwynans or Gwyans. See *Galys*.
Gyonde or Gyande, 302, 551, 637.
Harwy, 2853, 3206, etc.
Herynes (*i.e.* Hermes), 436.
Hundred knights, king of, 1545, 1554.

Jhesu, 2046, 2096.
Kay, 254, 355, 3081, etc.
Lady of the Lake, 220, 223.
Lancelot (*passim*) ; appears as the *red* knight, 991, etc. ; as the *black* knight, 2430, etc.
Logris, 2301.
Maleginis, 806. See *Malenginys*.
Malenginys,2873,3151,3155. See also *Hundred knights, king of*.
May, 12.
Melyhalt, 283, 895.
Melyhalt, lady of (*passim*).
Moses, 436.
Nembrot (*i.e.* Nimrod), 435.
Nohalt, 255.
Phœbus, 24, 2472, 2486.
Priapus, 51.
Round Table, 795, 3213.
Saturn, 2474.
Scilla, 2483.
Solomon, 1378.
Sygramors, 3083.
Titan, 335.
Valydone, 3249. See *Walydeyne*.
Vanore, 575. See *Wanore*.
Virgin (Mary), 2049, 2087, etc.
Venus, 309.
Wales, 599, 2153.
Walydeyne, 2879.
Wanore, 230.
Wryne, 2867.
Ydrus, 2851, 3152.
Ywan, 2606, 2618, etc.
Ywons, 2861.

Richard Clay & Sons, Limited, London and Bungay.

www.ingramcontent.com/pod-product-compliance
Lightning Source LLC
Chambersburg PA
CBHW030840270326
41928CB00007B/1142